CALLED TO WAR

Series

Out of the Stands...Into the Arena

By Art Hobba

Book 1: Called to War: *Out of th*

Book 2: The Battle-Priest: *Bo*
into Victory! (Available in 201

Book 3: The Shepherd-King: *Bou Service...Crowned
into Dominion!* (Available in 2013)

Wade Westfly

Out of the Stands...Into the Arena

Art Hobba

Art Hobba

JOM L!

The Lord will go forth like a warrior,
He will rouse His zeal like a man of war.
He will utter a shout, yes He will raise a war cry
He will prevail against His enemies.

-- Isaiah 42:13

New American Standard Bible

Contents

Praise for Called to War:
Out of the Stands...Into the Arena

"Women, buy this book for the men you love! **Called to War will most assuredly be compared with Wild at Heart,** *Healing the Masculine Soul and Raising a Modern Day Knight. Art Hobba's resourcefulness takes new ground earning inclusion in this unique fellowship of unabashed Servant Warriors. Men-of-God, saddle up; you have been Called to War!"*

-- Marc Stein, President, Gospel Light Worldwide

———————————————

"American Christian men in these troubled times require antidotes to extricate us from ignoble material ends. Art Hobba's experience with a church crisis in 2007 and his studies in Gideon—is a profound work of God—that is the "medicine" for men's souls—perhaps even for salvation from death.

"As he rightly says, Christian men are made for glory in heaven as a reward for acts of integrity and courage every day."

-- Sam Jackson, World Vision

———————————————

"God does not call the "equipped". He 'equips' the 'called.' And that is why men need to pick up this book and use it as a 'tool' in their arsenal of weapons to fight the battle of the day with care, compassion, and due diligence.

"Toynbee once said 'the real battle of the day is fought on the fields of inner attention' - Whatever can assist us men to engage, and stay in the arena of our joys and our struggles, whatever can help us to see that the formation of the being of Jesus was intimately focused in obedience to the Father's Will, whatever can call us to a maximized Christ-centered manhood, I want to 'go for it'"!

-- Fr. Joseph Scerbo, S.A., Ph.D., Franciscan Friar of the Atonement, former Dean of Trinity College of Graduate Studies, past president of the Association of Christian Therapists.

"I am a man and love being one because of what this book talks about. **This is a powerful book**. *If you read it, pray to the God mentioned in it, and take the next steps Art Hobba recommends,* **you will be a changed man**. *And, while you are at it, put on your seatbelt right now . . . because you will surely need it. The ride you are about to take will take you over terrain you've never be on.*

"Writing from his own experience, Art will not give you quick, simple, band-aid answers. He's honest and courageous as he offers powerful, life-extending (eternal) truths – truths that bring a man into his manhood and the freedom he so desperately seeks after.

"Having personally witnessed God's transforming grace in action in Art Hobba's life compels me to recommend this book to you."

-- John Tolle, Supervisor, Pacific Coast & Valleys District, The Foursquare Churches

*"**Every man needs to be exposed to this book**. We are at war and **Called to War** is a refreshingly honest analysis of our war with Satan, our enemy, and shares with us how to deal with the struggles we as men face. Then it shows us how to win!" It is time that the church demands that we become the men that God has called us to be. **Read this book, recognize your enemy, put on your armor, and get into the battle.**"*

-- Kent Humphreys, Ambassador and Former President, FCCI /Christ@Work

---

*"**This book is so needed by men today**. It helped me realize how much I needed to stop standing alone against the spiritual battles I face, and lock shields with a few good men. Read it...it will strengthen you as a husband, father and as a man... 'So others may live!'"*

-- Dr. Terry Schroeder, Head Coach Men's USA Water Polo, Beijing Olympics 2008
Triple Silver Medalist, Member, NCAA Champion, Water Polo Hall of Fame

---

*"**Called to War** is a poetically inspiring, yet substantial book critical for men in our time. It awakened in me a passion to become who I want to be versus who I am. If we men can't identify with the need to go to war for God today, as presented by the author, then the image in the mirror that looks back at us tomorrow may merely be a dead man walking."*

-- Ted Bagley, Vice President of Human Resources, Amgen

---

*"Art Hobba's **Called to War** is not just a book but a road map that every man should use to align himself with other men to stand their course. It not only challenged me personally, but it opened my eyes to how important we are as men to our families, community, churches, and to one another."*

-- Chris Hayes, former NFL Super Bowl Champion, Green Bay Packers

*"You're tired, hurting, and convinced you're alone. Your wife doesn't understand what you're going through and your children have become a burden. Work is drudgery laced with fear of losing your paycheck. Your glances at other women have become lustful stares and you can't wait until work is over so you can have a drink. You've lost your way. Then along comes a book that extends its hand to you and wraps you in the armor of God...protecting you with the shield of faith. Suddenly, you awaken the Warrior within! Art Hobba has crafted the remedy that will bring men back from the brink and restore their soul. **This is a groundbreaking work that every man must read!**"*

-- Dave Tofanelli, Vice President, WellPoint-Anthem, Professor of Business, California Lutheran University

*"As a Christian therapist I see men every week who have lost their way due to a false masculinity that abdicates their role as a servant-warrior who loves and protects his wife and children. **Called to War is not about macho, but about freedom**. Art takes a man through the journey of Gideon from a fearful farmer, to mighty warrior. Men can be freed from the very false and often toxic armor we put on for self protection, and learn a new openness before God and other men. Men who read this book will discover their divine destiny and the courage, in Christ's armor, to fight and win, their spiritual battles."*

-- Rick Blackmon, Ph.D., Adjunct Professor, Fuller Theological Seminary, co-founder Pacific Psychological Resources

*"Art's ability to rally men around the idea of stepping into the arena, and out of our comfort zones, is just one of his leadership attributes that draws us into his sphere of influence and man-to-man accountability. **Called to War** is a polished, well organized, and extremely inspirational message. He is able to mix his vast biblical knowledge with a lifetime of pertinent personal experiences and challenges. His use of scripture and often disarming transparency speaks to Art's firmly grounded Christian faith."*

-- Bruce MacDonald, President, OSI Electronics

"Art Hobba is effectively tapping in to what is needed to engage American men in powerful kingdom-focused ways in their families, churches, and communities. Using Gideon as a case study, he uses the biblical themes of the warrior to challenge us to "get into the arena" -- first by building interdependent relationships with other men, then freeing us from the dark bonds that drag men down, and finally by 'spurring us on to love and good deeds' in practical ways. Both the content and the approach are motivating and transforming."

-- Steve Adams, Christian Associates, Latin America Director

"Even though it was originally written for men, I find it even more challenging for me to dig deeper. I have learned so much about myself as well as others, and God has used this book to challenge me in areas of my life that I have been shoving in the back corner of my heart, and also challenged me with my relationship with my boyfriend...we have both grown because of this study. I have had to make sacrifices, BUT I love it! And love learning how to be a Warrior in the arena!!"

-- Kaila Shull, Catcher, UCLA Women's Softball, All Pac 10

---

*"**Called to War** has taken the Core 300 training plan to other churches so that other churches may enjoy the fruits of inspiring men to engage His Kingdom through the local church.*

"I highly recommend Art's book... this incredibly motivating message for men to "Rise-Up!" Your church will never be the same!"

-- Larry Carignan, President Carignan Construction, Elder, Calvary Community Church

Dedication

This book is dedicated to my lovely wife Sharon, who has had to endure the adventures and foibles of living with me during the last decade and a half. It has been wonderful having you as my partner, counselor, and best friend.

I also am indebted to my band of warriors, 180 strong, who were hungry to hear, along with me, the trumpet call of Gideon as God moved the heart of men at our church in a time of crisis. You made me strive to do better and clarified my calling in the arena. You will always be in my heart.

Finally, I dedicate this to my dear sons Nathan, Garrett, Justin, Steven and Jordan. My boys were often on my mind as I remembered the past and looked to the future. I more often was writing to them versus any other. These men, and the generations to which they belong, will soon rule our world. They will need more courage and devotion to their Creator than any of the generations that have preceded them.

Acknowledgements

In compiling this book, it has truly been a team effort and inspired by a wonderful and awesome God who is the Author of all things! I also wish to thank all of the people on the "Called to War" team who have contributed their time, talent and love along the way.

First, I must thank my dear friend Steve Abarta, who was the catalyst for writing the book and then partnered with me along each and every step as my head cheerleader, confidante and senior editor. He also skillfully filmed and edited the video vignettes for each chapter. There is no way this book could have been written without him.

Mark Stein, Mark Clark and Dave Tofanelli provided timely advice and support…and helped me navigate through the straits of author hood.

Others who offered their unique skills include the creative editor, Garrett Hobba (my son) who helped me broaden my audience, and Melissa Tonery who offered her diligent technical editing expertise.

The amazing team that generously offered their amazing skills in developing the **Called to War** website and the supportive **Core 300** website was comprised of Murray Whiteman, Tal Bahir and Bob Andrews.

Book cover design and internal graphics were beautifully created by my talented friend, Dean Clark. Dale Koscielski edited and produced the audio CD for chapter 4 and 5. Our "Readers" reviewed the book in its near final state and helped make it *much better* with their feedback. They include Madeleine Butler, Mark Clark, Ross Ellsworth, John Gardner, Flora Gordon, Bruce Hobba, Nate Hobba, Sam Jackson, Brian Lee, Steve Stebbins, and Marissa Thielen.

Finally, I wish to recognize the amazing breadth of practical wisdom that was brought to bear by my wife Sharon. Her loving fingerprints have touched me every day of the last fourteen years of my life, and she patiently partnered with God in making me the man I am coming to be. Thus the echo of her presence is felt, but not seen, throughout many of these pages. I am also thankful for her loving patience through the frequent blank stares and sometimes mindless disengagement that resulted from too many late nights!

Prologue

The life of a man upon earth is a warfare
Job 7:1

The Christian radio talk show host asked the well known women's
ministry leader the question, "So what do you think about the statement
that men in the church have been feminized?" Her immediate response
was, "I totally disagree. Men in America have not been feminized at
all...they have been *emasculated*. Men don't feel a need to be more like
women...they just have lost their identity as men."

This book begins with the true story told by a washed up minister
whom God forgave, restored, and reenlisted in His service. The real story
lies, however, with what the Holy Spirit did in a few men who were
discontented with the state of men in their church. We discovered a
pathway to re-engagement as God's men in this ever darkening hour.
What unfolded was not a program, but a divine *movement* that radically
changed the lives of hundreds of men. It has since been made clear to us
that what has transpired in our church was not an anomaly, but is at the
very heart of God to mobilize men in this hour.

1

With the encouragement of several friends close to me, and the urging of the CEO of one of the world's largest Christian publishers whom I met through a chance meeting, I felt compelled far beyond my zone of comfort or ambition to write of both the movement and its focus on the timeless biblical story of Gideon.

We need to start in the year of 1976. I was sitting in church, a recent college graduate, with a new job, wife, mortgage, and a brand new baby boy. I struggled to focus on the pastor's morning message. My father, a mountain of a presence in my life, had just been prematurely taken from us in a fatal accident, and I had never felt so alone and unequipped for this sudden call to responsibility.

Our church was in the midst of a burgeoning revival, lead by my pastor, who, after 15 years in a somewhat obscure ministry, found himself shepherding a movement that had grown from several dozen to 2,500 worshipers.

More people were committing their hearts to Christ and were being added every week!

My Pastor had just said something that snapped me back to the present moment: "Don't take this the wrong way ladies, but the single most important event that we have here this year is our first men's breakfast this next Saturday. Men, you need to be there so you can respond to God's call to leadership in your life." He concluded this thought with, "Wives, you need to encourage your man to be there for both his sake, and yours!"

That next Saturday morning I feasted on bacon and eggs with about 70 other guys, a few of whom I recognized and knew by name. There was an excitement about being a part of the first group to meet and hear about what was so important to our pastor. I sensed we were on the ground floor of something special. My Pastor then said, "Every man here today is called as a leader. And that leadership is woven by God into your very fabric as a man. Turn to the guy next to you and tell him, 'You are a Leader, and so am I.'" I don't remember anything else of what was said that morning but the call to be a leader...and it stirred some old memories.

As my Pastor spoke, my mind journeyed to a time twenty years earlier. I was a young boy in the first grade and the leader in my class. It seemed as though I was the tallest and (so I thought) the brightest...the fastest runner and teacher's helper. I felt destined for greatness and walked with a seven year-old's swagger, full of confidence that, given the time and opportunity, I could do anything.

That summer we relocated to a New York suburb about 30 miles east of Manhattan. I tested well for entrance into Timber Point Elementary School and because of my precociousness and size, my parents and the school administrators decided it would be great for me to skip a grade.

I went from the top dog in my comfortable neighborhood in rural Pennsylvania to the bottom, "pecked" upon as not only the new kid, but one who was a full year behind. The confidence and swagger was replaced with fear and insecurity, and my self-esteem and confidence took a dive from which it did not fully resurface until 20 years later.

Now, following My Pastor's exhortation to me that I was a "Leader," his words reached to where that dormant part of me had been driven to the basement of my soul. I felt an *awakening*. That re-ignited ember would soon be fanned into a blaze by the wind of the Holy Spirit over the months and years that followed.

Soon we were a group of 200...then 400, then, 2 years later, 1,500 men! We began to identify with those 12 men and others who followed Jesus in the adventure of birthing the early church! They were men who prayed and worshiped God out loud and with boldness. They were men who were unafraid to cry...or to serve in the nursery and change diapers. They were men who began to give away their lives in service to their wives, believing that they were called by God as an instrument of His beautification. And, they were men who would choose their children over ambition...family and faith over the brass ring of worldly success.

Some of you who are reading this book have suffered through some debilitating failures. We have much in common. This call to lead launched me into a two decade journey that included obtaining a degree in Pastoral Theology, several ministry appointments and 8 years as senior pastor at a southern California church. We spent much of this time in the teeth of a spiritual battle, but both my wife and I were ill equipped, inexperienced and too immature to navigate the barrage of assaults successfully. From ministry assignment, to ministry assignment, the state of our marriage deteriorated, even though we both worked hard, with scores of hours of counseling, to repair it.

After 22 years of marriage, I hit a wall where I could no longer minister. Thankfully, I was given the grace to have wise and caring

3

denominational leadership around me that helped facilitate a very healthy and peaceful transition to a new pastor. However, after, attempting to bring our marriage to a place of health, we finally separated and 12 months later, divorced.

One of the recurrent themes of this book is the scars, wounds, infections we pick up along the way...and the healing process. We all have soul scars...it is the stuff of life. What a man does with the injury, however, makes all the difference.

I take much of the responsibility for this failure, and I offer no advice for any man or women in the midst of a failing marriage, other than to stop any ministry and get godly counsel. Ministering in Christ's light attracts the darkness of the enemy, along with the increased fatigue that assuredly comes with serving others. The other vital step is to become a part of a small circle of brothers and sisters with good marriages, so they can pray and love on you both.

My direct Supervisor at that time was a good friend and wise counselor. He told me, *"Art, you will need to recover and heal for at least 7 years before you will be ready again to resume your calling."* That "prophecy" turned out to be spot on.

My failed marriage remains the deepest scar of my life. It took the full seven years before I could believe that God had purpose for me again. During that time, I met and married Sharon, who with my church family and the relentless patience and grace of the Holy Spirit, became a wonderful channel of God's healing to me. She is a big part of how I have come to write this today, but that is another story. After an appropriate amount of time "in the stands," the embers of my calling were ignited afresh in my spirit.

The problem

The condition at our church is common to many churches in America, A majority of our men were "in the stands" like I was. For my years of "rehabilitation," I was content to sit in the stands and watch life go by, accompanied by my other male spectators. But something was missing...I sensed that my colleagues were bored...all the while many were being picked off by peripheral and direct hits from some unseen enemy's artillery…or worse yet, disabled by phantom demonic snipers hidden in the many traps placed in our paths.

There is a great invisible cosmic war against Christian men. Most men I knew were good guys but they had no real practical way of living out their faith in the world. *But, until recently, many of us had our work and toys to salve our souls.* However, God has planned a new "game" for us. It is "in the arena" advancing God's purposes on earth. It is beyond success…a call to significance…and it is why you were born.

Sometimes what we don't know can really hurt us. The Bible teaches us that were all born into an invisible but deadly war against our souls and the souls of those we love. Like it or not…admit it or not, as long as we have breath, we will struggle against the aligned strategies of World System, Human Carnality and the Cohorts of Satan's Kingdom. As real, yet invisible as the air we breathe, you and I awakened to war this morning…and we will tomorrow, every day, until we die or return to Christ in glory.

> *"Those who trust in me will never be put to shame." Who can snatch the plunder of war from the hands of a warrior? Who can demand that a tyrant let his captives go?*
>
> *But the LORD says, "The captives of warriors will be released, and the plunder of tyrants will be retrieved. For I will fight those who fight you, and I will save your children. I will feed your enemies with their own flesh. They will be drunk with rivers of their own blood. All the world will know that I, the LORD, am your Savior and your Redeemer, the Mighty One of Israel*
>
> -- Isaiah 49:23b-26 New Living Translation

Boot camp is 24/7

Many of us have never heard about the reality of spiritual war. Nor has it been preached clearly from many of our pulpits. This book is a necessary boot camp training manual to prepare you to understand this unseen battle and train you for victory…equipping you and those you enlist, to engage and win in the adventure of the arena.

Why men? A **Focus on the Family** study stated that if a child is the first person in a household to become a Christian, there is a 3.5 percent probability everyone else in the household will follow. If the mother is the first to become a Christian, there is a 17 percent probability everyone else in the household will follow.

But if the father is first, there is a 93 percent probability everyone else in the household will follow his example of faith.[1]

Many have seen the breadth of devastation that impacts a church and community when a pastor or elder fails to guard their spiritual and emotional thought life, becomes isolated, and then falls prey to sexual temptation or some other moral sin. It is a strategy Satan has employed with many leaders because he knows that if he can *"strike the shepherd, the sheep will be scattered"*[2].

But everyday, common men like you and I have been *marginalized* by gender blending, *paralyzed* by the assault of sexual perversion, and *hypnotized* by the promise of fulfillment in achieving success in their work. In addition, many churches have overplayed the quality of "niceness" as a sanitized substitute for godliness and exchanged church-centric "ministry" conscription for the calling to the adventure of a dynamic faith walk in God's Kingdom.

Men in Crisis[2]
- Only two out of six American men who profess a faith in Jesus Christ attend church on a given Sunday. The average man accepts the reality of Jesus Christ, but fails to see any value in going to church.
- Fewer than 10% of U.S. churches are able to establish or maintain a vibrant men's ministry.
- Midweek church activities often draw up to 80 percent female participants.
- Churches overseas report gender gaps of up to nine women for every man in attendance.

This is why men are the focal point of this book...and also why men are the fulcrum upon which Satan leverages his war on this planet. Unless the individual man recognizes that he is called by God to prepare, act, think, and respond as a warrior in this life, he will fall far short of his created potential.

With so many pulpits focusing on only the more popular New Testament writings, the American Body of Christ has been for too long fed a pabulum rich diet based on taste alone, while two-thirds of Old Testament references are relegated to excerpts that include the Ten Commandments, the Genesis story, Psalms of comfort and Joseph and his "technicolored dreamcoat!" The fact remains that a full one-third of the Bible was written in the context of war. The victories and defeats of God's people, often leading to bondage followed by victorious deliverance were achieved as men went to war for, and with, Yahweh.[3]

The New Testament continues the theme of the breakthrough of the Kingdom of God into the human sphere by revolutionary and sometimes *violent* emissaries who come to free those who are bound and execute authoritative liberation in Jesus' Name. When we examine Christ's sacrifice on Calvary, we often miss the nature of the violence done to Him in order for God to win human "Prisoners of War" back to Him. Understand that the coordinated attack by Satan through his array of demonic forces, religious hypocrisy and human jealousy all were in the context of that Great War that has been raging since the Devil sought to lead a rebellion against God himself eons ago. And it rages still today.

> The fact remains that over one-third of the Bible was written in the context of war.

The timing for calling men into the arena could not have been better. Books like **Why Men Hate Going to Church,** by David Murrow and **Revolution** by George Barna indicate significant paradigm shifts among Christians...and men in particular. Add to that the traditional low percentages in male church attendance versus female, and the loss of masculine identity presented by a depraved society and a contracting economy, and you have what could be called the "perfect storm" of need.

As a father of five sons, the most sobering news is the lack of connection that exists between the older men and the younger. Published statistics show us a trend of boys in the American church generally walking away from the roots of their faith when they become men. In fact, surveys indicate that anywhere between 85-92% of high school students fail to return to church after they graduate and the percentages are higher for young men than for women.[4] We are losing tomorrow's generation to this cosmic war.

In this "War Manual" you will:

- **Learn and understand** the nature of **the unseen war** that you have been born into and *how to win that war*
- **Experience spiritual "boot camp"** and discover your mission as a mighty warrior.
- **Humbly, but surely step into leadership in your home,** lovingly leading your wife and children
- **Learn authenticity** and to find real protection, as you bond with and "lock shields" with other men.
- **Be freed** from debilitating sin and the influence of dark spiritual forces, and walk as an unfettered, free man

One final challenge before you read on is to look at these pages with a different lens than what you normally use when you read spiritual growth books. Most of the time a book like this will require me to use my "general disciple" lens. But you will most benefit if you read each chapter as a **new recruit**…drafted into a Corps of men that are being trained and conditioned to stand, and fight and advance together. Prepare for a violent, life changing encounter…and a battle that you must now face. This journey is not for the faint of heart, but for those who hear the clarion call of the Horn of Gideon. Prepare for the adventure of your life *"so others may live"*!

Engagement

A boy went to a church one day
To hear of a Mighty Lord
He left perplexed and disappointed
Feeling 'nice' and mostly bored

He grew into a teenage boy
Full of hope and strength and guilt
They showed him Jesus…gentle, meek, and mild,
While he, enslaved, was stilled

He wandered for a season, lost
Not knowing who he was
Is there someone who'll blow the horn?
To that noble, worthy cause?

He heard a quiet sound one day
He turned aside to see
Appeared his Captain, on stallion white
Bid "Come to War with Me!"

A flaming sword came from his mouth
Words sharp and deep, Alive!
Freed now with Spirit fire within
A warrior, bringing Life!

Chapter One:

Beginnings

What started as a crack in the dam became an avalanche of men sharing...many confessing some of the more darker scenarios of sin you can imagine: five figure online gambling debts, kept secret from the wife; an addiction to spending too much money at strip clubs; an addiction to heroin for 6 years...all of those years spent coming to church, week after week. There was a single man in his late fifties that had been divorced three times with a current girlfriend, and he confessed to anger management issues with his grown sons with whom he could not have a civil conversation. And there were two guys who asked for prayer for their marriages because one was just separating and the other was on its way to divorce court!

Yet these men had been sitting in the church services week after week, alone, hiding and disqualified from service to God. When it was over, at around 2 AM I retired to my sleeping bag on the top canopy of our houseboat under the stars. As the strong chaparral winds blew across the lake all through the night, time troubled by, in tune with my restless night's sleep.

The postmodern church in America today is on its heels, reeling from culture wars on the outside and generation gaps within. All this is magnified by additional financial pressures as giving has plummeted due to an extended global economic crisis. Yet, in many churches, attendance and needs are on the rise. Many churches have been squeezed close to, or beyond, the breaking point as staffs are cut and programs left unfunded. There has never been, in this writer's lifetime, a greater need, or *opportunity*.

We have all, it seems, been placed upon a mandatory "fast" of sorts, where the once attractive pursuit of opulence and acquisition has faded to Spartan black and white. Most guys I know are playing defense or ducking for cover.

A few things I learned the hard way

A couple summers ago, our family went up into the Colorado Rockies for a week of adventure based out of a Dude Ranch at 9,000 feet. For one of our days, between horseback lessons in the arena and riding in the woods, I had the chance to talk my wife Sharon and son Jordan, into a white water rafting trip down the upper Colorado River.

The rapids were "only" Class III and IV and the water level was very low so there were many more exposed rocks and boulders than other years. I attempted to convince Sharon that it was just fine. She was pretty nervous...not only for her life, but for our eleven year old son as well. She tried to persuade me to go it alone so she and Jordan could make a gentler decent down the class 1 and 2 river segment. She said, "*Honey, look at you...you have scars all over your body from these kind of adventures...a titanium hip, both your shoulders and one of your knees has been rebuilt, but that doesn't mean we have to follow in your footsteps!*"

I assured her, "*We have helmets, wetsuits, lifejackets, and an expert guide...what could go wrong?*" Being practical and wiser than me, she retorted back that if we had to wear all of that stuff, it must be pretty dangerous. Anyway, my son and I prevailed upon her best judgment and the three of us armored up and, equipped with paddles, launched downstream.

Fortunately, we only capsized once. It occurred when I was launched into the air from my station in the port bow as our "expert" guide ran us up on a huge boulder. Apparently, I inadvertently took both my wife and son overboard with me with what amounted to a cross body block. We were invigorated, wet, and safe again on dry land. In the gift shop, they were selling some mementos of the experience and I found a great tee shirt that said, ***"Scars are Tattoos with Better Stories."***

Unfortunately, I have rarely been one to be content with watching and learning from others. My seasonal penchant for arrogance blended with an almost unreal optimistic outlook has gotten me into some pretty bad skirmishes with circumstances beyond my control and not a little loss of blood and... scars with stories.

Why are men so disengaged?

I think there are several reasons why this happens to men more that it appears to happen to women. If we are to learn how to step into the arena, we must first clearly understand what God's objectives are and the nature of our enemy.

A study from Hartford Seminary found that the presence of involved men was statistically correlated with church growth, health, and harmony. Meanwhile, a lack of male participation is strongly associated with congregational decline. (source www.churchformen.com)

Strategy makes a better woodcutter than strength. -- The Iliad, Homer

One of our most basic reasons for disengagement is that we have not been taught the nature of the forces and entities arrayed against us, or the seriousness of our adversary's intent. In this book, we will walk together through an unfolding process of discovery regarding the ultimate goal of the Church and the ultimate goal of our adversary, the Devil. Scripture teaches us, magnified through the lens of history, that the Devil's ultimate objective is to destroy the Church[1].

As is true for any military boot camp which breaks down the soldier for several weeks and then builds him up again, but also makes him stronger, each of these chapters builds upon the previous chapter. So resist the temptation to jump forward or you may find yourself careening downstream with a pole instead of a paddle! A few chapters ahead, we will delve in more detail about the dimensions of war so we can be prepared and form a strategy for victory. Chapter Nine, Ten and Eleven bring us to the Armor of God, its tactical usefulness and strategic application for preemptive and victorious warfare.

Lack of modeling

Some men remain in the stands for much of their lives because they have never seen a model of an authentic spiritual man. The called, trained, and paid professional minister often gets distanced from the rest of us guys because he can easily be elevated to such a height as to become an untouchable anomaly of manhood. "Called," yes...admired, absolutely, but not someone to practically emulate in my "dog eat dog" world." Men need a tangible, Christian model to mentor them; someone to show them the ropes of a masculine faith. Most Sunday school teachers and schoolteachers are women. Many men, even in the church, don't pray at home or read the Bible. Many fathers today, and in past generations, are absent from involvement in the lives of their sons and daughter even if they do come home every night.

Churchianity

Other guys stay disengaged because they just can't buy in to the church program. A couple of years ago, while visiting a church outside our city, the pastor asked for a show of hands on who in the congregation were in the ministry. Out of some 1,000 adults in attendance, about five or six raised their hands. He went on to describe how scripture called *all believers* as ministers, full-time, *"prepared in season and out of season."* (2Timothy 4:2). At the end of the message, he asked the same question and the vast majority of hands went up.

This message needs to be brought to all believers and reinforced often...and then lived out. However, at that church, they continued to call those active in ministry "volunteers." When I think of volunteering at church, an image of stuffing envelopes comes to my mind, or ushering.

Both are noble and needed tasks as well as meaningful functions of service that benefit the church. But for many believers of action, or who have developed gifts and experience, those who are given opportunities to serve are often relegated to the inconsequential status of little or no influence.

When this happens to a gifted man or woman, they can often feel that they are being placated or herded, like sheep, often asked to perform some rote task. They may have front-line responsibility as a leader of scores of employees, or are a successful small business owner. At work, they are highly esteemed as an equal partner on the management team, and have trusted direct access to the CEO's office or have deeply honed skills working with their hands. They are significant and would love the opportunity to worship God in their spiritual gifts and vocational skills.

One of the most unfortunate terms used to describe non-professional Christian adults today is "laymen." Even "volunteer" does not do most of the role justice. I think the best biblical descriptions of all Christians, whether professional, staff or active church participants are "saints," "the called," "members," (as in critical parts of one body) or "ministers."

> *"When you come together, **everyone** has a hymn, or a word of instruction, a revelation, a tongue or an interpretation. All of these must be done for the strengthening of the church." (bold is mine)*
>
> --1 Corinthians 14:26

Professionalism

Church staff leaders live in a culture where it is hard to discipline or fire employees. The "grace" aspect of the Gospel can weaken requirements for top performance by managers. Per the astute and experienced observations of organizational expert Patrick Lencioni[2], these workers often function at a higher level of "team dysfunctionality" and a lower level of performance than most secularly engaged employees in similar jobs. On the other hand, as a church staff member at four churches for over fifteen years, and with another 25 years in lay ministry, I have often observed that those called and paid to serve the body, can subtly take on an attitude of spiritualized "ivory tower" superiority over other members of the body of believers.

14

This is yet another reason why most men remain disengaged. Since "dumb sheep" are not dumb at all, when the gifted and impassioned volunteer senses staff condescension, they quietly go back into the stands to take a seat, or find another place where they can find fulfillment. The church has lost another warrior resource because of the subtle yet prideful class system of staff (or clergy) versus laity.

Many churches have lost the participative community gathering and abdicated it too often to the professional staff. They are the "called" ones and are paid to draw us into God's presence in praise and worship (with state of the art video/audio technology) and then entertain us with witty stories, well-timed humor, and inspiring biblical exposition. I wonder what the poor archaic early church did without these seminary-trained pastors, children's educators and music programs leaders with master degrees?

Purple hearts

Other men have joined the stands due to broken dreams, which have then resulted in a kind of spiritual apathy. It just hurts too much to hope again. Others are wounded...a casualty of spiritual warfare or from becoming isolated and then picked off by "snipers" of darkness. Still others have been neutralized and constricted by personal bondage to sin, a debilitating divorce, or some other personal failure. Most of these believe they are disqualified due to their wounds...feeling unworthy or ashamed. We often simply put our heads down and lose ourselves at work.

Some men *need* to stay in the stands until they are healed or rested. But this is for the purpose of returning to battle readiness. I needed seven years. Others are like Lazarus, silently in a deep sleep, waiting for the call from Jesus to "come forth!" and shed the constricting grave clothes of their past. Any one of these or several may exist in your life today and every fiber of my being would love to look you in the eye right now and tell you that God is in *NO WAY* finished with you!

I *know* this is true. I have seen men just short of their eighth decade, like Caleb of old, become reignited for service of the King, and take a new hill for God. I have seen twelve-year-old boys, step into the arena, like young David, to do the same. He calls you to step up into significance, and once you have your gear on, with paddle in hand, launch out into the white water adventure of your life!

> *The Bible tells us to "put on the full armor of God." Upon graduation from The Warrior class, I was presented with a majestic Core 300 coin that I carry in my wallet at all times. This coin reminds me daily to put on the armor of God and be prepared to face each day. What this experience gave me was a profound insight into myself. The courses were not easy, and in fact, I had several classes where the subjects were downright uncomfortable. It made me look in the mirror like never before.*
>
> --Jim McMichael, Lt. Colonel,
> US Air Force RES

Here is how the movement happened. In the spring, our church went through a very trying and difficult time. Our leading pastor had just suddenly resigned and soon thereafter came stories of moral misconduct. We learned weeks later that he was also separated from his wife and had filed for divorce. Some of you have had that experience in your church and you know something of what we went through.

Others of you may have fallen as well or suffered through the breakup of your own family, like I did. The loss can be debilitating. For any sense of future ministry, a real sense of disqualification can haunt you like a second skin.

Please know that this book was written for you. If God could redeem a much-scarred warrior like me, He can and will do the same for you!

A few men began to pray

Three weeks into our leadership crisis, an emergency men's prayer meeting was called by some of the elders. The meeting was attended by about 40 men. Thus began the men's "movement" which originated with two to three of those men feeling called to continue to pray for our church together for one hour, on an every-other-Saturday morning basis. These men believed prayer was the most necessary and primary activity we could do because of dire need. Without a head shepherd, we knew the strategies of Hell, which were already declared in scripture, were bent on "scattering the sheep" of our congregation[3].

Leadership did their best to respond to the crisis. Elders faced accusations and questions courageously and met together often, working and praying through a variety of pressing issues. Our staff leadership looked to where cash reserves might be better conserved and jobs eliminated or transitioned to volunteer status. Our men's prayer group dug in as well, rapidly increasing to ten, then to about fourteen men, and the certainty of our mission and focus never diminished, but increased month after month. We knew others were at prayer as well, but we chose to pray as if no one else was praying but us.

Our prayer meetings continued through the summer, during which I coordinated communications and the prayer agenda. The church staff offered me the list of some 450 men who had gone through our membership class over the previous four years with the caveat that it was to be used to communicate around the prayer needs alone. Every other week, every man on this list received a prayer bulletin and invitation to the meeting. The prayer group grew modestly to about 18-20 over several months, though many who could not be there on Saturday agreed to pray through the concerns shared via the email.

We prayed for our elders who were sacrificially navigating the complex and treacherous straits of political fallout, fragmented trust, broken hearts, and reduced giving. We prayed for protection, for a spirit of forgiveness and healing in the church.

We prayed earnestly for women who felt betrayed by our former Pastor. To those who were married, his failure represented their deepest fear ("Will my husband leave me for another woman?") We prayed for those who were single, whose hope was challenged as to whether God could bring a truly trustworthy man into their lives...and for those who had suffered divorce and the temptation toward cynicism about men, and spiritual leadership in particular. Yes, we prayed for our women.

We prayed for our incredible staff...people who not only served sacrificially, but now also had to deal with the uncertainties of their church and of their own jobs. And we prayed for our youth, daughters and sons who were being challenged to walk in purity, and now were faced with the fall of a key representative of God's authority in their lives.

Finally, I began to introduce the idea of spiritual warfare to these men, many of whom had never even heard the term. Most, even if they had heard it, had little understanding or experience in engaging the enemy in intercessory prayer, but I began introducing scripture around the subject and these men were eager to learn, and we began practicing authoritative, Kingdom power releasing, prayer. The offensive had begun.

The telltale retreat

At the end of the summer, the leader of our men's ministries and my good friend, Bart, asked me to join the leadership team. The first order of business was our fall Men's Houseboat retreat, lead by Retired Los Angeles Police Chief Bob Vernon. "Chief Bob" was going to teach on the nature of and call to servant leadership. I had not gone on a men's retreat for over a decade and was not too thrilled to be on this one…but I had a breakout session assigned to me on mentoring and as a member of the new team, I signed up.

Did you ever consider that David, who God honored long after his death and who wrote many of our favorite psalms, was an adulterer, murderer and, at an old age, as pride caused him to number his army against God's directive, seventy thousand people died as a result of his sin. His son, Solomon was endowed with the greatest wisdom of anyone who had ever lived and made the wealthiest man in all history. His proverbs have inspired and instructed hundreds of millions of people and yet he was a polygamist and a polytheist in the end. Who, then, am I to count myself out of the game? If anything, I am inspired to *finish well.*

As we gathered after dinner around 10 PM Thursday night for introductions, our leader and Boat "Captain," Ross, led out with the icebreaker question, asking each of us to share what we were hoping God would do in our lives over the four-day weekend. This was the first night, so typically, 11 guys are going to "pose" for a day or two to get a comfort level before they might consider sharing some authentic pain in their lives. As the men, mostly strangers to one another, talked, phrases like, *"I want to learn to serve my wife better,"* and *"praying for deeper understanding of the Bible."* And the stories droned on and on.

When it was my turn to share, I figured that I'd just go for it, so I said the truth; that God had been dealing with me about my anger with one of my older sons, who was drifting away from church and the things of God. I said that I needed to get him back into my life and I was driving him away! I further shared that I suspected that my attitude needed some serious adjustment and that I was hoping God would do that in me before I ventured down the mountain.

What started as a crack in the dam became an avalanche of men sharing…many confessing some of the darker scenarios of sin you can imagine: six figure online gambling debts, kept secret from the wife; an addiction to *strip clubs*; another had been a secret heroin junkie for 6 years. There was a single man in his late fifties that had been divorced three times with a current girlfriend, He confessed to anger management issues with his grown sons with whom he could not have a civil conversation. And there were two guys who asked for prayer for their marriages because one was just separating and the other was on his way to divorce court!

Yet these men had been sitting in the church services week after week, alone, hiding and disqualified from service to God. When it was over, at around 2 AM, I retired to my sleeping bag on the top canopy under the stars. The strong chaparral winds blew hauntingly across the lake all through the night an echo to my restless night's sleep.

If you have read thus far but have not found freedom in Christ, it may be that when you came to Jesus initially, you were not given the essential understanding of what it means to be converted as a Christian and disciple of Christ. You may also not fully understand what it means to have *experienced* God's loving adoption as a son of the Father. Too many churches, it seems to me, have so watered down, or formalized the conversion experience as to make it impotent.

The Wound

Some of us had fathers who were present but abusively so, executing seismic reigns of terror in the souls of both wives and their children. William Manchester, noted biographer and author of **The Last Lion,** devoted significant text to the painful relationship between Sir Winston

Churchill and his father, Randolph. *"Randolph actually disliked his son,"* he writes at one point where he describes how often the father's harshness had hurt young Winston as a boy. Churchill later wrote of his childhood:

> *"[My father] wouldn't listen to me or consider anything I said. There was no companionship with him possible and I tried so hard and so often. He was so self centered no one else existed for him...He treated me as if I had been a fool; barked at me whenever I questioned him. I owe everything to my mother; to my father, nothing"*

It's not difficult to feel the pain of a broken and rejected heart and unfulfilled dreams of intimacy with his father in Churchill's words. Best Selling Christian writers like Gordon Macdonald (**When Men Think Private Thoughts**) and John Eldredge (**Wild at Heart, Waking the Dead**) have well developed treatises on what is referred to as the "wound" of the father....and many readers have found direction and healing in their messages. If you feel a deep stirring regarding this subject matter, both of these authors, MacDonald in particular, offer deeper discourses to help you explore the landscape of your own unique "wound." It may be that Father God has a gift of healing for you to discover as you seek Him as your Father.

A few of us have had awesome, fully functional earthly fathers. I have found this to be truly rare in my experience with men and women. Other dads, like mine, were missing key components...their presence...or words of love, affirmation, instruction, and needed correction. These missed deposits or "blessings" created vacuous holes in our souls that later caused some to dredge internal harbors of resentment, often leading to harmful behaviors...all trying to fill the voids. The substantial absence of these pillars of sonship that we all so desperately need also has a universal way of alienating us from our Father in Heaven. Like Churchill's father, we don't really believe Father God even *likes* us.

Other well meaning Christians have discovered the truth of *serving* God...but have never experienced the best part; living close to God as your *Father*...in *His* embrace under His constant gaze of love and knowing the confirming inner voice of God as your ***personal*** adoptive

Father. Paul takes the time to write to two churches this all important distinctive of experiencing life as God's beloved child:

> *For you did not receive a spirit that makes you a slave again to fear, but you received the Spirit of sonship. And by him we cry, "Abba, Father." The Spirit himself testifies with our spirit that we are God's children. Now if we are children, then we are heirs—heirs of God and co-heirs with Christ" (Romans 8:15).*

Again, in Galatians 4:4-7 Paul further emphasizes;

> *"But when the time had fully come, God sent his Son, born of a woman, born under law, to redeem those under law, that we might receive the full rights of sons. Because you are sons, God sent the Spirit of his Son into our hearts, the Spirit who calls out, "Abba, Father." So you are no longer a slave, but a son; and since you are a son, God has made you also an heir."*

Even during the final years of the ministry of Jesus, His Father in heaven affirmed His love and affirmation of His Son, both publicly and privately (Gethsemane and Christ's many forays into the desert alone). Jesus needed to hear from His Dad that everything was going to be okay (see Matthew 3:17 and 17:5). He was affectionately addressed by His Father as his *"Beloved Son* (New American Standard Bible)."

I know many men and women of authentic faith who are looking ahead to a time when they will stand before God one day, hoping to have finished well...hearing those words, "Well done my good and faithful servant." I too treasure a hope of sharing this experience with my fellow laborers in the Gospel.

But, at some intersection of our life, there is a unique journey of inner healing that we must all share as we're taken into the affirming arms of the Father. "Abba" (as we are instructed to call Him), meaning "Daddy God," wants to deposit into our souls, here on earth, a validation in real time, just as He did for his Son Jesus long ago. Sadly, most of us never take the time to allow God to convey this blessing that heals these often deepest wounds of subliminal rejection we carry in our soul.

21

I was *floored*. I was sitting at the supper table after church one Sunday afternoon with my ex-wife and two boys, Nathan, who was six, and Garrett, who was a precocious three. We had been discussing our joint experiences of what we had learned at church that day, and Nathan had just ended his theological recollection of the courage of Moses and the wonder of God's power in parting the Red Sea. Garrett had never entered into these conversations before, but wanting to contribute like his big brother, he suddenly blurted out, "I know who God is!" We all looked towards his beaming face and with a niceness that only mothers can conjure, she said, "Oh really, sweetie, who is God?" He then looked directly at me and pointed, "Daddy's God."

The profound truth of those words echo with me still today. Daddy is God to so many children. And it has always been so. These young hearts so often see their father (and of course, far too often less appreciated, their mother) as their only real perception of God the Father. This is God the strong…the nurturer, the protector and the provider. Beyond all of these is a God who sees them as real people of significance and gives credence to their voice…and wings to their dreams, however silly or unreasonable they may seem to others.

For those few men and women I have had the privilege of truly knowing through counseling or relationship, I have never met one who did not have to deal, at the deepest levels, with the issue of this "wound" of their earthly father. Even Jesus talked about how our fathers, being *evil* (literally twisted, incomplete), still desire to give us good things (Luke 11:12-13).

The Spirit of Adoption

I was driving home on the 101 freeway just outside of the San Fernando Valley one early summer day in 1975 and the memories of what had happened just a short six months before, involuntarily began to swell in my breast…and the tears began to flow again.

It was December 19, 1974, and we are all anticipating Christmas together at mom and dad's place in a few days. Presents were mostly bought and wrapped and homes were decorated for the joyful festivities only Christmas can bring. That day, after work in the field handing out cards and gifts to customers amidst background songs of Christmas carols, I returned home around 5:30 to an empty house. A note was on the kitchen table that simply said, "Call your mom...something terrible has happened."

My heart flashed to what was the deepest dread of my heart...that my Dad was dead. I dialed and my older sister answered the phone at my folks' home and she quickly passed it on to my mother. "Arthur darling, your father has passed away...and I am so sorry," her voice breaking up between each phrase.

What followed was four days of Hell. First, we were told he had suffered a heart attack in Monterey, California the night before. Then, bit by bit, we heard of a fight of some sort...and finally we came to hear from the local police that he had been brutally attacked and murdered on his way to his car after dinner.

For days up until the funeral on Christmas Eve, we wept as a family...and we wept as individuals...all in disbelief. Yet the Holy Spirit moved among us in unexplainable ways as we bolstered each other up and began to memorialize this good man, taken at the age of fifty-five. Several hundred came to mourn his death with us...and celebrate his life. Then slowly, healing had begun in each of us as we were simultaneously pulled even closer to one another. The closeness has diminished only a little over the past several decades, and God has done some beautiful things in the lives of each of my siblings and their families since that life changing event.

Now, on the freeway, I was weeping openly, barely able to control the wheel of the car and in anguish of spirit I cried out, "Daddy, I miss you so...I miss you so!"

The tears continued unabated for several more miles. Then there entered a divine warmth...a movement, like a warm covering over my soul, that could only be described as the very palpable presence of God. His love began flowing over me in the cockpit of my car. It became a Holy place...an intimate sanctuary...and healing balm began to cover my heart as God spoke these words into my mind;

"My son, today I am adopting you as my son...today I am now your Father, and I will be all you have ever needed...or desired...and more."

He held me then as I found my way to the side of the road, and for the first time, I basked in his loving presence and strength, and I was healed. God was no longer just my Savior and King...he had then *become* my Father.

The critical nature of this level of comprehension of God as Father in our salvation journey *cannot be overestimated*. This is where we all, men and women alike, find our **true identity** as adopted heirs of all of God's person and resources...and where we find our new nature (or DNA) as sons of God. This is who we are...sons of the Father...and there is no position, title, height, echelon, or degree of achievement in all of creation that can come close to what we have already inherited as sons of god. Yea, even the angels stand in awe at what God has done in us;

> *And God raised us up with Christ and seated us with him in the heavenly realms in Christ Jesus,* [7]*in order that in the coming ages he might show the incomparable riches of his grace, expressed in his kindness to us in Christ Jesus. For it is by grace you have been saved, through faith—and this not from yourselves, it is the gift of God*
>
> -Ephesians 2:6-8

Much of the balance of this book is about your and my calling **to the role of** Warrior. It would be amiss for us to venture forth as Warriors, even in the full armor of God...if we did not first stand firm on the bedrock foundation that Christ Jesus' perfect sacrifice purchased sonship, with Him, before our Father in heaven. We are identified forever as members of the Divine family. This stands true for other roles we may need to walk in such as father, husband, worker, church member, and good neighbor.

The gateway to adoption as a son or daughter of our Heavenly Father begins with repenting (forsaking) from your sin and acknowledging both His leadership over your life and His ability and desire to forgive and cleanse you from every blemish of sin in your past. If you are not sure this is true for you...that your name is written in the Lamb's book of life as one of God's beloved children...and that Jesus Christ is your Lord, pray this simple prayer to gain that assurance:

"Father God, thank you for the gift of the life of your Son Jesus. I set my will to turn away from a life of sin, going my own way, and I repent, giving myself to You. I believe in my heart that Jesus died for my sins and rose from the grave to conquer death. I need Jesus now to be my Savior and ask you to forgive me of all of my sins. Wash me whiter than snow.

I receive the spirit of adoption as your son, and choose to follow Jesus and your Word through the Holy Spirit, for the rest of my life. Thank you Father for calling me your son, Amen."

If you prayed this prayer, it is important that you call or meet with a few folks whom you know are Christians to explain to them what just happened. They will rejoice with you and encourage you to be baptized in water and with the Holy Spirit, and to get involved regularly with a strong Bible-teaching, Christ-centered church. Remember that a small group of men who meet regularly will give you guidance, friendship and accountability so you can learn to live and love like Jesus....and find your unique destiny in Him.

As we conclude this chapter, let's return to my restless sleep. Looking back on that night, something in my soul slipped out of joint (or maybe back into joint?). The source was like the beginning of a small tremor that became a catalyst that changed my life's direction. I felt the rise of anger...not at the men and their stories of disobedience and bondage, but against the insidious penetration of the kingdom of darkness into the lives and homes of men who are called by the Name of Christ. My spirit was grieved at the certainty of the echo of their actions, mine included, upon those around them...some would be damaged for generations to come. I was also grieved for the broken abdication of men from their priestly role of prayer and service to those they loved and were accountable for...and the loss of possibilities for them and their wives and children who so desperately needed them to be men of God.

In times like these, often God's Spirit will bring hope upon which we can rebuild our faith in His ability to bring repentance, liberty and restoration of the messes we have made.

Your playing small does not serve the world.

-- Marianne Williamson

I had been "playing small" and had, like many men I knew (there *is anonymity* in mediocrity), believed that simply because I wore a baseball hat and brought a glove to the ball game, that somehow I was a key player on the field!

That Sunday afternoon, as I descended from the mountain lake with my good friend Bart, we talked in earnest about what the men on our leadership team could do. A plan began to formulate in the front cab of his SUV, attended by the Holy Spirit, who more than any, sought to bring freedom to these and many more men in our church--men who have been marginalized into spectator status in the stands of life, while their dreams and destiny of significance awaits in the arena they yearn to enter, but cannot.

I attended my first men's leadership team meeting right after the retreat and discovered a group of 10 men, many of whom were already friends, who were dissatisfied with the apparent disengagement of some 1,000 men in our church. There was a Spirit led "itch" for change, no senior pastor at the helm, and no existing program to hinder us from trying something new. We set a date for an offsite, full-day retreat to seek God for a fresh call…and a fresh vision for men in our church.

Five key things happened that day:

1. We became more self-aware of how God uniquely made our personalities through some DiSC assessments. They were fun and helped unite us.[4]

2. Each man was anointed (yes, we used oil) with prayer for a new level of consecration and service by the other men.

3. We began to crystallize as a team with one heart

4. We all felt the beginning of a new movement for men's ministry at our church and articulated a new vision; we were to call men "out of the stands…into the arena!"

5. We laid the initial framework for a unique men's breakfast kickoff event

Now, for years, we had been having 3-4 men's breakfasts every year, complete with full lumberjack cholesterol clogging vittles, a worship team and a marquis guest speaker. But this breakfast was to be like none we had ever seen before. We would launch a to-be written teaching series that would call men to significance…to be identified as core…to be warriors for God.

Walking through some red tape

The big question was; do we wait until we bring in the new pastor? Or go ahead and launch? We prayed about and debated this for a full month. The risk takers in the group were for full steam ahead. Others wanted to wait, while about half of the guys were on the fence.

Just after the group leader proposed that we should wait, looking for a vote, one of the men (with a more prophetic edge to him) went to the whiteboard and made a passionate appeal to **go now**. It would probably be another six to twelve months before the search was completed. Then it would be yet another 18 to 24 months before a new pastor would be ready to take on such a risky project. How can you launch a radical new program to a church on its heels waiting for the new pastor to come in on the "white horse" and lead us?

The question he posed was, *"What if we fail?"* We all realized it was no big deal if we did. Men's ministry had about 15% of the men who attended the church participating in three breakfasts per year and another 5% for the annual retreat. We had nowhere to go but up! We unanimously decided to go forward with our plans to the Elders.

Our team leader did an amazing job of coordinating our motley crew of go-getters and troublemakers! The presentation was well thought through and featured our mission statement, three year vision and the launch of "Out of the Stands…Into the Arena" Breakfast (with a "Mystery Speaker"). The follow-on 9-week teaching series on Gideon (which had yet to be clearly defined by yours truly), would be developed along the way. We were going to have to sail the ship as we made the mast, sails and rudder!

The elders received our presentation with exuberant joy and confirmed to us that we were indeed hearing from God. They also confirmed that the timing was now. We all sensed we were on the adventure of our lives…and we bonded and banded, planned and prayed together as brothers, readying for the challenge ahead.

Table talk

1. In what ways do you feel you may be "in the stands" spiritually? Why?

2. What kind of spiritual model was your father? How do you think that may have impacted your walk with Christ? If you hold back on whom God is making you to be, who may have not been blessed because, to a certain extent, you have been afraid to boldly be that man? Do you think God will hold you accountable for what could have been if you shrink back?

Core conditioning

I have been learning to set "stretch goals" for every major relationship and for every significant person in my life. An example would be: What can my son become? What is it that God envisioned in him when he was created? How am I contributing to God's dream for him? Am I taking away from it? Write in your Bible or journal about what it might mean for you to become a leader…that man of God you sense He is calling you to be. If you are already leading others, how might God want to expand your vision of service to grow in your influence in the lives of others? Write down some "stretch goals for yourself and those you love and serve.

Chapter Two:

Gideon: Alone, Hiding and Disqualified

The Lord is a warrior and the Lord is His Name
-- Exodus 15:3

Scene XV: The Battle of Carthage

The Gladiator, once called Maximus, flanked on the right and left by a score of other warriors, ascended the dungeon stairway, moving as one cohort from the dank subterranean darkness, to the brilliant sunlight that reflected off the white sand on the floor of the Coliseum. Under a clear, cloudless blue sky, forty-five thousand voices rose in unison lauding these would-be Champions in anticipation of much bloodshed. It was the troop's first time ever in the great stadium and each warrior's heart quickened at the involuntary surge of adrenalin that flowed through them.

Standing at the center of this ill-fated band was the man who had endured the glories, trials, and injustices of several lifetimes. In a previous life, he had earned the love and loyalty of the fierce legions of Rome and the affection and trust of Emperor Marcus Aurelius, who was murdered by

29

his evil son, Commodus, and who had also usurped his throne. Commodus now stood to greet these armored entertainers.

Considered dead by treachery, the Gladiator, previously known as Maximus Decimus Meridus, was the secretly appointed and adopted heir of Emperor Caesar Aurelius and would have been Caesar, if it were not for the treachery of Commodus. He stood with the other men, who were mostly criminals and deserters. All of them were supposed to die on this day.

The crowds hushed as the theatrically-costumed Orator raised his voice to tell the saga of the famous Battle of Carthage, which depicted the superior Roman armies laying siege to the African city of Carthage they would ultimately annihilate the Phoenician Barbarian Hordes who were holed-up inside.

The Gladiator, well-educated in battle history and strategy, knew the outcome of this "reenactment" which was about to occur. He understood that he and his fellow combatants, men he had lived with and trained with, and fought side-by-side over the last few years, were to play the fatal role of the slaughtered Carthaginians as the choreographed drama was about to unfold.

"Anyone ever been in the army?" he asked his fellow soldiers, as they moved into the center of the arena. Several voices assented. *"Whatever comes out of these gates, we*'ve got *a better chance of survival if we* work *together.* Do you understand? *If we* stay *together we survive,"* said Maximus.

Suddenly, several gates of iron and timber simultaneously swung open on their hinges and out came six armored chariots manned with expert drivers and marksmen, and they bore down upon the small gathering of men who were moving towards the center of the arena. Maximus called the men to form a tight circle, with the outer ranks placing their five-foot tall rectangular shields on the sand, locked side by side so no arrows could pierce the phalanx. Those in the center stooped down behind them, raising their shields overhead to catch the barbed missiles that fell from above.

Some arrows quickly began to find their marks, but none of the men behind the phalanx of shields was harmed. Those who had not heeded Maximus, however, quickly became casualties, not because they were poor fighters, but because they made the deadly mistake of being isolated from their fellow shield-bearers. Being alone and unprotected on the right and left, they fell quickly to the rain of deadly arrows.

If you saw the film **Gladiator**, by Ridley Scott, starring Russell Crowe as Maximus, you will remember this scene. It was just moments later that Maximus directed the men into offensive tactics and, in chorus, "As one!" began systematically orchestrating the offensive, gaining an upset victory of these would-be trained assassins.

The bloody scene ends gloriously with Maximus, now upon a white horse, sword upraised in triumph, and his men raising their weapons with loud battle cries of victory!

The film stopped and I walked to the stage as the house lights were brought up. Two hundred and twenty-five men sat in silence, stirred in their spirits by the violence and heroic leadership of Maximus. Most had seen this film. Some, like me, had seen it several times. In the USA, since it came out in summer of 2000, Gladiator had been voted by a majority of men as one of their all-time favorite films. A more recent production, **300**, the story of the heroic stand of 300 Spartan warriors at the pass of Thermopylae in 480 BC, has also been ranked as a favorite film, especially among younger men.

Is it the violence? The blood? The weapons? Yes, we would probably say much of these characteristics have a kind of attraction to many men. However, not all men are drawn to battle scenes and swordplay, but we *are* all drawn to grit, courage and nobility…and the quest for justice. Women often don't get it, but guys do.

Those who had not heeded Maximus, however, quickly became casualties, not because they were poor fighters, but because they made the deadly mistake of being isolated from their fellow shield-bearers.

It was true for the men in this room as well, but by lifting out a single scene, there was something more. I asked the guys what they saw and there were several responses. One finally said, "The guys that listened to Maximus lived and then won." Yes, I said, but why else did they live and win? Another guy shouted out, *"Because they were protected by each others' shields!"*

Bingo.

If we travel back yet further in time, we find ourselves in the book of Judges. This book narrates the stories of twelve leaders who, for a season, were used by God as "Judges" ("judge" means "deliverer" in the original Hebrew language). Eleven of these Judges were men. One, Deborah, was a woman, and she kicked some serious behind!

I think it is important to put a side journey on Deborah in Judges 4. Deborah was a highly respected and courageous Prophetess who "Judged" Israel at the time. Many would come to her for insight, wisdom, dispute resolution, and to hear the "Word of the Lord" for their lives.

It is inferred in this story that God had appointed Barak, prophetically called through Deborah, as the appointed General-Deliverer of the army of the tribes of Naphtali and Zebulon. He was to lead the attack and conquer the Canaanites who had subjected Israel to "cruelty and violence for twenty years" (v.3).

He refused to lead, but instead said he would only go if Deborah were also by his side. *She* became the Deliverer and Barak's glory and privilege in history was eclipsed by this amazing Prophetess-Warrior. For me, I see so many guys out there that have told God the same thing. *"God, I will go and follow you, fight the good fight, and step out in faith if my beloved wife says I can (gives me permission). You see, Lord, as I understand my role, I must keep her happy first. That is what a loving husband is called to do in the Bible. If she goes, then, you betcha, I'll go too, with all of my heart."*

Now I understand I am on some seriously dangerous ground here. It will be easy to be misunderstood, especially by female readers.

Too many men have, in the name of scripture, disregarded their wives' opinions, warnings and God-given intuition that often uniquely allow them to see the whole picture better than we do. Leveraging the doctrine of submission and obedience that has been taught in many churches that women are to "submit to their husbands" (Ephesians 5:22; I Peter 3:1), some men have used the Word of God like a hammer to "wear the pants in the family" and have it our way most or all of the time. I have done this in the past, and I will confess that some of the scars that I bear tell the true story of how God disciplined me because I did not listen to, or honor, my wife.

However, we are clearly called to lead, nurture, serve, and protect our wives and children. This is actually pretty simple to do. Love and obey

God with all of our heart, soul, mind, and strength first and foremost. Wife and family come a distant second as a standalone priority. However, in that total loving of God is the role, duty, and even mandate of loving our wives in the same way as Christ loves His church…and died for her[1]. Yet we must monitor the *primacy* of our devotion to God. Look at Luke 14:25-27 where Jesus is about to deliver one of his tougher statements:

> *Large crowds were traveling with Jesus, and turning to them, he said: "If anyone comes to me and does not hate his father and mother, his wife and children, his brothers and sisters—yes, even his own life—he cannot be my disciple. And anyone who does not carry his cross and follow me cannot be my disciple.*

Jesus was pretty clear that our love for our families should be *such a distant second* in our hearts that it can be described as the chasm between "hate" and our love for God. I wrote it was *simple*, not *easy*. It is the simple things that are sometimes the most difficult to put into practice! We will explore the fine line of sacrificially serving our wives and families, while simultaneously following Jesus with humble courage in later chapters.

The call to repentance

> *Again the Israelites did evil in the eyes of the LORD, and for seven years he gave them into the hands of the Midianites. Because the power of Midian was so oppressive, the Israelites prepared shelters for themselves in mountain clefts, caves and strongholds. Whenever the Israelites planted their crops, the Midianites, Amalekites and other eastern peoples invaded the country. They camped on the land and ruined the crops all the way to Gaza and did not spare a living thing for Israel… they invaded the land to ravage it. Midian so impoverished the Israelites that they cried out to the LORD for help.*

> *When the Israelites cried to the LORD because of Midian, he sent them a prophet, who said, "This is what the LORD, the God of Israel, says: I brought you up out of Egypt, out of the land of*

slavery. I snatched you from the power of Egypt and from the hand of all your oppressors. I drove them from before you and gave you their land. I said to you, 'I am the LORD your God; do not worship the gods of the Amorites, in whose land you live.' But you have not listened to me."

--Judges 6:1-10

Forty years of peace follows because of Deborah's influence and leadership. It might be a good idea for you to open chapter 6 and carefully read it before continuing with this book.

The first verse in Judges 6 begins with the words: *"Again the Israelites did evil in the eyes of the LORD."* Later verses describe how the worship of Baal and Asherah had replaced or co-existed with the worship of Yahweh[2]. God had either been abandoned by idolatry, or He had simply been "included" as one of several deities. God sends a nomadic horde of Midianites, desert pirates, to inflict pain and suffering upon Israel.

For seven years, at the time when the crops were planted and growing, the Midianites would swarm into the land of Israel and destroy the promising produce. Then they would steal their livestock and move on. It grew so bad, year after year, that many of God's people had been driven permanently from their homes and villages and had built hiding places in the hillsides and caves. Essentially, many were what we would call homeless. And like so many other times in Israel's history, they cried out to God for deliverance, and He heard their cries.

I have observed many people who seem to want to be airlifted out of their troubles, to shortcut across the stadium grass to avoid difficulty, or be able to avoid the consequences of their foolish choices or disobedience to God. I have been guilty in the past of taking advantage of God's grace and had found myself looking for a kind of "get out of jail free" card from Him. *"Make it go away, Father, and I won't do it again,"* I promised. *"Make my harsh words be forgotten by my wife or help my boss to overlook me, yet again, for being late to his meeting,"* or more commonly, *"I'll read the Word or pray...tomorrow."*

God's mercy is overwhelming, as is His unmerited forgiveness, because of Christ's pardoning and atoning blood, but He is also committed to spare no expense for us to grow into Christ's image. Let's look at a tough passage:

My son, do not make light of the Lord's discipline, and do not lose heart when he rebukes you, because the Lord disciplines those he loves, and he punishes everyone he accepts as a son. Endure hardship as discipline; God is treating you as sons. For what son is not disciplined by his father?

-- Hebrews 12:5

We do not often hear or read messages on how He validates His Fatherhood to us as sons by rebuking (*"scourging"* in the NKJV) every son He receives with training and discipline.

Yes, sometimes reaping what we have sown must occur. It is a precept of the Word of God. And it can *really hurt,* hurt so much that you never, ever, want to take that pathway again. The good news is that He walks lovingly with us through those consequences along the way.

This is the condition of "discipline" that the Israelites were experiencing at this moment in history. These were times when His people, like you and me, must see and understand the reality of our circumstances, take responsibility, repent in our hearts before the Lord, receive mercy and forgiveness, and walk in a new direction. Many times for me, He has also made me bear the consequences of my choices, as well as provide the grace and forgiveness I needed to walk upright without guilt before Him.

Among our Christian friends there is a married couple that has gotten in big trouble by over mortgaging their home. I watched them refinance over and over, go on expensive trips, throw large social events, and join an expensive country club, mostly with non-earned borrowed money. When the mortgage crisis came and their interest rates began to climb, they cried foul because the large banking institution that sold them this debt did not require proof of income and loaned them too much money! They were praying for God to "deliver them," yet would not own up to their foolish and irresponsible management of an asset, their home, which God gave them to steward for Him. If they get bailed-out now, it is likely that they will again resort to the same frivolous behavior.

So, God did not send the Deliverer to Israel. Instead, He sent a *prophet.* We don't know this guy's name, but he apparently traveled through many villages, to the caves and temporary shelters, to deliver

God's message. He first reminded them of how God had saved them as a nation, out of Egypt, by His power and goodness. He then gave them this country, their land of promise, flowing with blessings. The messenger then delivered the diagnosis of why they were in such hard straits. God *allowed* them to be ravaged by the Midianites due to their disobedience and worldly idolatry. He let them stew in that for awhile.

Next scene we see begins in verses 11-15:

The angel of the LORD came and sat down under the oak in Ophrah that belonged to Joash the Abiezrite, where his son Gideon was threshing wheat in a winepress to keep it from the Midianites. When the angel of the LORD appeared to Gideon, he said, "The LORD is with you, mighty warrior." "But sir," Gideon replied, "if the LORD is with us, why has all this happened to us? Where are all his wonders that our fathers told us about when they said, 'Did not the LORD bring us up out of Egypt?' But now the LORD has abandoned us and put us into the hand of Midian."

Figure 1 – the distribution of the Tribes in post occupation Israel around the time of Gideon (about 1100 BC)

God, in his wisdom and foreknowledge, had decided to seek out this young man. God proclaims the good news that He is with him, and then, incredulously, calls him a "*mighty warrior!*"

This reminds us of when God sent Samuel to anoint a son of Jesse in I Samuel 16:7 as Israel's new king. Samuel assumes the first born son was the Lord's choice, but God corrects him and says, "*Man looks at the outward appearance, but the LORD looks at the heart.*" Then, as David came in from the field, the Lord said in verse 12, "*Rise and anoint him; he is the one.*"

God does not make bad choices. He did not with Gideon, and He did not with you. We often are tempted to "pedastalize" Bible heroes. We far too often do the same with our pastors, priests, worship leaders or elders. Historical men and women, especially those who participated in God's miraculous activities, are touchstones of inspiration for us. Too often, however, they become so highly revered that we unconsciously detach ourselves from the very real possibility that they are there to call us to similar, or even greater, actions of faith and sacrifice.

No one who ever lived inspires me like Jesus. Yet He expected His followers to surpass His powerful ministry on earth. In John 14:12, He says to His Disciples,

> *I tell you the truth, anyone who has faith in me will do what I have been doing. He will do even greater things than these, because I am going to the Father*

Wow. For a minute, I thought *I* was on the hook, but good thing Jesus was talking with His disciples, the *mighty* twelve. Now there are some "Studs" of faith!

Not. There I go, "pedastalizing" again! They were common men though chosen by Jesus. Like God chose Gideon…like God chose you and me.

The words are clear and to each one of us who knows Christ, "*he who believes in me*" is the *only* prerequisite.

Could it be that the God who chose David to be King as a youth, and who sought out Gideon hiding in the winepress in his mid-twenties, would choose you and me? I believe so. And, if you have not heard the soft, penetrating voice of the Spirit of God before, I believe that today He calls *you* to be a mighty warrior!

Alone

Let's take a few minutes and explore Gideon's condition. Firstly, he was alone. Men, like you and me, know immediately what this means, because we are often alone in a crowd. We have all been raised in a culture that praises individualism like it is a religion. Songs like **My Way**, lyrics written by Paul Anka, ring true to this philosophy, and it has shaped us more than deep tissue plastic surgery. It has carved patterns of behavior into our souls to the extent that it is difficult now to differentiate it from real masculinity.

And it is deadly. We are far too often, alone, flying solo. It is also *lonely*. Men like women, were designed as interdependent social beings.

Who me? Yes you! Read what Solomon wrote:

Two are better than one, because they have a good return for their work: If one falls down, his friend can help him up. But pity the man who falls and has no one to help him up! Also, if two lie down together, they will keep warm. But how can one keep warm alone? ***Though one may be overpowered, two can defend themselves.*** *A cord of three strands is not quickly broken. (bold is mine)*

-- Ecclesiastes 4:9-12

In the book, **The Friendless American Male,** the author offers a test to see whether or not our loner style is from God. He writes, "Is this aspect of my personality a positive attribute or destructive? If it is destructive, you can bet that God did not make you that way."[3]

You might say, "But I can't seem to find any friends." Well, I believe God calls you to have at least 2-3 close Christ-follower friends. In addition to what he writes in Ecclesiastes, Solomon writes in Proverbs that "A man who has friends must himself be **friendly,** there is a friend that sticks closer than a brother" (Proverbs 18:24, New King James Version) so ask Him to intersect your life with the friends that He has for you, then go out and be friendly, press in to a small group or Bible study, and expect your efforts and prayers to be rewarded! It could save your life.

Hiding

Men are especially gifted at hiding, more than women. When God visits Gideon, He not only finds him alone, He finds him hiding, keeping his head down in case he is discovered by the Midianites who are due to return at any time. He also emulated many of us by hiding in the winepress of *work*. When you are alone, it is much easier to hide. Men can also compartmentalize almost anything, so while we might live in one compartment, we grow expert at hiding in another; mostly we build our winepresses to hide from ourselves.

I learned to hide early on. I was nine years old and had gone to see a double feature with some buddies on a Saturday afternoon. The first was **"The House on the Haunted Hill"** and the second was **"Thirteen Ghosts."** That night I could not sleep. Shadows turned into beings of darkness; headless monsters came for me with groping hands. My only solution was to dig down deep under all of my sheets and blankets and cringe, waiting for my brief life to end. I knew it was over.

When I awoke in the morning, alive and well, I convinced myself that it was my hiding skills that had protected me—not the fact that there were no real creatures roaming my room at night. I learned to cover up pretty well.

One dynamic of management is that one manager can only truly give oversight and coaching to five to seven direct reports. We see some similar ratios when it comes to family units. Yet many of us have somehow been persuaded that church units of 300, 1,000 or even 10,000 are capable of growing strong disciples with far fewer leaders providing care and mentoring for those who need it. Is this one reason for the anemic condition of so many churches? Who will step into the gap?

When I turned thirteen, the night terrors faded, but it was replaced with a deeper hiding in the dark. I was hiding from myself, my family, and others; and deeply ashamed of the onset of habitual masturbation. And I was fearful of the young man that was emerging and confused about my sexuality. Finally, I covered up my lack of courage, and lived in a naked fear that others would somehow discover what a poser I really was.

God had clearly rejected me for my evil behaviors. Looking back, I had actually dug down deeper under the covers.

As I grew larger and taller, I discovered football. My size and developing speed allowed me to get plenty of playing time, and the camaraderie of the team combined with the physical blocking and tackling of other young men helped shore up my teetering confidence. A steady girl friend did wonders to lift my self-esteem as well. However, all of these were only a substitute to replace the bed covers. My hiding became more sophisticated…but God had a better way planned for me.

Developing the Squad Leader

Our men's leadership team identified that the tendency to be alone and hide behind the armor of our self-fashioned winepresses, was a major obstacle to overcome if we called men to become real with each other. Therefore a few of us trained for what we later called "Squad Leaders." More than just a facilitator for five or six men at the table, we saw this role as that of an under shepherd, with a responsibility to love and nurture these men beyond the ninety minute weekly gathering. We practiced learning how to create an environment for authentic dialogue in a small group setting. And, we laid out a rule that *"what is said at the table, stays at the table."*

After the time of teaching, usually 30 to 40 minutes, our Squad Leaders would open up with a subject-related question that gradually required *real* conversation for the men. For the first couple of weeks, the Squad Leader often had to lead out by transparently letting his guard down, so the men could see that the table was a safe place for them to open their hearts with one another. Gradually, the whole group found themselves opening up, many for the first time. There were serious moments, mixed with laughter, and sometimes tears shed as the men began to realize that they all shared experiences akin to one another.

Disqualified

Gideon's less than enthusiastic response sounds a great deal like us. First, he immediately questions God's judgment: "God is with me? Are you kidding? Where have you been? Do you have any clue what we have been going through here, Lord? I heard the prophet's words but its clear God has abandoned us to these barbarians! This is going to be the eighth year in a row that these accursed Midianites are heading into town to steal and destroy; can't you see that I am working down here trying to make a living for my family? Do you see how I fear for their lives? Do you have any idea what it feels like to be a constantly terrified man? Me... a mighty warrior?...sure!"

In order for us to understand Gideon's cynicism and disbelief, we have to try to get into his sandals for a moment. Let's look at Gideon's body language and where he is standing. He is alone in a winepress, his head is down, and he is bowed over, hiding. As best as he knows it, he is doing his job as a husband and a father. Since he was a young teen, he had been living with a sense of danger, powerlessness, and despair. And we thought Jr. High was tough!

Each year, the layers of shame, injustice, and impotence had accumulated with no relief and no hope in sight. Even though God had sent his prophet to call the nation to repentance, explaining why the Lord had lifted his blessing from Israel, he still must have felt that his life would remain in the shambles forever. His wife and son probably saw him as a coward at heart, but what could he do? He was the least in his family, the lowest clan in his tribe, and it was the lowest tribe of Israel. God had the wrong address and the wrong guy.

> We are all in the same human, carnal bucket. Yes, I may be able to declare that I am dead to sin, but last I checked, sin is not dead to me!

The point is: Gideon was just a guy. Actually, by his own description, he was a loser. Perhaps he felt like you or me. He was alone, he was hiding in his work, and he felt incredibly disqualified as a man and follower of God.

I was a washed-up pastor. To make things worse, when I got back into the business world and began to succeed, a marriage that had been on the ropes for years, failed...or more accurately, I failed in my marriage.

Disqualified? You bet. Finished for significance with God?? I believed it was true for me.

Bullies can *really* hurt

I awakened to a clear winter morning, as a fresh canopy of snow embraced the ground. We heard school was cancelled on the radio…it was a "Snow Day!" I was twelve and my baby brother, Bruce, was five. He looked up to me, and I knew it was my job to look after him, even though he could really be a brat at times. Brothers can share a special bond; we did then, and thanks to our common faith, it is even stronger today. We like to talk on the phone and play golf or go scuba diving together, whenever time or budgets, permit.

After breakfast that morning, my mom was relieved that we were headed outdoors, overstuffed with thick wool coveralls, black rubber buckle boots over our shoes, and even heavier jackets.

Today instead of setting up snow forts in our *cul de sac*, and having snowball wars with the neighborhood boys, we were headed to where many of my junior high schoolmates were, the Turnpike Bridge. It was Bruce's first time and our first real sledding adventure together.

Long Island, New York, where we spent most of our childhood, was pretty flat. You needed hills for sled runs and the only hill close by was at the freeway interchange one and a half miles away. So with our two double-rail Flexi-flyers, we set off for the bridge.

When we arrived, there were already about thirty or forty kids of all ages making runs down the hill. I knew many of them. There was one kid there who I was not fond of, Robert Pilsner, a thirteen year old, with his nine-year-old brother Jimmy. You may have had a Robert Pilsner in your life growing up. He was not the prototype oversized bully; he was good looking, an amazing athlete, and smart, but he had a mean streak. His brother was even worse. Because I was bigger, Robert liked to belittle me or, on rare occasions, shove me around sometimes. Seeing him filled me with apprehension and I felt my stomach begin to churn.

The sledding rules worked like this: since there were only one or two good launch points, you had to wait in line to gain access to the steepest, scariest spots. No cuts. One kid was stationed at the center of the bridge as lookout. The snow was still hard-packed and had not melted on the freeway lanes in both directions, so if you really wanted a good ride, you had to descend down the steepest hillside that was closest to the eastern end of the bridge structure, and then traverse two lanes of turnpike, cross the center island median, and then cross the other two lanes going in the opposite direction. Then we would walk up the west side of the bridge and get back in line. Of course, if you were a metal-rail sledder, none of this silly round disc or plastic toboggan stuff would do. We're talking sharp red rails, fastened under an oak plank platform. These were poke-your-eye-out rails, impaled through your spleen, rails. You knew you needed to wax the blades to get the speed right so as not to get stuck in the middle of the far lane. Timing was everything. The possibility of being flattened by a Semi truck made it all the more fun!

I had to first do some "soft" training runs with Bruce. He had never seen such a hill like this and he was a bit cautious. After a couple of times, we climbed back up the hill, breathing heavily, and got in line. This was going to be the real deal. Bruce and I were going to run the gauntlet together. There was nothing to be alarmed about because the extra weight of his body on top of mine would give us enough speed to go the full distance.

Did I mention that mothers were not allowed near the bridge?

My brother set his sled to the side to ready for our tandem launch and just then, Jimmy Pilsner stepped into our starting position. Now Robert was there, as was my little brother, so even though I was scared, I told Jimmy to get back in the line. He just scoffed at me and then reached down and grabbed Bruce's sled and threw it down the hill where it whizzed by the heads and feet of several innocent children and stopped some 50 yards at the bottom of the hill.

My response was instant: I grabbed Jimmy's sled from his hands and was going to toss his down the same way. But Robert grabbed my arm and threatened to do me serious bodily harm if I followed through. This was the moment of truth. As I looked at my crying brother, who was obviously looking for some sort of justice from his hero big brother, I made the choice.

Down went Jimmy's sled. Now I was close to the edge of the hill, and suddenly Robert was on my back and we were tumbling down the hill for what seemed an eternity, rolling over and over each other. In the fall, my knit ski cap came down and completely covered my eyes and nose...I was totally in the dark when we stopped. Immediately, punches began to be rained on my head and back as I tried to stand but could not. I yelled *"I give, I give!"* and it was over. The "fight" lasted 10 seconds, max.

Removing my cap, I stood, surrounded by classmates, some smirking at how easy it was to "take" Artie Hobba. Some were looking now with fear and admiration at Robert. I was a beaten boy. I put my head down, gathered my brother's sled, and trudged up the hill taking Bruce's hand as we turned towards home, a thoroughly vanquished "wanna-be" hero.

My sadness and shame joined forces raining their own kind of punches on my soul. As I ascended the four concrete steps to my front porch and opened the door, my mom was surprised we were home so soon. I could tell she was a bit put off by the scene she was taking in. As I wept, I told her the story, hoping for some small affirmation for at least standing up for Bruce. To my chagrin, she refused to let me back into the house. She demanded, with sternness, that I go to Robert Pilsner's house and call him out onto his front yard and give him a beating he would not soon forget. In my humiliated condition, she might as well ask me to fly. Weeping, I put my head down one more time and pushed my way into the house, escaping to my room to nurse my wounded soul.

Now my mom was a great lady. In fact, as she aged, she got sweeter and more caring. She became not only my favorite personal cheerleader as a boy, but also throughout my adult life. More importantly, she was a faithful and godly woman of intercessory prayer for me, my siblings, and our kids. She recently "graduated" full of years to be with her Jesus, and her husband who had preceded her. At her memorial service, we all honored her love and her legacy.

This day, though, she did not understand that her eldest boy had become, over time, a "chicken," and that Robert, and a couple other seventh and eighth graders, had taken the fight out of me soon after we had moved to this town five years earlier. It was not until my mid-twenties, after some pastoral counseling including deep inner healing by the Holy Spirit, and walking through forgiving each of the bullies in my life…by name, that my courage returned.

Courage is resistance to fear, mastery of fear, not absence of fear. Except a creature be part coward, it is not a compliment to say it is brave.

-- Mark Twain

At the precise moment that God called Gideon a mighty warrior, I bet he felt like a chicken. For seven years, he had taken a beating. Maybe you have memories, distant or recent, of being beaten down. Maybe there lingers a destructive habit in your life that controls you. Maybe the leadership of your home has been abducted by your wife, or even your children. Has your boss or a past boss been a bully? This wound in a man's soul runs deeper than any I know. It shapes what we see every day in the mirror. As a man, I am still embarrassed today to write this story of my public defeat. I wish I could go back in time and reclaim my honor.

Joshua was afraid when he arrived in the Promised Land, so much so that God had to personally tell him *four times* in one sitting to *"be strong and courageous,"* and He had to make some big promises to get Joshua off the dime. What about Jesus, the Son of God? While never sinning, He still asked His Father three times in His final night to change the game plan. Do you think he was scared? I think so. But He, like Joshua and eventually even Gideon, overcame their fears with transcendent courage from God.

For you and me, God stands before us right now and calls you a "mighty warrior." No matter what your age or place in life, He has "game" for you…to be a difference maker…a Kingdom expander…and a deliverer to the oppressed. This is a good time to close the book and pray alone. Open your heart to Him, as your healer. Let Him affirm you as His son. Let His hope and courage flood softly into your core being. Listen for the whisper of His presence.

Here's what Mike Gregory, Leader, Men's Prayer Ministry wrote:

The major change that occurred in my heart and attitude from before the Core 300 program and after was that, for 30 years, I had tried with all my heart to follow Jesus, but I kept my head down and tried to avoid conflict of any kind…especially in the spiritual realm. When pressed upon by the darkness in and around me, the best I would do is play defense and yield as little ground as possible.

Today, I am a warrior. When I wake up, I awaken to the invisible battle on this fallen world that surrounds me, and I willingly take

*it on, equipped with God's power and His armor. And I take it on
offense not defense. Although I do not win every fight, I have set
my face for and found victory as God's mighty warrior!"*

Table talk

1. Why do men repeatedly try to solve their problems on their own?
    How well has that worked for you?

2. What is the greatest fear you have about disclosing to another
    those things from which you have been hiding?

Core conditioning

Gideon was renamed (Jeru-baal), God changed Abram's name
(Abraham), Jacob (Israel), and Saul of Tarsus (Paul) as well. Get away
from your home or workplace, turn off any technology, and find a place to
be alone with God. Maybe the desert works best, or a beach or lakeside is
convenient, or taking a walk in the depth of the woods. Read a few
passages in scripture about these great men. Be still in quiet thanksgiving
and worship for a while. Wait on Him and then ask God your true name.
Listen for the whisper or impression for the Holy Spirit. Let Him love on
you a while, and write that name or impression down somewhere in your
Bible. If nothing comes, continue to ask Him to show you...and wait
patiently on His answer.

Chapter Three:

Blood on the Floor

"Called to War" contains the much needed "medicine" to heal men's souls today. For some, it may be their lifeline for salvation from death"

— Sam Jackson, World Vision

The dialogue between the Stranger and Gideon continues: in chapter six, verse thirteen:

"But sir," Gideon replied, "if the LORD is with us, why has all this happened to us? Where are all his wonders that our fathers told us about when they said, 'Did not the LORD bring us up out of Egypt?' But now the LORD has abandoned us and put us into the hand of Midian." The LORD turned to him and said, "Go in the strength you have and save Israel out of Midian's hand. Am I not sending you?" "But Lord," Gideon asked, "how can I save Israel? My clan is the weakest in Manasseh, and I am the least in my family." The LORD answered, "I will be with you, and you will strike down all the Midianites together."

47

--Judges 6:13-16

Gideon's situation, like that of most good men I know today, was complicated. Firstly, he wanted to provide for and protect his family. Secondly, he could not do that if he was not a good farmer-businessman. He had to make sure his *assets* (food, livestock, farmland, shelter, tools, and supplies) were producing what he needed and that they were protected from the Midianites.

Gideon was facing the most awesome being to ever place foot upon the earth, the "angel of the Lord," and they were having a chat as if they were casual acquaintances! Gideon did not realize that this was what many theologians believe to be a pre-incarnate visitation of the Son of God, commonly referred to as a *Christophene*. His response, however, indicates that he had been giving thought to the prophet's recent call to repentance, and that he had even possibly wondered how *he* might become a leader to drive the accursed Midianite horde from his people.

Regardless, his response to this stranger was to bring well-rehearsed arguments that had passed through his mind many times before. This messenger had appeared, uninvited, in the midst of a mundane workday to convince Gideon that he could play the key role in utterly defeating a seemingly unbeatable foe, an enemy beyond numbering. In the recorded dialogue, "But sir"... Gideon complains about how God had done all of these great things in the past, but that now He had abandoned His people. The surname Gideon used here was "sir," or one of a man showing respect for another. The Hebrew word is *adon*.

Then a profound change occurs in Verse 14. It says, "The Lord then *turned to him...*" which literally means that He turned towards him and faced him directly, face to face.

My family was a part of that first generation that grew up watching TV. In 1963, we had the first color TV on our block. After eating dinner and washing dishes, the ritual developed for the six of us to gather in the living room where my dad and I would lie on the floor, my brother and two sisters would sit on the couch, and my mom would sit in her chair.

Until my brother got big enough, my role was to carry the two galvanized trashcans from behind the kitchen to the front yard sidewalk on Sunday night after dinner. It was a Sunday night and I was a typical pre-teenager...just beginning to suffer from a unique kind of deafness to parental direction. I had forgotten, again, to put out the trash. The show went to commercial and about thirty seconds into it, my Dad, his back to me said, "Art, did you put out the trash?" I said I had not, but would do it on the next commercial. I watched in amazement as a Timex watch was bound to the propeller of an outboard motor and immersed into a clear tank of water by John Cameron Swayze. He turned on the motor and revved it up into a frothy soup. Lifting the propeller, the camera zoomed in to the watch and we could all see that it was still working. "Timex takes a licking and keeps on ticking," Swayze said. The show returned and about five minutes later my dad said, *"Son, did you take out the trash yet?"* I said, "Sorry, I'll get it on the *next* commercial."

When the commercials came again, there were a couple of the funny ones and we all laughed together. When the show returned, my dad said, *"Art, did you take out the trash yet?"* I said no, but I would on the next commercial. At this point, my dad *turned to face me.* I had noticed that his face had begun to redden…that was not a good sign. The direct eye contact I encountered would have melted metal. Then he said it simply, forcefully, *"**Take the trash out, NOW!**"*

He turned to face me. …Like God turned toward Gideon. At that moment, my father *grew* in size and authority to his full stature. He became that person who I respected, loved, and feared above any other...and the one man who could put a world of hurt upon me. My attitude and hearing improved dramatically. I had no option and without hesitation, responded immediately.

This perspective change happened to Gideon as well. There was a distinct difference seen in the narrative in how he saw this visitor. Gideon stopped addressing him as a nosy bystander and began addressing "Him" as Lord or Master using the reverent Hebrew word for God (*adonay*). His complaining about God as a third party in the conversation moved to giving his "Lord" reasons why *he personally* was not a good enough candidate for the immense calling God was placing upon him.

It may be that God is using this moment now *to face you directly.* Maybe His piercing gaze and thunderous whisper are speaking to your heart. Above the white noise and trivialities of life, eyeball to eyeball, He is calling you to the next level. You are made of better stuff than what you have settled for. I know this has been true for me and the many men who have experienced the **The Warrior** series. I pray this is so for you as well.

The angel of the Lord is now fully recognized by Gideon as God, and Gideon changes his tune in two significant ways. Firstly, he addresses Him as the **Lord**. He uses the word that is only reserved for God in scripture. Secondly, he goes from complaining about his current conditions to a series of humble statements as to why he was disqualified for God's calling. His confession is a vital step here…and it is a vital step with us as well.

In the last chapter, I referred to Ecclesiastes where Solomon wrote, *"two are better than one."* Gideon realized that he was utterly weak in his independence and aloneness. Gideon confesses his sense of powerlessness, and then God again prophesies to Gideon that he now sees him becoming a man partnered with God, *"I will be with you, and you will strike down all the Midianites together."*

> *Gideon replied, "If now I have found favor in your eyes, give me a sign that it is really you talking to me. Please do not go away until I come back and bring my offering and set it before you." And the LORD said, "I will wait until you return."*

> --Judges 6:17-18

Gideon is out of excuses, but encouraged by God's third affirmation and willingness to partner with him. However, he needs some time to process all of this and to respond appropriately, so he asks if God would wait while he prepares an offering of worship. God says he will wait and Gideon hurries off to make preparations.

I find it humorous, and yet heartwarming, that the Lord *waited* for him to prepare his offering. Funny because we see God apparently spending hours "killing time," sitting by a broken down winepress in some hole in the wall town in ancient Israel. Heartwarming, because he was committed to give Gideon the time he needed to reflect and think about the consequences of believing His message to him—that he was not what he believed himself to be, but what he had hoped and dreamed he could be, a Deliverer for his people.

Gideon goes home to prepare a sacrificial offering for his Divine guest. Now, this meal was *not* on his wife's menu for the day. Food and supplies, especially meat, were scarce. Scripture says, however, that he prepared a *substantial* meal of bread and a young goat.

Gideon went in, prepared a young goat, and from an ephah of flour, he made bread without yeast. Putting the meat in a basket and its broth in a pot, he brought them out and offered them to God under the oak. Let's pick up the story at verse 19:

> *The angel of God said to him, "Take the meat and the unleavened bread, place them on this rock, and pour out the broth." And Gideon did so. With the tip of the staff that was in his hand, the angel of the LORD touched the meat and the unleavened bread. Fire flared from the rock, consuming the meat and the bread. And the angel of the LORD disappeared. When Gideon realized that it was the angel of the LORD, he exclaimed, "Ah, Sovereign LORD! I have seen the angel of the LORD face to face!" But the LORD said to him, "Peace! Do not be afraid. You are not going to die."*

The revelation of divinity is now complete. Gideon moves from seeing the messenger as "sir" (*adon*-v.13) to Lord (*adonay*-v.15). However, Gideon now sees God revealed and is *afraid*. He addresses him as *Adonay Yahweh*. Lord, I AM, the ever present One. The God of Moses. For the rest of the story this young man's devotion, courage and powerful anointing finds its roots in this full and multidimensional appreciation of God.

The bread offering

The flour, which was the ultimate objective of the work he was doing when God interrupted his workday (sifting raw wheat in the winepress), was *precious*. It not only represented his work, but survival itself. In these times, money was not commonly used for commerce. The three most common things used for commerce and trade were: livestock, which varied in value by utility, such as pulling power or ability to produce milk or eggs; oil, made primarily from olives; and grain, most commonly used for making flour.

Flour was more valuable than sifted wheat, because it had already been ground for making bread. We already know that food and livestock were scarce, and now with the season of the Midianites yet again upon them, families were surely in the midst of hiding and hoarding their foodstuffs.

The story describes Gideon preparing one ephah of flour. An ephah was roughly three quarters of a bushel or 4.8 gallons. This amount of flour would make approximately 72 one-pound loaves of bread! The typical family, depending on its size, would consume two loaves per day, meaning Gideon prepared a gift of *over a month's supply of bread*, their core source of sustenance. Think of it as a full month's pay for your household during a recession.

The bread was unleavened, which in scripture, symbolizes an inner condition of the soul which is without guile or hypocrisy. Gideon's direct response to go home and prepare the sacrifice shows no hidden agenda here, not, *"I'll give You this, so You can give me more back."* There were no strings and it should be the same with us.

The "Prosperity Movement," as it came to be called, which swept our country in the 1970s and 1980s did much damage to many innocents. Again, when the **Prayer of Jabez** topped the New York Times Best Seller lists for several months in 2000, many people tried to read into Bruce Wilkinson's brief, contemplative masterpiece, a promise for wealth and expansion of properties and possessions. What the book spoke to my heart was to look to God as the one to expand our leadership and influence…to make a way through a childlike, submissive prayer. But unfortunately, many took it as a canned formula to strong arm God to cough up the goods through the supposed "magic" of repeating a prayer formula for 30 days.

One critic wrote insightfully:

> *The formula Wilkinson is teaching leaves no room for God to say "NO" or "WAIT." Faithfully pray the prayer of Jabez, and you've got God in a box. Yet the Bible teaches that when one trusts Christ, a relationship is begun with Him that is in part defined by submission to the will of God and recognition of His absolute right to do whatever He pleases with us.* [1]

This is not a positive or negative treatment of Jabez' prayer or Wilkinson's book, but of how people often pander towards shortcuts and alternatives rather than following a responsive, day-by-day obedience to the Word of God. As we shall see, that kind of authentic obedience will always, at some point, require *some blood on the floor.*

The young goat

Archeological records have shown that goats, lambs, and even young fawns have often been beloved family pets in ancient civilizations. The goat was, of the three, the most practical of family pets because it was an excellent source of milk and butter for the family with a mature goat providing a gallon or more of milk per day.

The young female goat here represents, at least to Gideon, *potential investment in the future.* Yet while the kid remained young and "cute," it would often become a favorite of one or more of the children, roaming the house, looking for affectionate head scratching from various family members, much like a dog or cat might today. The expectation of every family member was, unless the young goat was stolen by the Midianites or suffered an accident, it would be with the family for many years, giving birth to many kid goats and providing daily nourishment for the family.

We must try, as best we can, to imagine this scene as it was written by the scribe to an audience that would have the historical context of agrarian living in Middle Eastern 11th century B.C.

Gideon has an important guest waiting, a guest who could be divine and the bringer of hope to him and his family, maybe even an entire nation. He surprises his family, coming home early from work, and informs his wife that he needs a 30-day supply of flour baked into loaves right away, and then proceeds to personally haul the beloved goat outside, most probably to its bleating protests. The bleating was joined by one or more of the children who, at minimum, are fearful of what their Daddy is doing to their pet, and at worst are weeping and protesting profusely!

His wife is distraught because she sees a look in her husband's eyes that she has never seen before...and fearful, because it is the season of the Midianites. Now, more than ever, they need to hoard and hide what they have, not waste it on some stranger!

Gideon takes the kid (the *goat,* not one of his children) in his left arm pulling back the neck to expose the internal carotid arteries and cuts deeply with the knife in his right hand. The ground turns crimson as he captures the animal's life essence in a pot and begins to butcher the meat to prepare it for boiling. This same pot is what he will later bring to the Lord as his prepared meat offering of worship.

What was Gideon thinking and what must the conversation have been like with his wife, using up their precious supplies and murdering their family pet?

My wife and young son cringed when they heard me read this paragraph to them. My son identified the goat with his new puppy and immediately asked if God would require him to sacrifice his pet in order to prove he loved Him! Of course, I responded that his dog was safe. Jesus had become, once and for all time, the sin sacrifice for all who believed in Him.

The sacrificial letting of blood—the brutality of slitting the throat of a valuable animal is anathema to us today. But in the days of Gideon, it was commonplace, both because living on a farm required the butchering of animals to provide the protein they needed in their diets, and because the god of Ba'al, whom they worshipped, required the sacrifice of not only animals, but children as well.

God needed Gideon to offer up a sacrifice of worship…*costly* worship to Him before anything else could transpire. We all know intuitively that hardship for a disciple of Christ makes him or her all the stronger. History shows us that this was also true for the church throughout history. It was the blood of slain martyrs that spurred many European Christian outcasts to flee the persecution of the institutional Church during the immigration to the United States in the early formative years of our country.

Since then, we have watched our country gradually go soft. During my lifetime, being a Christian has lost it edge…its sacrifice…its cost. The new gods of pleasure and prosperity vied for our offerings, to which we readily sacrifice our earnings. Many teachers mix theologies to create a "mammonized" version of abundance and season it into a more popular version of capitalistic faith. Giving sacrificially, as well as church attendance and the acknowledgement of membership in a local community of believers, becomes optional.

But it was not so for Gideon. He gave at an intensity rarely seen in scripture. And he gave at a level that would embarrass most devoted American followers of Jesus.

As I write this, I am on a private retreat looking out my window at the silver green peaks of the breath taking mountains of Montecito California. My sanctuary is one I have visited often for the last twenty-five years…a holy monastery called the Immaculate Heart Center. This place has saved my life more than once and I find communion with my Savior at newer and deeper levels at every visit.

I arrive as usual, emotionally and spiritually drained and in need of a healing encounter with the Holy Spirit. He has never failed me in my quest for refilling and reorienting in my walk with Christ. Another common perspective that I bring to my retreat is an often smug internal unarticulated opinion of how spiritual I am…and advanced in my walk with God as compared to other men I know in these uniquely shallow times.

After an organic and sumptuous dinner prepared by the sisters who attend us, my first stop is always the great library. It is filled with thousands of books, many of the liturgical and monastic writings by men and women who have followed the calling to a life of quiet yet sacrificial service to God, inspired by the Desert Fathers of the 4th through 6th centuries A.D.

The next morning began with prayer and sacred reading from a wonderful devotional book by Sister Jeremy Hall. In her discourse was the modern application of the lifestyle prescribed by Saint Benedict, the Father of Western Monasticism. She is known by her constituents as one of the living "Great Ones"…a living Catholic legend.

After a short fourteen hours here, I am suddenly abased in the knowledge of how truly superficial and self centered I am. Sister and God have successfully tag teamed to take me on a clear descent into reality. As a sharp, 89 year old sage, she writes:

Chapters 4-7 of the Rule (of Benedict) indicate the essentials that are to be learned in this school (of monastic living), first in the general listing of the tools of good works and then in three discreet chapters on obedience, restraint of speech and humility. These are virtues of Christ himself and are far more surely and authentically acquired by those who seek to be possessed by Christ than by those who seek to possess the virtues.[2]

How truly humbling it is to realize that the life I have lived as a follower of Jesus for forty years is one marked primarily by me inviting the Spirit of Christ into MY day—seeking His aid, assurance, forgiveness, and provision as I seek to accomplish my hourly and daily agenda. The idol of a "day well lived" guides me on my pilgrimage, seeking to maximize the time God has so graciously provided. How noble of me! How *wasteful.*

The protestant movement that began in earnest under the inspiration of Martin Luther five hundred years ago has systematically buried and abandoned the ways of Catholicism so far away that we have interred the good with the bad. Benedict's disciple speaks to me as a prophet today when she gently calls me to be *"possessed* by Christ." I am *not* to bring Him along on my journey...He seeks to bring me along on His, living through me. I see how God needed to bring Gideon to a similar realization.

> I am *not* to bring God along on my journey...He invites me to come along on His...

At the time of the weekend of my retreat, our world was submerged into the midst of a serious recession. It has been dubbed "The Great Recession" by the media and analysts due to how deeply it has violated the historical trends of annual economic growth and its global impact. Time will tell if we can pull out of this downward spiral, back into a semblance of nationwide prosperity, or if we must adjust to a new norm of "less is more."

One thing is certain: life, for almost all of us, has profoundly changed and most likely will never revert back to the consumerism that preceded the turndown. Values and priorities have shifted, and for many—notwithstanding the harsh difficulties that arise for those of us who have lost jobs, savings, and even homes—I believe it has been for the better.

Many of the women I know seem to be more susceptible to fear than men, or at least they are more expressive of their anxieties. We all share concerns...for the security and the welfare of our households, but men are more likely to feel the agony of being disconnected from the unhealthy umbilical lifeline between career success and self-worth.

If we are feeling the pinch and pain of our current economy, imagine how Gideon felt! Seven years of having *all* he had worked for, all he had inherited from generations past, put at serious risk. The threat of loss each year from the Midianites was significant and life threatening. Hunger and death were at the door at all times. If God knew Gideon's dire circumstances and still called him a mighty warrior and the instrument of deliverance for a nation, what does He say to you and me today?

Another way Gideon is like many of us is that he most probably had dreams of freedom...or maybe fantasies of greatness. He may have plotted for revenge and retribution upon his enemies who had deeply harmed his village and family. These dreams and hopes must have come alive when he heard the stories of great men and women of God, like Moses, Joshua and Deborah, overcoming insurmountable odds and bringing deliverance to a downtrodden people who were enslaved and abused by pagan taskmasters. These great leaders were again brought to mind with the message of the prophet, calling the people to repent of idolatry and to return to the authentic, monotheistic worship of the Lord.

For us, dreams of significance are often spawned in our hearts as we watch great men portrayed in films, or perhaps we are inspired by a sports hero we admire. The Bible is also filled with incredible, even miraculous, feats of courage and faith done by common men like you and me.

In his book, **Crazy Love**[3], Francis Chan writes about a level of giving that defies financial planning logic. In a recent radio interview, he said:

What I have normally done

When I feel God tugging at my heart to make an extraordinary sacrifice or even an ordinary one, the first thing I think is: "What will my wife think of this idea?" I walk through the scenario in my mind. If it does not look good, I begin to negotiate with God. "What about a partial down payment, Lord?" Then I'll explain to Him why I can't pony up what He is asking for. If I still sense Him quietly standing there waiting for me to say yes, I might even whine a bit, or delay further.

Finally, oftentimes, I commit to do what he asks. It often does not result in an easy-to-see "one hundredfold" blessing, but there is a settling...an easy peace with God, and the fresh presence of His partnership. I feel a kinship with God as the Spirit walks alongside me. He brings an abundant peace when I walk as a simple steward of His assets.

God is looking for people who take him at his Word and who are "crazy in love" with Him. I am meeting more and more people who are totally selling out for God

Francis takes his own advice, choosing an almost Spartan lifestyle for him, his wife and four children, and giving away all of the seven figure profits he gained from his recent best sellers. He has discovered the freedom and deep joy of giving as an act of pure worship and gained the richness of internal satisfaction that his generosity, wisely invested in others much more impoverished than himself, has its earthly and heavenly rewards.

In the following passage, the prophet Malachi records what God has said through him. Here, God chooses to role-play with himself as the speaker, playing both sides of a dialogue between God and Israel:

"Return to me, and I will return to you," says the LORD Almighty. "But you ask, 'How are we to return?' Will a man rob God? Yet you rob me. But you ask, 'How do we rob you?' In tithes and offerings. You are under a curse—the whole nation of you—because you are robbing me. Bring the whole tithe into the storehouse, that there may be food in my house."

-- Malachi 3:7b-10a

The diagnosis is made. God discloses that Israel, most assuredly exemplified by her leaders, had compromised in their *devotion* to God as displayed in their lack of giving thankfully to Him. Can you sense the *pain and sadness* He is communicating here at being robbed by His own children? Malachi writes in this last book of the Old Covenant that God's people had become self-deluded into thinking that they were meeting God's requirements for giving.

God continues His solo dialogue with a challenge filled with hope, and a promise which stands firm to this day:

"Test me in this," says the LORD Almighty, "and see if I will not throw open the floodgates of heaven and pour out so much blessing that you will not have room enough for it. I will prevent pests from devouring ("rebuke the devourer," in the KJV) your

crops, and the vines in your fields will not cast their fruit," says the LORD Almighty. Then all the nations will call you blessed, for yours will be a delightful land."

-- Malachi 3:10b-12

In this passage is one of the cardinal cornerstones of *defensive* spiritual warfare and a foundation of protection that is missed by many believers who have rejected the concept of tithing as a *starting point* for giving. If we will be *thankful* to Him as the provider of the 100%, and give Him the tenth (literal meaning of tithe), He will bless the 90% that remains so that there is a crazy (there is that word again) level of abundant provision! These Jews were uncovered and exposed to the "Devourer," much like the Israelites were during the days of Gideon. The additional protection comes as a bonus. Look at what God says here: *"He will 'rebuke the devourer' for our sakes, nor will untimely circumstances rob you of the fruit of your labor or your vine prematurely drop its fruit before it is ripe."*[4]

"Rebuke" is the same word that was used another time in the Old Testament when Moses "rebuked" the water of the Red Sea so that it became dry ground.[5] The "Devourer" can be figuratively interpreted as including the operation of satanic forces, because its meaning is far beyond the NIV substitute word, "pests." It also includes the meaning of "that which wastes away," "slays by the sword," and that which "consumes or devours as in a roaring fire."

Some of us are reminded at this point of painful losses in investments or other assets we had thought of as "safe" in barns and silos laid up for retirement or college funds. This is why Jesus said our labors should be for treasures in heaven, not earth.

Finally, allow me to wade in a little bit deeper on this point. Some teachers are of the persuasion that tithing is an Old Testament practice that was done away with by the New Covenant, which "swept away" the Levitical Law. This is not entirely true. We still honor and treasure the Ten Commandments and much of God's wisdom, precepts, and principles given to us by Moses and found in the Old Testament canon. Let's be reminded that the new "Law of Love" ushered into the New Testament by Christ's death and resurrection is a law that *fulfills* the Old Covenant, and, as Paul writes, even *exceeds* that of the Law[6].

59

Gideon's sacrifice, in the face of seasonal famine and after a seven-year depression, cuts me to the quick when I compare it to my level of giving. How do you think God felt at the generosity of Gideon's offering at such a dire time in his life? The rest of the story shows us that Gideon not only experienced unprecedented success in battle, but that he and his family were abundantly blessed as well, and the nation of Israel experienced 40 years of peace following the annihilation of the Midianites under his leadership.

Why is giving at this level so discomforting to us? When was the last time you gave until it hurt...until there was some of your own "blood on the floor?" When were you and I last *cut deeply* in our worship to God? Does God own our operating capital only, or our retirement nest eggs as well? We know the answer: He owns all of the buckets.

I must not fear.
Fear is the mind-killer.
Fear is the little-death that brings total obliteration.
I will face my fear...
And when it has gone past I will turn...to see its path.
Where the fear has gone there will be nothing.

--Paul Atreides, **Dune**
by Frank Herbert[7]

That God was pleased with Gideon's offering is apparent in the way we see him walking with amazing favor and protection throughout his journey. When Gideon had brought the meat and the bread to the Lord, He told Gideon to take the meat and the bread and place it on a rock. God then extended his staff and the tip touched the offering, and from the rock itself flared an intense flame, totally consuming the offering placed upon the stone.

Gideon was terrified at what had just happened. It was understood that if a human ever saw God, he would immediately die. The Lord comforted Gideon, sharing one of his great Names with him, *"Jehovah Shalom,"* or *"The Lord is Peace."* Gideon spontaneously built an altar there and worshipped God.

Setting up your altar

In our group sessions, this is where our Squad Leaders normally distribute a 1-2 pound rock to each member of his squad. As a part of this group experience, go ahead and join them by finding a good-sized rock to set up your first prayer altar to God. Follow these easy guidelines to setting up an "altar," or special place, where you and God can connect every day. The rock can be round or flat, it is up to you. It is simply a symbol, like it was for Gideon, of that holy place where God encountered him and where Gideon worshipped God:

1. Find a place in your home where you can be alone every day for 15-20 minutes or more. Maybe that is not possible where you live. Maybe it is in your car or a private place at work. Also, it is okay to start with five minutes if this daily discipline is new to you.
2. Set the rock on a shelf or on the floor where you can begin worshipping God each day. The first day, place your hands on the rock and pray to the Lord something like this:

Lord, I am here to meet with you. This shall be our special place...a place where I can come to worship, read your Word, and seek your face. This will be a place where I can get to know you better and even learn how to hear your gentle voice. Here is where I will regularly pray for those I love and care for.

Show me, as you did for Gideon, the fullness of Adonay Jehovah.

Here is where I will bring to you my deepest sorrows and where I will sit silently in times of confusion to find your peace. I consecrate this rock...and ask you to make it a holy place for you. Amen.

3. Set your daily calendar to go to this place first ...before you begin any work. Give Him the best and first part of your day and watch how He blesses you and those you pray for.
4. After prayer, prepare to give *an offering at church that hurts,* and that shows you that you have given Him control of all of the buckets. He owns them all anyway!

Table talk

1. Why is important for our giving or service to God to hurt…to really cost us something?

2. Discuss how your table might take a step of obedience in real, bloodletting sacrificial giving.

3. Share the place you have chosen for your prayer and why it is the best spot for you.

4. Challenge and hold each other accountable to be at their rock every day

Core conditioning

1. Take a stone and establish an 'Altar' or Holy Place in your home.

2. Make an appointment to visit there with God every day in worship.

3. Pray and then give God a sacrifice that cuts deeply this month

Chapter Four:

A Primer on Spiritual Warfare

You then, my son, be strong in the grace that is in Christ Jesus. And the things you have heard me say in the presence of many witnesses entrust to reliable men who will also be qualified to teach others. Endure hardship with us like a good soldier of Christ Jesus. No one serving as a soldier gets involved in civilian affairs—he wants to please his commanding officer

-- 2 Timothy, 2:2-5

If you have navigated as far as this chapter, it probably means that you have decided to step it up, and if you had not done so before, to commit to at least a season of daily Bible reading and a daily time of prayer. Welcome to boot camp!

This and the next chapter might be good ones to read together with your wife, if you are married. As you agree together in your perspectives on spiritual warfare and the priorities of winning the war together, major changes for kingdom expansion can happen in the two of you and then through you both as well.

The salutation of "mighty warrior" is for you and me, not some historical hero. If you are going to become a warrior, you must first learn to fight. Consider the rest of this book as a warrior training textbook. In training camp, the soldier goes through rigorous conditioning, learning hardship and the art of war. Then he must apply himself to developing his skills in hand-to-hand combat, survival, weaponry, and the various tactics employed with those weapons. Moreover, he learns the critical value of the buddy system and building trust with his fellow soldiers in a small fighting unit called the Squad.

We already looked at the battle scene from **Gladiator,** which underscores the indispensable need for fighting men to act "as one" and quickly form the interlocked shields, or tortoise formation. Aligned close together we see the model of what we seek to create at the tables during our sessions.

This chapter will lay the biblical and practical foundation that articulates the anatomy of a very real war, which impacts every one of us. Furthermore, it will outline the strategy and tactics that you will need to know in order to *win the war*, one battle at a time. The more awareness you have into the nature of this war and what's at stake, the less actual fighting is needed. In the United States because of the superior training and equipment of our armed forces, it is relatively rare for us to have to make a show of force to hostiles. An **attitude of readiness**, plus the **investment in superior weaponry,** and **disciplined training** are the chief deterrents that prevent our enemies from attacking in the first place!

Every trained soldier knows that if they venture out alone into enemy territory, they will likely face death or be captured.

A wild boar was sharpening his tusks on a tree trunk one day. A fox asked him why he did this when there was neither huntsman nor danger threatening him. "I do so for a good reason," he replied. For if I am suddenly surprised by danger, I wouldn't have the time to sharpen my tusks. But now, I will find them ready to do their duty."

--Fables, Aesop, 6th Century B.C.

The attitude of readiness

I love a great Sci-Fi movie. Many of you may have seen one or more of **The Terminator** movies. I have seen every one of the series, some more than once, and I can't wait for the next one. The plot involves a dim look at the future where super-intelligent machines become self-aware and revolt against their human creators by launching a global nuclear attack, they wipeout the vast majority of the human population.

But pockets of people remain who begin to organize with the intention to survive and ultimately regain control of the planet. The future world is mostly barren of life. Men, women, and children live in bombed-out shells of rubble that resemble Baghdad a few days after our US and allied forces first invaded Iraq.

Back in the present day, the first movie begins when a "Terminator" and a brave member of the human resistance militia both travel back in time through a portal to a present-day American city.

The Terminator is a pure, indestructible killing machine programmed to destroy a woman, Sarah Connor, who will one day give birth to a male child that will rise up to be the heroic leader of the underground resistance against the machines in the decades ahead. The boy's name will be John Connor.

In each film, the riveting plot is essentially the same, though staged at different times in John Connor's life. Scenes move from the present, to a nuclear holocaust, and then to the age where machines rule the world. In this world, men, women, and children all fight courageously and strategically against monstrous odds to regain the planet. In each film, John Connor grows older and wiser.

In the opening scenes of the second movie, John comes to understand the threat on his mother, his own life, and that of humanity. Once he fully accepts his destiny, a deep change comes over him and his countenance changes. Life becomes deadly serious, and every action and decision matters. With acute alertness, he masters the craft of subversive warfare. Connor ruthlessly, yet compassionately, leads his followers to win back the planet...and to turn back the momentum of fate. Like the faithful warriors in an active combat zone, they execute the art of warfare without hesitation or compromise. These soldiers are "on duty" and cannot allow their judgment to be compromised in any way. It is a given...no one drinks while on duty....and duty is on 24/7.

Connor's personal mandate was to endure "Spartan" hardship and that meant living in an at-risk, dangerous world, and doing without many things considered a luxury or recreation today. In contrast, many today live an over-busy life where we juggle work and life priorities, mixing business with pleasure. Most of us harbor hopes for a peaceful retirement. This is entirely alien to Connor and his followers.

Men who follow the ways of Christ, like Connor, are living in a world at war. Our war is not visible.

Do not think that we wrestle with flesh and blood (people) but we wrestle against spiritual wickedness in high places, against principalities and powers, thrones and dominions.

—Ephesians 6: 12

But our war is pervasive and can be as dangerous as a constant barrage of three-way machine gun fire. The coordinated dimensions of the *carnal nature* of man, the magnetic draw of this *world's system,* and the activities of various demonic entities or *evil spirits* under the hierarchy of Satan are committed to systematically hunting down and killing everything that is good and godly in humanity.

This evil cosmology is working in a coordinated fashion to destroy your marriage or, if single, your wholeness. Each of your children, and other beloved family members and close friends, are marked targets as well. Think through your life and your surrounding sphere of influence and make a tally of the successful assaults by Hell. Think of friends and loved ones whose marriages and other relationships, even their mental and physical health, have already been assaulted by dark forces within and without. Satan has leveraged and launched a three-dimensional

A Perspective with spiritual connotations...
"Without war, human beings stagnate in comfort and affluence and lose the capacity for great thoughts and feelings. They become cynical and subside into barbarism."

-- Fyodor Dostoyevsky 1821-1881

game of chess for keeps, while we seem to be dinking about with tic-tac-toe.

Paul assumes that we understand the realm of the invisible and of the nature of spiritual darkness in particular. He states, "We are not ignorant of his devices."[1] Yet many American Christians today have never heard a sermon on, nor have they participated in an exposition of, this very present darkness.

As a young Christian, I felt that my schooling in the realm of our invisible enemy was pretty biblical and fairly robust. I first made acquaintance with the Armor of God, from the great passage in Ephesians 6 in a Bible study when I was 18 years old. I was excited about suiting up for God and getting in on some real action!

I remember as we got into the teaching series, which lasted several weeks, we were taught to put on the armor one piece at a time. Then the game plan was to "resist" the devil, our universal adversary. "The shield of faith is for you to hide behind so the fiery darts of temptation don't take you down," the teacher said. "The girdle of truth is so you can gird up your loins quickly in order to run away and 'flee youthful lusts.'" He went on to explain that the "gospel shoes," which in Roman martial design had nailed cleats in the soles, were to help you hold fast and resist giving ground to the enemy.

"What about *the sword*?" a young man asked.

"That's so you memorize scripture to use like Jesus did when he overcame the temptations of the devil in the desert," replied the teacher.

As a college football player in my second year, I *knew* the purpose of cleats on the gridiron. I understood the purpose of the helmet and how the shoulder pads allowed me to inflict the maximum damage upon an opponent without breaking my own frame. Drive the man back was the objective, and *beat* your man on each play from scrimmage. If enough of us won the play-by-play battles against our opponent, we would win the game.

Over the years, with different coaches, I played on both the offensive and defensive lines (I don't think they often knew what to do with me). While playing offensive guard, I led sweeps, trapped, pulled, screened, cut, cross-blocked, and protected the Quarterback. When on defense, our objective was to penetrate the line and maybe cause a fumble by trying to knock the running back into yesterday.

I understood that you cannot really win a battle on the gridiron without a grinding, ground gaining offense and a relentless, ferocious defense. I remember how disappointed I was as a new believer, to hear that the *Christian* "warrior" was relegated to "resist and to stand only. I spent the next twenty-five years resisting…standing…*playing not to lose* and eventually, by gradual attrition, lost almost everything.

Origins of evil

The Bible teaches that eons ago the devil, or Satan, had attempted to take over the throne of God in Heaven. He raised a following of one-third of the angelic host and together they were cast down from heaven by God.[2] Sometime after this, according to Genesis chapters one through two, God created man in his image, male and female, and placed them in a glorious garden. He then gave man dominion over all of the earth and everything it contained. However, it was an authority delegated by God to Man, not intrinsic to Adam. Over this world called Earth, he was made the ruling steward.

Because jealousy is characteristic of Satan's nature (he had already shown his true colors by wanting God's position and power), this new wrinkle in creation—a being, fashioned like God—really ticked Satan off, so much so that he declared a personal war on all mankind and sought to usurp man's authority and bring him down. He did this by [3]enticing Eve and then Adam to break the single statute God had given them. By disobeying their Creator and tasting of the fruit of the Tree of the Knowledge of Good and Evil, man's delegated rulership was relinquished and defaulted to the Serpent. Man has profoundly suffered from this fall ever since.

Let's take a moment and examine the nature of our adversary. This list below was difficult to write…and may be difficult to read, but we cannot hope for a victorious lifestyle without facing directly the truth of the one who desires the destruction of you and your family. Here is what scripture tells us about our ancient foe, his system of evil, and his agenda:

1. **His power over Christians has been broken.** The biblical teachings of Jesus and other New Testament writers clearly affirm that we have inherited the positional and earthly authority of Christ

in the church through faith. This is both for the present and future. We are **now** seated with Christ in heavenly places with all powers in creation submitted under our feet.[4]

2. He is an old, patient, and **relentless schemer**. His plans take the long view and he will patiently weave his web over the decades of our lives, chipping away at our resolve while he plans a great fall for every man and woman and child. But he is not really interested in you or me personally, except for how he can leverage your weaknesses (or sometimes your strengths) to destroy you and those you touch. Like an expert bowler, he will strike the head pin (you or me), which then is able to adversely impact those around you and even multiple future generations through the echo of sin in our lives.

3. He is the **original rebel against authority** and the source of the spirit of rebellion in all of society. *All* of what Satan has and does, and his kingdom, is fully corrupted. Hating God's designed authority, he seeks to corrupt those who have power and then, as usurper, cultivates the lust of power in human hearts to pull down or supplant those powers he is corrupting. Though he seeks to do this at every level of society, his focal point is and will always be the church.

4. His **heart is filled with war**[5]. When Japan attacked Pearl Harbor, the appropriate reaction of our government was the formal declaration of war. However, much of the American church has taken a more pacifist, conciliatory approach to the enemy's attack on believers. **Know this:** *There will be no truce, no rest, and no reprieve in this war against the Saints until he is finally cast into the Lake of Fire. Wrapped in lies and self deluded, he actually thinks he can win, and as the end of these times approaches, his wrath will escalate against the Saints and the Bride because he senses his time is short.*[6]

5. He is a liar and **the father of all lies**. The first lies that come from within us are voices of exaggeration, self-defense, and rationalization. If he can train a child to avoid the truth regarding their personal responsibility for their actions (often, regretfully,

with the parents' cooperation), then the child will be raised with the eventual inability to perceive truth. Once lying to yourself is established, it becomes the means of operation with others. The Father of Lies relentlessly seeks to breed his lying seed in us.

6. He is **not omnipotent**. The Devil is a broken shadow of what he once was. He remembers his previously powerful and lofty position as the most beautiful, and probably even favored, of heavens' angelic beings[7]. The first great setback was when he was cast down to earth due to his rebellion against God. Filled with new jealousy of mankind after God poured his image into Adam, he wrought great destruction upon humanity with an almost free reign over death, disease, and war. The second great breaking of his power was when he was fooled into murdering Jesus. In Jesus' post crucifixion descent into Hell's domain, much of the enemy's power was broken with a profound wound inflicted by Christ as the last Adam. This is when many believe the Lord seized the "keys to death and Hades"[8] from Satan's hand, redeeming mankind through his righteous sacrifice.

7. He is **not omnipresent**. As a singular created being, he must work strategically through the tactics of shoring up an evil world system that plays to erudite, high sounding proud philosophies and the basest parts of our carnal nature to get most of his work done through people. The balance of his forces are demonic entities assigned to key individuals and leaders, political arenas, or strategic organizations.

8. He is **not omniscient.** But he has the benefit of many thousands of years of *experience* with the predictable fallen nature of the human race and knowledge of how we can predictably be manipulated, tempted, and intimidated.

9. He is the **author of Death**.[9] The apocryphal book of wisdom, written a century before Jesus' birth, aptly says, "*...by the envy of the devil, death entered the world, and they who are in his possession, experience it.*"[10]

10. **He is a murderer** and the source of all thoughts and actions of hatred. Gangland violence, wars, sociopathology, armed robberies,

demonic possession, abortion, drunk driving, brawling, terrorism, physical abuse, sexual abuse, cancer, AIDS (and other deadly diseases) and suicides all have the spirit of murder at their core. It is the ultimate end to the means of Hell and he is busy in his planning and execution.

11. He is much **smarter than a fifth grader**...and thus you or me. As Eve discovered, it is dangerous to dialogue with him. Even the most powerful of angelic forces, the archangel Michael, when God assigned him to retrieve the body of Moses, did not affront him directly, but had to employ Gods direct authority by declaring *"the Lord rebuke you."*[11] There is no place for glibness or testosterone-induced moxey when dealing with the enemy directly. Jesus himself used the scriptures ("It is written") to combat Satan on the mountain of temptation. The spiritual weapons we have been given, along with a total dependence upon God's power, are sufficient to prevent attack, or, if need be, to protect us...and to win!

12. He **hates women** and has active plans to destroy their humanity, femininity, motherhood, beauty, glory and the female gender's great influence for love, courage, wisdom and all that is good. (Genesis 3:15; Rev 12:13-15)

13. He **hates children**. The passion of *his* fatherhood is to make liars first and then, into disciples of Hell. Just as the great evils of the Khmer Rouge, Fascism, Nazism and Communism take the young and inoculate them with their poisonous doctrines, he knows that if he can bend them through their childhood years, they are likely to never meet nor learn to love their Creator and Savior. (Genesis 3:15; Revelations 12:17)

14. He **hates men (and boys) most of all**, which is, of course, one of the primary reasons for writing this book. As we have discovered, he also knows that the linchpin of society...and of the growth and health of the church, is men.

15. Lastly, we need to **understand his overarching strategy**. Like in the great game of chess, he seeks *to take out the Queen*. Like chess, the King (Jesus Christ) has empowered the Queen (the

Church) as the ultimate power player on the chessboard of this earthly realm.

Jesus conquered death on the cross by overcoming all temptations and living a pure life without sin. He was crucified, though innocent, and rose from the dead. Through his sacrifice, he gained the "keys of Death and Hell" from the enemy. Christ has now pressed them into the hands of the Church, his bride-to-be. These keys are the metaphor Jesus uses for the real power He acquired and then gave (bequeathed) to his church with the full rights to either open or lock…prevent, free or bind… on earth.[12]

Wherever there are believers who will ask boldly in faith as Jesus instructed, you will find the power of the miraculous at work…not hindered by latter-day theologies or scientific philosophies. God continues to confound the wise through those who simply believe.

In the United States and other modernized countries, we have not only to deal with the powerful philosophies of humanism and spirit of unbelief (a demonic entity) that work together to shrivel our faith in a God of power. But many of us have seen the excesses of Charismatic manifestations, often dramatically paraded on platforms across North America.

Others have observed (maybe even experienced) people swaying or falling "under the power" in churches or auditoriums. These events often include healings orchestrated by a man or woman with what seems to be miraculous powers. Unfortunately, our cynical suspicions regarding the validity of these occurrences are often validated when we hear confirmed reports of super affluent lifestyles or fractured morality from one of these leaders. Are these dramatic experiences sometimes real and from God? Yes, some are. But mostly, we doubt…or scoff.

Other believers I know would just prefer to leave things alone. The "seeker-sensitive" movement of the late eighties and nineties went so far in some cases to recommend eliminating the use of "seeker-offensive" words from the pulpit like "the devil," "Lucifer," "Satan," and for some, even "repent" and "sin" were no-no's! Many church leaders, who valued packed pews and growing budgets funded new building programs and saw expansion as the key signs of success. Many were enthralled at the new marketing approach and made celebrities out of those who did it better than others.

The philosophy was, "what we don't know can't hurt us. And because there is so much good stuff to preach on anyway, let's keep this *all positive*." The idea was get them in the door, warm them up, and eventually get them to make a decision. The marketing message of the church service, along with follow-up fun-filled events for youth groups and families, were the operational mechanisms *to make them a customer for life*!

In our country, I have seen a gradual adoption of dumbed down expectations that have minimized the power of God to move in the miraculous realm. Even the definition of a miracle has been seriously watered down. The argument I have heard is that "the dynamics of the book of Acts were for those historical days because they did not yet have the Bible." Tied in with this is the neo-scientific view that demonic spirits have somehow all been explained away by psychological labeling remedied by pharmaceutical cures or years of therapy.

For the benefit of control, and to avoid rocking the boat of controversy, it seems that far too many church leaders would rather allow their members to remain in their comfort zone than deal boldly with the matters of the Spirit.

Today, most contemporary church leaders have come to understand that this was the wrong way to present the gospel. The younger X and Y generations have left these churches in droves. We may be too late. They saw the "come-as-you-are," low barrier to entry, Christianity. Then they observed or experienced the highest ever divorce rates of their churched parents. The dissolution of so many families happened while rampant materialism (oftentimes disguised as a kind of theology that wealth represented God's approval) as destructive forces in their lives. They saw how "the god of more," or consumerism, brought irresponsible personal and government debt and deeply scarred the ecology of our planet.

> I believe that God weighs believers as well as counts them
>
> -- Dr. Jerry Cook

As non-believers and young people listened to this very "hip" gospel, they saw that there was no bite, little risk, and no high price to pay to become a follower of Jesus. All savvy consumers today know that what costs them nothing, or very little, has little or no intrinsic value.

I have had men admit to me that they'd rather not discuss the theology of evil or its invisible champion because it might draw unwelcomed attention to themselves, their family, and their careers. Like Gideon, it seems best to keep your head down and stick with what you know. It is very much like our gender to want to master and control our environment, and it is as if we say to ourselves "I can't figure out this invisible, demonic stuff so I'll just stay under the radar and try to live as good a life as I can."

But scripture does not teach that our invisible battle is with demonic forces alone. Nor does it give any indication that we should keep our heads down in fear, or merely "whistle in the dark," hoping evil will not touch us.

I'd like to draw an analogy from the physical realm of war. Figure 2 shows the three dimensions of physical war as it has always been fought throughout history. They are: the **Air**, the **Sea** and the **Land**. These spheres of offense and defense have existed for millennia. In modern combat, the skies evolved into a critical factor in victory or defeat. No commanding officer would have a chance at military victory if he disregarded the sky as both a threat and an opportunity to sway the tide of war in his favor.

Figure 2: The Three Dimensions of War

The same is true of the dimensions of the invisible war into which we have been born again (Figure 3). The Bible teaches we have three great adversaries, three theaters of war that are coordinated together against believers and the church as a whole. These are the *world system*, the *fallen carnal nature of man* (also called "the flesh"), and the realm of the "*Prince of the Power of the Air*," or Satan[13]. For brevity sake, let's call this multi-dimensional warfare CWD, for **C**arnality, the **W**orld, and the **D**evil.

Unless you and I are not aware of or trained for fighting in each of these dimensions, we will be consistently taken down by one or more of the enemy's attacks. In the pages that follow are the keys to understanding how you can discern, fight, and win the spiritual war and then walk in the victory for which you were made.

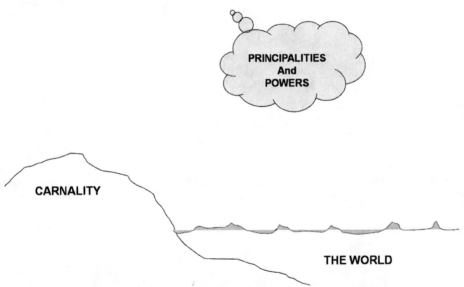

Figure 3: The Three Dimensions of Spiritual War

How do these three dimensions coordinate in our everyday life? The graph in Figure 4 shows a typical month in the life of many guys I have come to know, and what was typical of me for decades. I was mostly playing defense spiritually, either trying to protect my turf from these mystical, unseen forces, or I was simply trying to minimize the damage of my next unforeseen failure as a man of God. Blindfolded to the interplay of these dimensions, I was being knocked off my feet by blows that rained down on me from all directions. I would experience brief periods of peace in the presence of God... but mostly, I labored under all kinds of stress, staggering forward as best I could.

> *Get used to the fact that your life is lived in the context of war.*
> *Every breath you take is an act of war... You answer to only one*
> *Commander and Chief, and only you will give an explanation for*
> *your choices.*[14]

-- George Barna

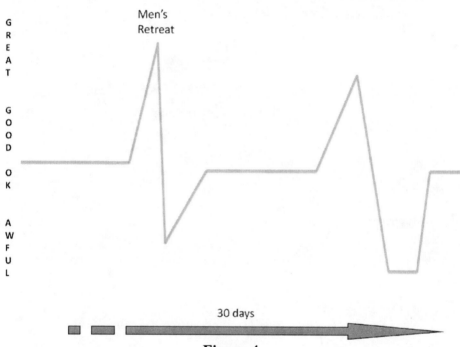

Figure 4

This diagram shows a typical guy who goes to church "flat-lining" in his spiritual life. Discontented, he goes to a men's retreat and comes back down the mountain inspired and all pumped up. God may have lifted him so high he thought he'd never come down, or perhaps a sinful habit was broken when he confessed and was prayed-over by a group of guys in his cabin.

It is important to remember that no matter how men posture around you, you can be assured that a vast majority of them share these feelings of spiritual delinquency as life beats against their feeble piers of faith, only to be followed by a crushing condemnation from the "Accuser of the Brethren." Words of shame roam around your head like a ferocious lion "seeking whom he may devour." He seeks to devour the warrior in us because together, we are the greatest threat to his power on earth.

Let's take a more detailed look at this timeline. After the peak of the men's camp retreat, this guy, (let's call him Steve) is feeling somewhat invincible. Freed from some habit or filled afresh with the Holy Spirit, he returns home brimming with spiritual confidence. He can't understand the lukewarm reception he receives from his family and friends. "They really need to get closer to God," he thinks.

Spiritual pride was one of Jesus' pet peeves. It stinks up to high heaven. The Bible *promises* that God will resist those with proud hearts. Steve is unaware of how his heart is steeping with growing darkness like a teabag in a cup of boiling water. It's just a matter of time before Steve loses touch with the fresh inspiration he has gained on the retreat. As the diagram shows, he might berate one of his kids or maybe bombard his spouse with Scripture. After the fall, he feels a pang of melancholy because the brief spiritual honeymoon is slipping away.

Back to earth, he returns and as the mountaintop experience fades away, it is quickly replaced with life as it always has been. A underlying sense of unbelief seeps in to Steve's soul like water in a basement with a busted pipe while the promised resolve for meaningful daily Bible reading, alone time with God every morning, and prayer with his kids each night, has washed away.

A few days later, after he repents and reads the Bible a bit, he returns to the steady road again. A week or two later, something awesome happens at work. Steve closes a huge sale, beating out the incumbent competitor. *"Who-hoo, Praise God (and, man, am I good at what I do[15])!"* He thinks. *"We can really use the extra money,"* he tells a coworker. Steve gets what's called that BIG feeling. It is time to celebrate! He makes reservations at his wife's favorite restaurant and then calls her with the good news.

That evening, they share the perfect meal together. Steve raises a toast (or three) and returns home secretly relieved he was not stopped by a cop.

He is still wired with adrenaline, but now with a buzz, he says goodnight to his wife and remains downstairs alone, in front of the TV[16] with that "big feeling" intact.

Steve has just spent an "unguarded" afternoon and evening, growing more vulnerable by the rush of glory at work, the esteem of his wife and kids, and a desire to buy more stuff. He is feeding his carnal nature. The corresponding demonic spirits of Lust and Pride may be aware, *but they may not need to do a thing* because of Steve's lack of self-awareness and discipline, which can be seen in his hasty impulse to spend future income and by his over drinking. Steve has *no idea* he is in the midst of all three dimensions of war.

James 1:13 explains the source of carnal temptation:

When tempted, no one should say, "God is tempting me." For God cannot be tempted by evil, nor does he tempt anyone; but each one is tempted when, by his own evil desire, he is dragged away and enticed. Then, after desire has conceived, it gives birth to sin; and sin, when it is full-grown, gives birth to death.

That next morning, his wife goes to Nordstrom and he goes to work as the "mighty hunter." Stepping out of the elevator, he catches the eye of the "hot" Executive Admin who works for a colleague down the hall from his office. Unconsciously pulling in his gut, she winks an admiring smile across the cubicle to him…and it was for him alone.

At his desk, after his blood pressure drops to a safe range again, he calls the buyer about the whereabouts of the promised email with the scanned, signed purchase order. There is no answer and no callback by 11 AM. His stomach lining begins to secrete extra acid. Then he gets the call right before lunch; it's a rumor from another vendor that a competitor has aced him out because the other company's salesperson played golf with the CEO two days earlier. The pit in his gut tells him the deal has started to unravel. Still there was no answer from his buyer.

He threw up some "Hail Mary" prayers to God, and then his boss got involved to try to save *his* deal. After Steve does his best, even emailing an invoice showing a lesser price by 11%, the rumor proves "spot on." The verbally promised purchase order was hijacked right before it could be faxed. The deal is dead.

Steve went home deflated, humiliated, and embarrassed to tell his wife. The loss of face with his co-workers and the premature spending in the last twenty-four hours, combined with the seeds of watching inappropriate television the night before, have made him feel utterly dejected and humiliated. The pain of reality drives him, like a lamb to the slaughter, to that dark place where both pain and God, consequences and duty, are all forgotten. This is that private, anesthetizing place where he can salve his need for masculine validation, that old familiar need to be esteemed by a woman of his dreams.

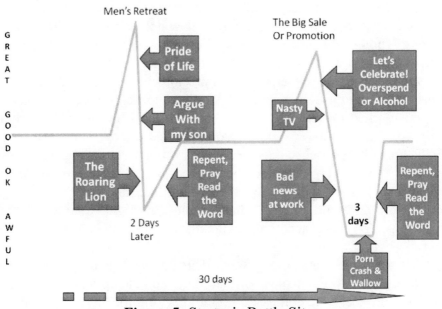

Figure 5: Strategic Battle Sites

But not all of us go there, do we? Michael was a good man, different and more disciplined than Steve. An engineer by trade, now in retirement, he found conversation with his wife, Marian, difficult. It seemed that ever since the nest was empty, they hardly even knew each other. His wife, in Michael's opinion, was always talking about things that had no practical value or whining about how she didn't have any friends. She missed her two children and, now, their older daughter's three grandchildren since they moved two states away last year. Her doctor had recently put her on Prozac for depression, to which Michael could not begin to relate.

He felt useless, unloved, and alone. Often by seven in the morning, after finishing his morning devotions, he would retreat to the garage where his expertly equipped woodshop gave him a place where he could design and create his beautiful guitars. Specialty highly-sought-after exotic maple, walnut, and Koa wood stock was transformed into refined works of art. Once finished and strung, there were few instruments that could match the tonal quality which resonated from one of his creations. One hundred and forty hours later, God, his beloved, his children, and his grandchildren all but forgotten, he would create one more guitar for his growing collection. These beauties were like his special children, for him and him alone. Tragically, his family hardly knew him.

The danger with Michael's failure is how deceptive it can be. There is obviously nothing wrong with a wholesome hobby. But this hobby is really a *hiding place*. It is his winepress...the same as it was for Gideon, but even more so. He is spending each precious hour, every golden minute of his remaining days on himself, lovingly caressing the dead wood as it was transformed into lifeless instruments. All the while he was depriving those who needed his love, his wisdom, and his legacy. They desperately felt the hole of his absence and the pain of his unconscious rejection.

Most guys today are too busy for endless hours dedicated to craftsmanship. They will exhaust their best efforts and creative energy at work, returning home an empty husk night after night. Like Steve, their private place is readily accessible at their fingertips just a click or a remote controlled TiVo away.

Let's get back to our buddy Steve. Three days later, he crawls back to God, and back into the stands. On Saturday, he gets up and can't believe how badly he feels. He confesses to God, begging for cleansing, and then reads three chapters of the Bible. Next day it's off to church with his family. He feels useless for advancing the Kingdom, but Steve holds his gaze firm, smiling at the other men he greets. He takes a seat to hear what the pastor has to say while he pushes the recent past into a compartment of his mind. There is that familiar and uneasy fear...and the unanswered questions: "Will I ever measure up? How many more times will God forgive me and take me back?"

Like Gideon, he is alone and hiding again in shame, feeling completely disqualified and buffeted by the bully tag team of CWD. Neither unaware nor alert or "prayed up," unseeing and undiscerning,

Steve simply feels deeply sad. With no one to help, he climbs up the ladder, back to the flat line of mediocrity.

Praise God that His never-ending fountain of forgiveness which flows to you and me from Jesus' sacrifice washes us clean, always. Our forgiving God whispers to you again, "You are right with me, my son. Re-engage, mighty warrior!"

However, most men in this cycle cannot hear God's courageous affirmation. They have just finished a disorderly retreat on an invisible battlefield to lick their wounds and hide their shame. The slow death of living a defeated secret life takes its toll.

> *Death is impossible for us to fathom...society is organized to make death invisible. As a warrior in life, you must turn this dynamic around. Make the thought of death not something to escape but to embrace. Your days are numbered. Will you pass them half awake and halfhearted or will you live with a sense of urgency? Feeling death at your heels will make all your actions more certain, more forceful. This could be your last throw...make it count. A warrior fights his greatest fight when there are only two options...death or victory."*
>
> -- Robert Greene[17]

Slowly, days later, most of us get back on the road. Not the road to victory, however, but a kind of maintained existence on the flat road of life.

The cycle continues; fatherless boys and girls grow up to raise a next generation that will look for substitutionary love, missing out, maybe for eternity, on the freeing salvation of Christ and the warm embrace of their adoptive, heavenly Father.

Gideon, too, must have felt this way. We shall take a closer look at his personal battle in this arena in the next few chapters. Like Michael and Steve, he was born into a cosmic conflict not of his own choosing. The deceptive heart in our breast and the world's voice that says we must acquire more power, more prestige, and more possessions to measure up, all harmonize to the ears of our soul, while demonic forces whisper and connive in symphony under the direction of the Maestro of Hell.

Table talk

1. When is it that men are most frequently attacked? How can we help each other be more alert and stronger to win these skirmishes?

2. Describe a repetitive area where you have a tendency to fall into sin. Are there any practical things you might do to avoid the circumstances where these failures come?

Core conditioning

Contact your two or three closest friends, and explain your desire to establish a 911 relationship, asking each of them to walk alongside of you and to pray for you daily.

Chapter Five:

From Fearful Farmer to Baal Buster

With the primer on warfare behind us, we can return to Judges 6. Gideon had passed his first test; by going against the grain of his own fears, overcoming low self-esteem and his own "common sense," and sacrificing deeply. The young man is then given a rare look into the very heart of the Father when he became the recipient of the benediction "Jehovah *Shalom*." One of the seven names of Jehovah in Scripture,[1] this blessing of hope has been repeated by Jews and Christians for 3000 years. Let's pick up on verse 23:

> But the LORD said to him, "Peace! Do not be afraid. You are not going to die." So Gideon built an altar to the LORD there and called it **The LORD is Peace**. To this day, it stands in Ophrah of the Abiezrites. That same night the LORD said to him, "Take the second bull from your father's herd, the one seven years old. Tear

down your father's altar to Baal and cut down the Asherah pole beside it. Then build a proper kind of altar to the LORD your God on the top of this height. Using the wood of the Asherah pole that you cut down, offer the second bull as a burnt offering." So Gideon took ten of his servants and did as the LORD told him. But because he was afraid of his family and the men of the town, he did it at night rather than in the daytime. In the morning when the men of the town got up, there was Baal's altar, demolished, with the Asherah pole beside it cut down and the second bull sacrificed on the newly built altar!

We should take a moment to drill down into what this word peace or *shalom* means in verse 23. Merriam-Webster's dictionary gives several definitions of peace:

1. A state of tranquility or quiet

2. A state of security or order within a community provided for by law

3. Freedom from disquieting or oppressive thoughts or emotions

4. Harmony in personal relations

Although there is a co-relationship between the commonly used words for peace (*eirene*-greek) in the New Testament, the Hebrew concept of peace is not touched upon by any of these definitions. In many ways, it is has a deeper and broader meaning that encompasses wholeness, completeness, wellbeing, and prosperity... even salvation. In Nehemiah 6:15 *shalom* is used to describe completing or finishing the repairs and reinforcements of Jerusalem's broken-down wall; and in Isaiah 42:19, it infers the meaning "made perfect." For Gideon, to whom God conveyed His blessing of *shalom,* it carried this deeper Hebrew meaning to him.

CS Lewis said:

If I find in myself desires which nothing in this world can satisfy, the only explanation is that I was made for another world.

Jesus instructed the disciples to convey a blessing of peace upon every home they entered, and He is referred to as the Prince of Peace in Isaiah.

We see Him often escaping the busyness of ministry by retreating to quiet places for contemplation and communion with His Father. On occasion, we see him gathering the children to His lap and, on another occasion, speaking the deep and profound truths in the beatitudes. He calls the common man, woman, and child to come to him to find rest and unload their burdens.

Just as often, however, we see him in acts of aggression or even violence like casting out demonic hosts into pigs, which brought a peaceful sound mindedness to the Gadarene demoniac.[2] We also see Him using a self-made Roman style scourge[3] to beat and drive out (literally *"to throw out violently"*) the animals and moneychangers. He destroyed their workplace, and harshly confronted the religious leaders of His day. All of these confrontational acts were performed *perfectly* by the Prince of Peace!

> We are faced with the paradox of following a God that is a warrior, a God of blood, and a God who establishes peace through victory.

Today, we live in the middle of a world at conflict with a much larger global population infested with the oppression of human rights, radical fascism, wars, slavery, and murderous genocides. North Korea and the entire Middle East constantly operate on the edge of chaos…all presenting dire global consequences too complex to predict.

Western philosophy is more sophisticated. Conflict averse, we march and carry signs with well-intentioned slogans calling for the universal end of war. Protesters singing "Give Peace a Chance" are common at public anti-war rallies and where once the two fingered "V" sign was for victory, it is now the universal peace sign. I saw a bumper sticker recently at the beach that read, "Peace Begins on Your Plate," referring to abstaining from the violence of killing animals for meat.

The modern church has often bought into this definition of peace as well: Peace is the absence of conflict. The Bride of Christ is expected to champion everything that has to do with peace and oppose everything that has to do with conflict. Yet, untaught and therefore unknown to many Christians, we are faced with the paradox of following a God that is a warrior, a God of blood and a God who establishes peace through victory.

Near the end of the Book of Job, God initiates a *direct* dialogue with Job, like no other in all of scripture. Job 39:19-25 says:

Have you given the horse strength? Have you clothed his neck with thunder? Can you frighten him like a locust? His majestic snorting strikes terror. He rejoices in his strength; He gallops into the clash of arms. He mocks at fear, and is not afraid; nor does he turn back from the sword. The quiver rattles against him, the glittering spear, and javelin. He devours the distance with fierceness and rage; nor does he come to a halt because the trumpet has sounded. At the blast of the trumpet he says, 'Aha!' He smells the battle from afar, the thunder of captains and shouting of war.

-- Job 39:19-25 (New King James Bible)

Can you sense the tenor of testosterone? God's joy in his majestic creation? With much of the Old Testament written in the context of oppression, bondage, and battle, we prefer to default to a kinder gentler God of the New Testament. Yet Jesus' gospel is one where His presence begins the new age of the Church, through which the Kingdom (government) of God is breaking into the human sphere in a violent fashion.

Many are surprised to read the gentle orator of the Sermon on the Mount later say:

Do not suppose that I have come to bring peace to the earth. I did not come to bring peace, but a sword. For I have come to turn a man against his father, a daughter against her mother, a daughter-in-law against her mother-in-law— a man's enemies will be the members of his own household.

-- Matthew 10:34-36

And, later, in the next chapter He continues the theme in verse twelve:

From the days of John the Baptist until now, the kingdom of heaven has been forcefully ("violently" or "carried by storm") advancing, and forceful (violent) men lay hold of it (literally, "to seize by force").

No wonder that God has designed us to grow stronger through the exercise of our faith in him through the trials of life and the agency of battle!

What is gained by spiritual struggle and why didn't the "finished" work on the cross suffice to destroy the enemy instead of just crippling him? Paul Billheimer's inspirational book, **Destined for the Throne**, answers this question. He brings a remarkably lucid viewpoint to the purpose and struggle of redemption…that the ultimate purpose of God's design was to create the Church through His Son's sacrifice. God is in the process of preparing us (including you and me), to reign and lead with Christ, by His side, throughout eternity! The struggle against sin and the warfares of our soul and spirit is our universal boot camp to strengthen our faith and resolve, and to teach us authority and rulership. Every believer who commits to follow Jesus has already been conscripted into His army for this purpose: so His Bride might be ready to rule with Christ as co-Regents in eternity.

Like Gideon, God has invited us to His battle in order to train us to rule and reign with Christ for eternity in what we know will include, at minimum, the judging of angels, and encompasses a future age full of wonder that far transcends our human comprehension… it is far beyond human ability to begin to describe! The immensely popular and stunningly beautiful movie **Avatar** stretched mans ability to visually create a world heretofore only reserved for writers of fantasy and science fiction. Yet the world of Pandora cannot scratch the real heaven and new world God has already designed in His mind…and will create at the rapidly approaching end of this age. These two verses underscore what God is preparing his men and Church for:

No eye has seen, no ear has heard, no mind has conceived, what God has prepared for those who love him.

-- 1 Corinthians 2:9

For our light and momentary troubles are achieving for us an eternal glory that far outweighs them all. So we fix our eyes not on what is seen, but on what is unseen. For what is seen is temporary, but what is unseen is eternal.

-- 2 Corinthians 4:17-18

What a paradox this must look like to God as he watches us crazy humans pridefully traverse history wielding the will of self-absorbed men. I must pause just to thank Him for His merciful patience!

How then, shall we fight? Let's look at Gideon's dream and find out in Judges 6.

The bull

Gideon was told to take the "second" bull from his father's herd, one that was seven years old, and use it to pull down the Baal altar and then use the animal as a sacrificial burnt offering on a new, "proper" altar to Yahweh. The energy source to be used to burn the massive animal was the wood from the Asherah pole, another pagan deity. It was to be chopped down and then killed as an integral part of Gideon's worship to God.

> "We are clearly accelerating into the end times. God's people need to wake up, then suit up with the armor of God. Thirdly, we need to begin to look up in anticipation of His imminent return as conquering King."
>
> --Greg Laurie

Looking at this powerful beast of burden, there are several facts which add significance to God's directive to Gideon. First, it was the second-ranked bull. This means that there was a higher ranked bull in his father's herd. It may have been the second strongest when teamed up for pulling heavy loads. The first-ranked bull may have been older, tougher, and less acceptable than the "second" bull.

It had also been *seven consecutive years* that the Midianites had ravaged Israel, and the eighth occurrence was literally preparing to invade a few miles away. This bull had survived seven years of hiding, nurturing, and serving under Gideon's father's household. When compared to Gideon's young goat, it was *priceless.* Priceless as the chief burden bearer of this farming society, precious as a symbol of the strength of an ox in its prime, and with an expected lifespan of 20 years, precious for its ability to procreate many times over in the years ahead. God, observing Gideon's sacrifice the day before, had significantly raised the ante and the risk, far beyond that of taking from his own household assets. His father was the chief priest of Baal and an elder in the community. The bull belonged to him.

Baal worship or "successianity"

Over a period of more than two thousand years before Christ, a Baal-type god was worshipped throughout Northern Africa, the Middle East, and southern Europe. Baal *(Assyrian-Babylonian "Bēl")*, which literally means "Possessor," "Master," or "Lord," had developed many different expressions over the centuries, as he was worshipped by diverse peoples[4].

There are approximately 89 references to the god Baal in the Old Testament. Baal was a Canaanite deity whose worship was organized. Significant temples were constructed in some larger cities. This deity also had priests and schools of prophets who would speak in his name.[5]

In the history of the nation of Israel, no god or demon came even close to rivaling the centuries of devotion given to this deity. From the exodus of God's people from Egypt around the mid 15th century B.C. where Aaron caved to the people's cry to fashion a golden calf-idol in the wilderness, through the years of the twelve Judges, all the way through the fall of Jerusalem in 597 B.C., this idol was a constant and compelling attraction for God's people. Prior to conquering the Canaanite nations as they were about to move across the Jordan River, God clearly and repetitively warned His people of the dark dangers of idol worship. Let's look at Moses' warning to his people in Deuteronomy:

> *...and after they have been destroyed before you, be careful not to be ensnared by inquiring about their gods, saying, "How do these nations serve their gods? We will do the same." You must not worship the LORD your God in their way, because in worshiping their gods, they do all kinds of detestable things the LORD hates. They even burn their sons and daughters in the fire as sacrifices to their gods.*

> -- Deuteronomy 12:30-32

This cult of Baal demanded the highest level of sacrifice imaginable, seeded with gross abominations. When paired with a female deity, worship included ritual prostitution to symbolize the fruitful "watering of the womb" of mother earth by the god. This next paragraph is historical, but graphic. My purpose here is not to shock, but to later draw important parallels on how proliferations of this deity are still active in our society today, and unfortunately, in the church.

The altar of Baal was in the image of a double-horned bull with the head and shoulders of a man. Later it evolved into a completely human form but retained the two horns on the head. Its arms extended outward as a stoked fire belched out from a hole in the chest. As a requirement of devotion for each family, and to receive the blessing of the god, the Priest of Baal would demand one of their children as a sacrifice. When the child was handed over, it would be placed on the outstretched arms of the idol, where the child could then be rolled into the fire. In Baal worship, as the child raised its final screams, the frenzied priests and priestesses would openly engage in hetero and homosexual intercourse. Finally, the balance of the worshippers would then complete the ceremony by engaging in an orgiastic ritual.[6]

In 1929, excavations began in Ras Shamra (the ancient port town of Ugarit) in northern Lebanon. The remains of a palace discovered in the first year of excavation yielded a library containing hundreds of ancient documents that provided a wealth of information about the Canaanite religion. What did these tablets reveal? The texts show the degrading results of the worship of these deities, with their emphasis on war, sacred prostitution and lasciviousness. Another more recent excavation of a site of Baal worship contained the remains of more than twenty thousand children. [7]

As the Israelites settled into the land, they encountered the cult of Baal in almost every city of the defeated. However, scripture tells us that several tribes of Israel did not thoroughly annihilate the Canaanites from their land, but cohabitated with them. In the case of Manasseh (Gideon's tribe), it says in Joshua 17:12:

Yet the Manassites were not able to occupy these towns, for the Canaanites were determined to live in that region. However, when the Israelites grew stronger, they subjected the Canaanites to forced labor but did not drive them out completely.

Due to the fact that this religion was much less morally demanding than their legalistic code given to Moses and the Ten Commandments, new generations of Israelites began to worship Baal rather than Yahweh. Baal was more "practical" with his lordship over the challenges of everyday life such as rain, fertility, crops, and livestock. In addition to the name Baal, he was also called the "Rider upon the Clouds," or the god of the storm or rain. For this reason, the Israelites often would worship both Baal and Yahweh throughout the calendar year. They had become polytheists.

Prophet after prophet (from Moses to Nathan to Jeremiah) brought dire warnings of harsh consequences if the people did not forsake their idols. But in their blindness and rebellion, they continued to conform to the practices of the pagans around them. Within this vicious cycle, the pain and suffering became so intense and the loss of life and property so debilitating, they would finally repent. Each time, God would require the pulling down and complete destruction of the altars (also called high places) and a full return to the true monotheistic worship of Yahweh, the God of Abraham, Isaac, Moses.

Throughout the written prophetic accounts, these men would passionately appeal to wayward Jewish leaders and citizens to forsake their "adulterous" ways and return to the God who chose them and loved them with an everlasting love. In this story, though many hearts were stirred by the prophet who brought the message of repentance (Judges 6:7-10), it took the responsive and remarkably courageous faith of a young man, Gideon, to catalyze and lead a revival to restore worship and freedom to Israel.

For many years, I was perplexed by the barbaric diversion of God's people towards idolatry during this time in history. It also seemed to me to be mostly irrelevant historical information, without practical implications for the Church in today's seemingly monotheistic world and, frankly, a waste of space and content in the Bible.

However, when Israel invaded and conquered the land of promise, they did not, per God's injunction, utterly annihilate the Canaanite races that lived there. These people were mostly followers of Baal. Many added the goddesses Asherah or Ashtoreth, which were sometimes worshipped as a consort, mother, or wife of Baal.

Although the Jews came with the best of intentions and sought initially to worship only Jehovah, slowly the races began to intermingle. Shrines to various divinities, which had been destroyed in the conquest of Canaan, became tolerated. Some of the Israelites took foreign wives, who brought with them their household idols. Observing the blessed and noble life of

King Solomon, we can observe how *in less than a single generation*, a great and wise man who had personally experienced the presence and glory of God, could become utterly corrupted, leading an entire nation into blended and polluted polytheism.

In the last eighteen months, after deeper study, I began to see some alarming similarities between Baal worship and today's modern world. I also began to see how Baal had infiltrated my own life and worship as a Christian man.

As recorded in the Bible, below are listed some of the more common names attached to the various Baals worshipped throughout the ancient world:

> **Baal-Tamar** "lord of the palm tree," Judges 20:33
> **Baal-Gad-** "lord of good fortune," Joshua 13:5
> **Baal-Hamon-** "lord of wealth," Song of Solomon 8:11
> **Baal-Hazor-** "Baal's village," 2 Sam 13:23
> **Baal-Meon-** "lord of the dwelling," Num 32:38
> **Baal-ze'bub-** "lord of the flies," 2 Kings 1:3; Matthew 10:25
> **Baal-Peor-** "lord of the opening," Deut 4:3

Baal-Tamar "lord of the palm tree," Judges 20:33

Worshipped in the book of Judges as well, this god represents the coveted place of rest. Palm trees were often places of safety or salvation (oasis). It could also mean the god of refreshing. Our family likes to getaway sometimes to Palm Desert, California, for some "R and R." I have a fantasy of one day retiring to a cabin in nearby Bear Valley, a place where the grandkids can roam and deer visit you by the back porch in the evening. My wife thinks of Kapalua in Maui as the place to finish our golden years. Another way to look at Baal-Tamar might be thought of as the beauty and relaxation we are supposed to feel when we see a Corona beer commercial.

Many people will sacrifice dearly to buy second homes, cabins, motor homes, and timeshares for a sanctuary away from the hustle of day-to-day living. We yearn for peace of mind…for quiet, and will often escape to a vacation spot, a great novel of adventure, or never-ending rounds of golf at some pristine private club. Of course, God himself ordained times of rest not only every week in the commandment of the Sabbath rest, but during specific holy days and feasts prescribed by God throughout the Jewish calendar year. Beyond vacations, depending on your vocation[8], it may be necessary for periodic, extended times of non-productivity to avoid burnout. We all need times to recharge.

Dallas Willard's book, **The Spirit of the Disciplines** speaks profoundly to this inside out paradox of seeking a solitary, desert experience with God:

> *In that desert solitude, Jesus fasted for more than a month. Then and not before, Satan was allowed to approach him with his glittering proposals of bread notoriety and power . Only then was Jesus at the height of his strength. The desert was his fortress, his place of power. Throughout his life he sought the solitary place as an indirect submission of his own physical body to righteousness.*[9]

Who is our daily source of rest…TV, the gym or a Scotch? The writer of Hebrews instructs his readers in Chapter Four about a Sabbath rest that has been purchased by Christ's priestly work on the cross. This is that *real rest* which fulfills our yearnings for inner peace and decompression. The fact that these yearnings almost universally exist in each of us is proof in itself of how our Creator has designed man to long for a place and state of rest. A place we can finally lay our burdens down.

It has been my personal privilege and practice for the last twenty-five years, during both the years as a Pastor and subsequent years in the secular workplace, to set aside two or three-day private retreats to simply be alone with God at a local monastery. I have to do this every six to nine months. Aside from it being my favorite days on earth, it has saved my life, several times over.

We can find this place today, if we will intentionally step off the treadmill and set an appointment to meet with God alone. Our ordained oasis is in the arms of the Father…drinking deeply of the living, yet still, waters of Christ.

Go to your calendar and set aside a half-day block of time in the next week, if possible, and make an appointment to be alone with God. When you get away, bookmark this page, grab your Bible and a notebook, and then drive, bike, or walk to a solitary place. Jesus did this often, and like water baptism, his regular example is a pattern of obedience for us. You may wish to listen to some soothing meditative music, a scripture CD, or some favorite worship tunes as you roll down the road. To prepare, I have made it easy for you. Go to www.core300.org/privateretreats and print out the "My Half Day with God" page and some of the scriptures to reflect upon. If you are a veteran of longer times away, we have some models for one, two, and three day retreats as well. Choose a quiet place where no one can find you (if it is *really* remote, make sure a loved one knows where you are). When you get to your destination (beach, mountains, park, or lakeside), turn off the cell (no, it can't be on vibrate!) and iPod so you can FOCUS. Now, after you have settled down, take five *deep* breaths, slowly counting 8 seconds breathing in, and eight seconds breathing out.

> *Come to me, all you who are weary (exhausted) and burdened (toil from weights on your shoulders or from grief and sorrow), and I will give you rest."*

--Matthew 11:28

Baal-Gad - the "lord of good fortune," Joshua 11:17

This deity was worshipped by the Northern Canaanites conquered by Joshua's army. "What happens in Vegas stays in Vegas" is a common mantra and a branding campaign for the city of Las Vegas. People from all social strata flock to this city or to other sites that promote the games of chance. The addictive rush of adrenalin for just the *opportunity* to be blessed by "Lady Luck" squanders billions of dollars every month. Others are content for a chance to win it big in the lottery. The world system will always throw in our paths a promised shortcut that invariably turns into a detour…taking you out of your ordained running lane so you might get rich quickly. God's word actually promises *punishment* to those who take this route.

Baal-Hamon - the "lord of wealth," Song of Solomon 8:11

Similarly, Baal-Hamon pulls us all to different degrees. Part of what my company does is provide executive coaching for senior executives and thus, I have often found myself listening to the problems, hopes, and challenges of business owners and executives who by almost any standard of economic measurement are raving successes. The 30 percent hit they took on their assets in the economic downturn of 2008-2009 still comprises more money than you or I will make in a lifetime.

However, close up, I have seen how wealth has become a *burden* for many of these men and women. As Jesus said in the Parable of the Sower, the seed that was sown among the weeds initially sprouted with promise, but soon found the "*cares* (anxiety) of this world and the *deceitfulness* of riches"[10] choking out all of the fresh, vibrant life that had begun to grow. There was to be no fruit for this soil...and no lasting legacy.

The wisdom of Agur, as recorded as a prayer in Proverbs, says:

Give me neither poverty nor riches...Lest I be full and deny You and say, "Who is the LORD?" Or lest I be poor and steal, And profane the name of my God.

--Proverbs 30:8-9 New King James Bible

However, just because you may not be "wealthy" at this present moment doesn't mean you're so easily off the hook here! The "American Dream" has grown since the 1950s to not only include owning your own home (mortgaged of course) and a car in every garage, but to acquiring three cars (in, of course the 3-car garage), a boat, and perhaps even a beach house (for some guys swap out the beach house for a private duck blind or ski condo)! How much is enough? Today's downturn has re-anchored many of our values by necessity. However, history has shown us that after a serious belt-tightening, a return to a prosperous economy will cause most of us to dive back into spending at an outrageous level.

I know many men who have paid the dearest of prices for chasing the brass ring, however you may define it. A dead or broken marriage often comes with alienated kids with holes in their souls, not because of divorce, but because their parents valued stuff more than they valued each other and their children. How quickly weeks turn into years because we bowed daily at the shrine of Baal-Hamon.

Baal-Hazor - "Baal's village," 2 Sam 13:23

"Conventional wisdom" is defined in Wikipedia as "a term used to describe ideas or explanations that are generally accepted as true by the public or by experts in a field." These commonly held opinions can also be referred to as "group thought" and reflect the popular, media supported viewpoints of the world. The idea of a superior "collective" group-thinking is assumed to be wiser than the individual or family unit, and arrogantly assumes what was best for an ever "evolving" society.

The voice of the village can be heard over the airwaves, TV, and in print. Free speech is tolerated as long as it agrees with the collective. For me, as a parent concerned about the future, humanistic philosophies are canned, quoted, and driven down the throats of our children from elementary school through higher education.

> If I have kneeled to Baal-hazor, I will feel either bigger or smaller, depending on who I am with or where I am.

Another way the "community" impacts us is through the amount of energy and resources we spend maintaining a standard of living that is often measured by advertising, commercials, and our neighbors. For young people they know this god as "peer pressure."

The Bible teaches that for us to compare ourselves with others is foolish,[11] and yet that is what I unconsciously do every time I go out into the marketplace. I think to myself, "How can Fred, my neighbor, afford the new, bright yellow Porche 997-series Turbo?"

When my wife and I recently went to a church family's house for the first time, I remarked to her on the way home, "I had no idea they lived in such a huge, well-decorated home (as compared to mine)...this guy must really be bringing home some serious money or they are in debt to their earlobes." To add further to my dwindling ego as a manly provider, my wife innocently remarked, *"Yeah, and did you see the size of the rock on Mary's hand? It must have been over three carats!"*

The tragedy, however, goes far beyond my bruised ego. As I unwisely compare myself to others, I also forget my glorious position and inheritance in Christ. When I buy into the world's definitions of happiness, the trickle-down effect penetrates the fragile veil between generations as well. The television and internet, as well as the

96

environment of our schools, shape our children and grandchildren. But research has clearly shown that the value system and lifestyle *of the parents* have by far, the deepest influence on a young person's life choices and direction.

Some long-term Christian friends of mine were over for dinner some time ago, and we were talking about their son Jason's choices regarding which college to go to. The talented high school junior had promise. Paired with a strong GPA and a sharp mind, he had that wide-eyed optimism that said to the world, "The sky is the limit!"

However, Jason and his best friend Mark had been deeply stirred in the last two years by the Holy Spirit and had become active disciples of Jesus, getting involved as mentors in middle school ministry and serving on the worship team. They had both prayed about God's direction for their lives and had decided to forsake a secular education and go to a local accredited Liberal Arts Bible College. Mark went to his mom, a single parent who was unchurched, and she was concerned about him "wasting four years" on an education that would not set him up to enter the high energy business world where he could make a life for himself and a future family. But Mark had an ace in the hole. Jason's parents, who attended the same church with the boys, had a significant influence on Mark's life and they were well-liked by his mom. He and Jason decided to seek their advice and then leverage the idea back to his mom to win her over.

As the boys sat down with Jason's parents and presented their hearts for serving Jesus and young people, and told them of their dream for Bible College and preparing for full-time ministry as their vocation, the atmosphere in the room changed. Jason's parents were not happy about where these boys were setting their cap. What did they know? With some strong arguments, they were able to persuade both boys that the nearby, high prestige state university was a much wiser decision...and one that they would support. They argued that if they felt called to the ministry after they graduated from this more "reputable" institution, they could pursue ministry then. But whose definition of "reputable" were they using?

We all knew this school had a serious reputation as one of the West Coast's leading party schools. There was even a special campus holding-lounge where publicly intoxicated minors could "sleep it off," providing amnesty to card-carrying students to exempt them from local law enforcement! I was dumbfounded at hearing of this decision, but unfortunately, I bit my tongue in cowardice, saying nothing. I deeply regret not risking the relationship for this window of opportunity in these young men's lives. In a few short weeks both had registered for the state university and that next fall, off they went to school.

The first year for these two fine men was a disaster. By mid-winter, they had learned to party hard almost every night. By year's-end, both had flunked out and returned home as failures. Both boys also became addicted to illegal substances for years. Today, one remains bound by alcoholism and despair. Neither one has voluntarily stepped into a church for a decade.

Why did these two Christian, church-going parents give such disastrous advice? Let's reflect on the previous chapter where we looked at the three arenas of warfare. Like many American men and women I have known, the world system, or village viewpoint, conforms their values to the lens of worldly success. Their worldview was not focused on heavenly values and the need for these young men to follow their hearts in obedience to God.

I know too many men and women who brag about how blessed they are because their son or daughter got into such and such school. And it can start as early as preschool! I confess that I too have done this, and I fear I was sometimes more proud of the name and rank of the school's pedigree in the world's eyes than I am of the quality of my son's heart and walk as a disciple of Jesus.

This battlefield between Godly values and worldly values has proved to be the place where many Christian parents have succumbed to weighing economic opportunity over God's calling, and career over taking up the cross and following Jesus.

Baal-Meon - "lord of the dwelling," Numbers 32:38

This idol harmonizes pretty well with Baal-Hamon. However, figuring out if you are hanging out with the home god can get pretty dicey. Firstly, as fathers, we want to provide a safe place for our family, and a home that is comfortable and provides both the space for hospitality and the privacy we each desire. I also want to live in a decent and safe neighborhood where people take care of their lawns!

Although it is easy to be misunderstood when making gender-based generalities, what complicates this further is that the man generally looks at the dwelling as a *house* and the woman as her *home*...an extension of who she is. It is a reflection of her decorating tastes, a sense of pride and security in her nest.

For men, it is sufficient to simply open our hearts and ask God if we are hung up on our home or not. Are you in a small apartment and unhappy...discontented with your portion? It may be because you have bowed to Baal-Meon. Do you wait for compliments on your home when someone comes over for the first time and feel badly if they don't remark about it? How much did you sacrifice for that compliment? How much father-daughter time was pushed aside over the years seeking to uphold the standard—not a standard of values, love, and fruits of the spirit—but of extraordinary landscaping, artwork, or impressive square footage?

Have you ever asked *God* if He liked your home? Is He welcome in every room?

Baal-zebub – the "lord of the flies," 2 Kings 1:3; Matthew 10:25

Zebub is the most familiar god surnamed Baal and literally means the "lord of the flies." Historical evidence as to what this means is sketchy, but on one occasion a King of Israel was sentenced to death because he sought the counsel of this demon instead of God.

The worship of this style of Baal may have been relevant to the farming-based economy of the day. Meat and produce were difficult to store and preserve for any length of time. Fly larvae, or maggots, were a very real danger to the future of this society.

The people, therefore, would highly value a god who could preserve or keep safe the storage of their harvest and livestock, in a

We may often be fooling ourselves that, in this enlightened, twenty-first century, we are unaffected by idolatry. I am convinced it is so pervasive that we often find it difficult to distinguish between our desires to serve and please the one true God, who demands all of our allegiance, and the polytheistic divinities that permeate every fiber of our world.

similar way that we may value a retirement account or investment advice from a stock broker or financial planner. Future posterity can preoccupy much of our time. Whether this was the reason why they sacrificed to Baal-zebub or not, I know the concerns that can often knock me off center in my day-to-day walk with Jesus...and the absolute struggle with fear of the future that can seek to oppress me and those close to me.

Similarly, insurance policies can be a warm (and costly) security blanket as well. I know a nationally well-known and respected man of God who refuses to carry *any* insurance for himself or for his family. His answer to what appears to be grossly irresponsible by many is that if Jesus said take no thought about tomorrow and to trust in the Father, we should take Him at His word and trust in His protection and provision.

These times can seem frightening...and for many they are marked with real times of want. I pray we never return to the days of opulence and outright irresistible borrowing and spending by many at the outset of this third millennium. Now more than ever, every day, I must cast all of my cares on Him, for He cares for me and mine. I cannot be successful in navigating my day unless I am also willing to tear down the altar of Baal that attempts to compel me towards *fear of not having enough* tomorrow or of the spoiling of that which I am now steward over.

Baal-Peor – the "lord of the opening," Deuteronomy 4:3

Peor was the version of Baal worshipped by the Midianites. Like lawless pirates, they simply took advantage of any opportunity or "opening" that presented an advantage to them. Their *modus operandi* was to bully and plunder whenever they could, using expediency as needed. The law was for the strong to dominate the weak and there was no remorse because survival and domination of the fittest prevailed. "Do unto others before they do unto you" was their motto. Pragmatic narcissism dictated their actions. Their form of worship was also marked by orgies and child sacrifice, forsaking both fidelity and the future generation for their agenda of success.

Some scholars believe that this represented the opening of the womb of fruitfulness for an individual, family, or community. Feeding the engine of materialism and commerce today is capitalism. For many years, capitalism has been identified with what is distinctive about the United States. When I was once in London on business, I was in a conversation with a British businessman and we began talking about the differences between "Yanks" and "Brits" in their approach to business. At one point he said, "You Yanks are much more willing to sacrifice everything for commercial success. I admire your work ethic…but most of the chaps I work with are not willing to pay as dear a price to win as you are."

Jesus warned of this deity as well, but He referred to it using a term common in His day. He called it "Mammon." In context, He warned His followers that they could not simultaneously serve God and Mammon; you must love the one and hate the other.[12] I am convinced that much of the conflict that has plagued Christians…much of the stressors we have tolerated… has been due to these two streams, the one pure and life-giving, and the other corrupt and polluted. The two can't flow from the same heart. James' letter reminds me that a double-minded man is unstable in all his ways indeed!

Baal Chronos in modern times

A final note on Baal worship is worth mentioning, though not directly referenced as a Baal in scripture. The Grecian Golden Age emerged between the writings of the Old and New Testament. As they conquered lands in the Middle East, they encountered the Canaanite Pantheon, centered around Baal. Having their own gods, they renamed Baal as Chronos or the god of time.

After I launched into the business world from the relative innocence as a Biology student at my *Alma Mater*, I soon acquired a monkey on my back. In the modern Chronos bucket, you'll find concepts like "competitive advantage," "goal achievement," "multi-tasking," and "high performance." The *edge* goes to the individual performer or industry leader who has the highest sales, profitability, or market share. In my day-to-day life as a businessman, I fight this "demon" monkey more than any other.

In the third century B.C., the conquests of Alexander the Great brought the Greek culture and value system to the Middle East, Northern Africa, Asia, and Southern Europe. One of these developments was the evolution of Baal into the god Chronos, or the god of *time*. Out of reverence for Chronos, the Phoenicians, and especially the Carthaginians, seeking to obtain a divine favor, would vow to sacrifice one of their children to the deity.

Today, Chronos has reemerged through the acceleration of technology as that hard taskmaster who demands more and more of our allegiance. Instead of parents offering their children as sacrifices, however, we have a much more civilized and enlightened approach. We provide them with nannies, television, computers, and video games, so that both mom and dad can press their shoulder to the wheel of time and extract every penny possible to achieve the American Dream. Add to this three generations (Boomers, X and Y) who have apparently been given over to investing great amounts of money and time to try to *slow the process of time* with plastic surgery, pharmaceutical virility cures, cosmetics, and extravagant spa diets.

After a long day at work, which was interrupted by a divine visitation from God, a costly sacrifice, and finished off with a miraculous all-consuming blast of fire, Gideon returned home and went to bed. I wonder what his last thoughts were as he fell asleep. A mighty warrior...me? How can such a thing happen? If I truly am a man of valor, where would I begin?

God visited him in his dreams, ordering him to do the unthinkable. Go up to the village shrine...the place of deadly sacrifice and orgiastic worship...to the altar of Baal and the totem of his wife (the goddess Asherah) and destroy them both! Do you see the process of God, leading Gideon through the gates, one by one, into his calling?

- He interrupts his work, addressing him with a new name
- He fully engages him, bringing the reality of his weakness to the forefront, and then affirms his leadership destiny as a Deliverer to his people
- He moves Gideon's heart towards priestly worship at a deepest level of sacrifice
- Gideon watches as God performs a wondrous miracle consuming the sacrifice with fire
- God affirms him again, and calls him to go cross-current with his parents and community

The raised ante here for Gideon goes beyond moving in obedient sacrifice in the midst of resistance from his wife and children. He would have to tear down the altar of his father and destroy the central focus of obeisance for his *entire community*. This shrine was the hub of their wheel. If somehow he survived the ire of his town, what would happen to his ability to provide for his loved ones if he obeyed God? It did not take a calculator to figure out that this was probably a one-way suicide mission.

We all know Gideon successfully accomplished exactly what God had commanded him to do. He and his ten men leveraged the power of the bull and completely destroyed the Baal shrine and place of sacrifice. What about you and me? Take a few minutes and review the different Baals described above and write down the ones that were quickened to you by the Holy Spirit. Be as specific as you can. If you are going through the book with other men, share openly how the enemy may have penetrated your heart with Baal-like worldly attitudes and carnal mindsets. How have these idols inadvertently, but strategically, taken up residence in *your* heart and mind?

As important, is the hard follow-on question...what has it cost me? What has it cost my family?

For though we live in the world, we do not wage war as the world does. The weapons we fight with are not the weapons of the world. On the contrary, they have divine power to demolish strongholds (lit. fortress). We demolish arguments (hostile reasonings) and every pretension (lit. elevated barrier) that sets itself up against the knowledge of God, and we take captive every thought (lit. evil purpose) to make it obedient to Christ.

-- 2 Corinthians 10:3-5

In this foundational verse on spiritual warfare, it sounds as if the great Apostle had just finished reading about Gideon's dream in Judges 6! Apply this teaching to your list of Baals and see where these "strongholds" and worldly pretensions come to lift themselves up above God, with evil purposes, for you and those you love.

Jesus is the great burden-bearer, who calls us to walk alongside Him, walking in the light yoke of laboring for Him. But, although you may not be hiding in the winepress any longer, you may be overwhelmed with the size and weight of the Baals in your life, and you can no more tear it down with your own strength than you could tear down a ten-story building!

Your pathway to freedom is one of *violently* casting down these altars, praying in the mighty Name of Jesus, much in the same way that Gideon had to use the full-grown ox to destroy the altar in his village.

Jesus' attitude about His temple

On two accounts, the scripture tells us that Jesus violently "cleansed" the Temple in Jerusalem. The first occasion was early in his ministry and the second was a few days prior to his crucifixion.

We know from biblical history that God demands the fidelity of his people and that, when they pollute their lives with the worship of other gods, it drives Him to a fierce jealousy. I believe the same was true with Jesus on these two occasions. For almost 1,000 years, He had observed His people entering the temple with divided hearts. He was bringing the New Covenant which would redefine the Temple as the individual body, spirit, and soul of the believer. Time after time, Jesus had cleansed the defiled temples of lepers, the ill, lame, and the demonized. Would it not also be appropriate for Jesus to claim that His Father's house should also be cleansed in order to make it a House of Prayer for all nations? Let us not forget the holy zeal of Christ as He entered into the temple square and began turning over tables like a scene from a bar brawl. It is healthy for us to soberly acknowledge that we have truly been "bought with a price" and that His jurisdictional rights of occupancy are complete.

Destroying the Baals

God *hates* idols in our hearts not because He is insecure, but because it strangles our faith, steals from our future, and severely handicaps our future generations.

"Men, the time for half measures and talk are over...
The deeds we do this day will echo in eternity"

> *-- General Meridus Maximus, Gladiator,*
> *meditations of Marcus Aurelius,* 170-180 AD

You may feel a kind of resistance or fear of tearing down of these entities in your soul. Don't be alarmed! This is normal. Who will I be without these idol(s) in my life? But you need to find the courage…then get angry at all you have lost…and like Jesus, get your game face on and determine to cleanse your temple!

To help you break through to freedom, we have found it psychologically and spiritually effective to ask the men to be willing to *involve their bodies*; their voices, their hands, and even feet as a part of this prayer. *Don't let self-consciousness prevent you from continuing.* It was violent with Gideon…it needs to be possibly the strongest prayer of your life. If you are alone, ask yourself, are you self-conscious in front of yourself? In front of God? Of course not.

First, cultivate an atmosphere of thanksgiving before God. His Word promises that He inhabits the praises of *His* people, so speak out loud **specific things** you are thankful for and then offer prayers of praise to Him.

When we are together in a group, the men will normally stand together to say a **Prayer of Releasing** to God. It is written below. Recall the specific Baals you have identified on your list. Then pray the prayer and begin tearing them down, one at a time. Try clapping your hands or even stomping your feet. With each clap, see that particular point of influence or control torn down, crumbling before you like an old building being demolished by sequentially timed dynamite charges. The dynamite is the power (*dunamis*) of the Holy Spirit in Jesus' name, and every demonic idol. Then see them shattered under your feet. After a minute or two of this, worship and thank God for your new freedom and ask for a fresh filling of the Holy Spirit.

NOTE: To help with this process it might be worthwhile to listen to the CD or MP3 called **Breaking Down Your Altars**, where I bring a message on Baal and Asherah and then lead in prayer to break down the altars of Baal and later on the Altar of Asherah. The balance of the message should be reserved for the end of Chapter 6. Included in the purchase of this book is a private link (free download) at www.core300.org/freedomdownload.

If you are participating together with a group of men, whether with a live teacher, or through the DVD or CD, get together to pray the prayer below. If you are reading this book alone (as many will be), pray the Prayer of Releasing below:

Prayer of releasing

My Lord Jesus...thank you for claiming my victory when you rose from the dead and for the present power of your resurrection right now. Thank You that you are also a mighty burden-bearer able to help me pull down any stronghold that has gripped my life.

I confess to You my sin of allowing other gods to influence and control me. Forgive me Lord and open my eyes to see the freedom that You have for me as your man of war.

I confess the following altars in my life:
1.

2.

3.
And I repent of serving them in any way. I forsake them and renounce their influence in my life forever!

Now in Jesus' Name, and in His power and authority over every high thing of darkness, and over the world spirit, I break down the altars by name (begin intense clapping as you name the Baals and as they fall down, or stomping your feet, seeing them crushed, entirely)

I cast them down, far away from my mind. I tear down every philosophy, every argument, every bondage, and every influence that these have had in my life and through me in my family.

Lord Jesus, I establish a new singular and proper altar to You in my heart...totally devoted to You. Heavenly Father, I come to

You as a free man, no longer hindered by the false gods of this present world. Thank you for setting me free! Amen.

In your new level of awareness and freedom, make sure you engage in the Word of God at a deeper level than before. Let God's Word fill those places that were once occupied by foreign influences and boldly walk in a new level of freedom.

Table talk

1. Which Baal do you struggle with the most? Why? How is Baal integrated into your self-image as a man?

2. How have we sacrificed our children? What does it mean to be a leader-servant-father?

3. Under what value systems are we raising your kids?

Core conditioning

Take your list of Baals and sit down with your spouse or your 911 buddies and talk through them together. Ask them where they see the fingerprint of these gods in your life.

Chapter Six:

From Asherah to Ashes

In my late twenties, I sat yet again in front of my mentor and pastor in his office for counseling, spilling my guts in humiliation of how I had been taken down by pornography. I felt so isolated in my carnality, *"Why has God cursed me with being so **oversexed**?"* I asked.

Daryl gently chuckled...not the reaction I was expecting. He replied, *"Art, one of the oldest tactics of the devil, and he has been at it for thousands of years, is to work closely with your inherent male desires throughout the day and then fan your lust into a flame while you reach for porn to complete your fantasies. Then, boom! He is instantly on your back, slamming you to the mat with remorseful, hopeless feelings of guilt and worthlessness."* My eyes locked on him as my mentor paused, *"He is hoping it will be days before you crawl back to God."*

"The second big lie is that you are somehow 'special' or a freak," continued Daryl, *"overloaded with testosterone to the extent that **you cannot win this battle**."* It has been a comfort to learn in my study of scripture over the years, that Jesus was hit with the similar strategy when

108

the devil tempted him in the desert with the preemptive, '*If you are the Son of God*[1]. I had believed that I was so unique as to deserve special treatment from God, and the devil played that card with Jesus because He was the Son of God. The outcome, of course was different...Jesus was *ready* for it. He *never* gave in...He *never* got beat in a fight."

I did not want to hear that I was not special. I had comforted myself in the lie that I was endowed with hormones...a biological mistake that was not my fault. But it was freeing to know that other guys had the same drawing to the fire...and struggled to gain dominion. It was also good to be reminded that Jesus had the same drawings and temptations as I did, but He never fulfilled them in his heart or body as I had done...far too many times to count.

I swear, the shame was so great, that I sometimes wanted to just let it roll, and yield some temporary ground in my soul, while I did my best to keep the rest of my walk with Jesus intact. But I feared that once giving in, I might never recover.

> *I believe that pornography is the gigantic "pink elephant" that the church must address, if the men are to be able to lead effectively. The Warrior course was an inspiration to all the guys and had a refreshing quality of openness, both from the teacher and at the tables. We learned how to share our mutual weaknesses...to be more genuine with one another as we joined ranks with our brothers.*

--Tom Erdman, Director
Everyman's Battle Ministry

In this chapter, we will attempt to take a full, Biblical "swing" at answering the following questions:

- What are the components and practices of Asherah worship as it relates to us?

- What is the big deal about sex? Why has Satan invested so much spiritual energy in sexual pollution and compromise?

- How do the combined three forces of evil, CWD (Carnality, World System, Devil), orchestrate warfare on your sexuality?

- How is your life and that of many others, at stake in the war?

- Why has *God* designed this unique battle to prepare you as a man of honor and power in ministry for His glory?

- How can we walk free in an ongoing, victorious lifestyle?

The Goddess Asherah

Asherah was the principal goddess at the time of Judges 6, and she was the personification of the reproductive principle in nature. Her name in Hebrew literally means 'Grove' and she was a Canaanite goddess often symbolized by a carved pillar or totem. As the "Queen of Heaven,"[2] she was supposed to have given birth to 70 gods of the Canaanite pantheon and personally nursed them as infant gods. Some cults today still honor her as 'mother nature."

Asherah is referred to 40 times in the Old Testament. As Baal's wife or consort, she was represented by an engraved totem pole next to his image, where they could together assure a tribe of worshippers that their efforts for fruitfulness and reproduction would be blessed.

Other names she was called by ancient peoples in the Fertile Crescent were Athirat, Aphrodite, Astarte, and Ishtar. In 1 Kings 18:19 there were four hundred active prophets of Asherah who ate at Jezebel's table. Although jealously forbidden by the God of Israel, oftentimes this idol was erected near centers of Yahweh worship. Once an Asherah was erected *in* the Temple in Jerusalem.

Temples of Baal and Asherah were usually found together in major cities or side-by-side in villages as they were in Gideon's town. Priestesses were temple prostitutes. Sodomites were male temple prostitutes. Worship often resulted in fervent, animistic orgies.

Archaeological diggings show many images and plaques of Asherah with rudely exaggerated sex organs. The cultures who worshipped this idol had gone far beyond simply appealing to these gods for a fruitful harvest; they were steeped in sexual preoccupation and perversions. Paul described a similar condition in the first chapter of his letter to the church in Rome, which had lived for decades under the decadent leadership of the two most lascivious Caesars, Caligula and Nero. Let's look at his description of the depravity of man:

For although they knew God, they neither glorified him as God nor gave thanks to him, but their thinking became futile and their foolish hearts were darkened...Therefore God gave them over in the sinful desires of their hearts to sexual impurity for the degrading of their bodies with one another. They exchanged the truth of God for a lie, and worshiped and served created things rather than the Creator—who is forever praised. Amen.

Because of this, God gave them over to shameful lusts. Even their women exchanged natural relations for unnatural ones. In the same way...Men committed indecent acts with other men, and received in themselves the due penalty for their perversion. Furthermore, He (God) gave them over to a depraved mind, to do what ought not to be done. They have become filled with every kind of wickedness... Although they know God's righteous decree that those who do such things deserve death, they not only continue to do these very things but also approve of those who practice them.

-- Romans 1:21-32

What is the big deal about sex?

Since the time that God made man and woman with the ability to procreate, Satan has been *enraged* with jealousy. We must remember that his aspirations are to be like God in every way and when God gave the ability for mankind to reproduce unique living beings imprinted with God's image his only recourse was to declare war on everything that surrounds this creative capability. What is the *net result* of overindulgence in sexual promiscuity and preoccupation by a society? Recent demographic and social studies have brought some surprising conclusions to the surface.

The decline in birth rates in Japan and other more sexually "progressive" nations have been linked to a decline in the frequency of people engaging in sexual intercourse. The irony is that, as pornography and preoccupation with sexual fantasy increase, real sex and birth rates decline. Multimedia exposure to sexual content permeated a society that resulted in shrinking intimacy and population! Populations are in decline with an average household giving birth to only 1.2 children among many European countries.[3]

Historically, the carnal nature of *men* has lead women and entire civilizations into sexual bondage. The Roman Empire during the years of the reigns of Caligula and Nero (AD 37-68) descended into massive gross immorality and it brought serious decline to the strength of the empire, giving place for laxness in the discipline of the military and the quality of public service. Famine and disease followed the gradual erosion of the integrity of this massive and seemingly indestructible empire.

The writer of Ecclesiastes wrote, "There is nothing new under the sun," so this is not a new problem. The eruption of Mount Vesuvius in AD 79 almost instantly buried the entire city of Pompeii under 60 feet of volcanic ash, sealing for modern archaeologists the contemporary first century lifestyles of the people in this city with remarkable accuracy. Pornographic painting, mosaics, and sculptures were pervasive, adorning the walls of homes, public places, streets, and temples of this city.

It has been long thought that, due to the nature of art in Pompeii, it was the sexual capital of the Roman Empire. Recent research has debunked that theory with findings that nearly every excavation from major Roman cities contained evidence of sexually-charged content.

What was clear in the *messages* conveyed by these ancient images is also clear in the message of pornography today: that a man can be elevated to an object of worship if a woman can be debased to an object of pleasure...at his whim, and under his control. Male porn for women accomplishes the same objective, elevating a woman to the status of a goddess through words spoken and acts of obeisance.

Ephesians 5:3-4 says:

But among you there must not be even a hint of sexual immorality, or of any kind of impurity, or of greed, because these are improper for God's holy people. Nor should there be obscenity, foolish talk or coarse joking, which are out of place.

"Flee from sexual *immorality"* (1 Cor. 6:18) The Bible tells us to "resist" or contend against, the devil...but to *flee* sexual immorality and youthful lusts. It is the only battle from which we are to immediately retreat. Don't stand around looking at it – if you do, it will snare you.

In a conversation recently with one of my sons, a college student, I was preparing to bring The Warrior series (the same material in this Chapter) to a group of coed Christian college athletes, at one of our nation's leading universities. We were half way through The *Warrior* track and the group had already doubled in size as compared to any previous gathering, and lives were being transformed. I had been speaking to men on this subject for some time, but never to a mixed audience. I asked my son, *"What is different about this new generation* (called the "Y" generation) *that is different than the way your mom and I think when it comes to sex?"* He immediately responded, *"We live with a daily pressure from our peers to engage in casual sex. We are not supposed to get attached to one another…it is supposed to be for entertainment only."* I tried to grasp his meaning…and then I saw it. How similar it must have been in Gideon's day. It, for them, was *perfunctory* worship…it was supposed to be no big deal. *Everybody* did it.

How much our western society resembles the altar of Asherah today! The hope for our youth…and yes for the church in America, depends upon those men who still fight. We must maintain and mentor young people in the truth that sexual intimacy is one of the most sacred, special and wonderful gifts of God. And that it is designed for a husband and wife to declare their love and fealty to one another. *This bond is at the very **core** of family.* The devil's strategies and the incessant waves of the world system have gradually overwhelmed the unwary and eroded the unprotected and fallen human nature in our culture. For many of our sons and daughters, it has become a part of an evening of entertainment; dinner, a movie…some texting…and sex.

It's all about worship

In the movie **Fireproof**, starring Kirk Cameron, there is a scene where he comes face-to-face with the life-sucking parasites of the duality of worshipping the dream of owning a boat and a disabling addiction to internet pornography. After a tug of war in prayer, his eyes are opened and his countenance changes. He gets "game face."

Moving quickly, he seizes the computer monitor and chassis and goes into his back yard, placing them both on top of a table. Picking up a metal baseball bat, he attacks both components with full swings, shattering them into pieces until there is no hope of repair. He then stuffs the remains in the trash can. The idol, for this man, is destroyed. Asherah has been chopped down to never rise again.

Sinning through sexual impurity is *the most powerful strategy the enemy has* because it uniquely accomplishes five things other sins do not:

1. The mental and emotional aspects of satisfying yourself sexually can lead to ever increasing forms of Hedonism and a perversion of the way we relate to women. It also causes a decline in our desire for our wives, (if married) or even over time to have children. If you are single, you will experience a decreased desire to wait for the partner of your dreams. Our loneliness, which we may have been partly trying to diminish by pornography or fornication, is *increased* not decreased.

2. *It burns us.* We feel an immediate separation from our relationship with the Father after we give place to sin. How could he want to be with me now? God is robbed of true open worship for a season…or longer, and we are robbed of the strengthening joy and communion of the Lord, with the beauty of His holiness. The effect of this burning is that our conscience can become "seared as with a hot iron."[4] With frequent enough cycles of sin, we can actually lose our sense of touch in that part of our soul that yearns for God. After a too-long season of habitual sin, the once pure, precious soul before God *can* become defiled, shipwrecked and even condemned to the lostness of having once been in sweet fellowship with the Holy Spirit…now an outcast, disengaged and disinherited from experiencing life in the Kingdom of God. Where does one cross the line? We must fear God and treasure His mercy enough to never tread that dark boundary.

Do not be afraid of those who kill the body but cannot kill the soul. Rather, be afraid of the One who can destroy both soul and body in hell.

--Jesus to the Twelve
in Matthew 10:28

3. As the living temple of God, it pollutes His temple. As living members of one body, the church, it links our participation in Asherah's rites to whom we relate in the church, and to defilement. Paul makes it clear when he writes in 1 Corinthians 6:14-20:

Now the body is not for sexual immorality but for the Lord, and the Lord for the body... Do you not know that your bodies are members of Christ? Shall I then take the members of Christ and make them members of a harlot? Certainly not! Or do you not know that he who is joined to a harlot is one body with her? For "the two," He says, "shall become one flesh," But he who is joined to the Lord is one spirit with Him.

Flee sexual immorality. *Every sin that a man does is outside the body, but he who_commits sexual immorality **sins against his own body**. Or do you not know that your body is the temple of the Holy Spirit who is in you, whom you have from God, and you are not your own? For you were bought at a price; (bold is mine)*

4. It subjects us, yet again, to the act of slavery and obeisance and increases the sense of hopelessness, disqualification, and isolation we feel as a man of God. Like Adam, we will cover up and hide in the woods lest God meet us on the path.

5. It compromises our ability and confidence to minister God's Word and His power to those we love.

Let's return back to Gideon. We see him in verse 25 being instructed to set up *a proper kind* of altar to God. Although Baal was to be torn down, the fuel for worship would be provided after he cut or chopped down the Asherah pole. The word for "cut down" of Asherah was the common word for "dismember," "to sever completely," or "decapitate." In this context, the cutting down of the Asherah totem most probably required severing into many smaller parts in order to use it for sacrificial firewood and then split with the axe to be used for kindling on the new altar of worship to Yahweh.

Take a moment and read this excerpt (with some paraphrasing) from the classic by C.S. Lewis, **The Great Divorce.**[5] This part tells of a man, who has died hours previously, is traveling on a very special bus towards heaven, along with others who had suffered the same fate. The bus had made a travel stop where he is now having to make a decision as to whether he wants to enter heaven or not.

One of the passengers, an unsightly man, has decided to leave and is headed back to the bus. Sitting on his shoulder is a little red lizard, twitching its tail like a whip, and whispering things in his ear. The man turns his head to the reptile and snarls,

"Shut up, I tell you!"

Just then, one of Heaven's radiant angels sees the man. "Off so soon?" he calls.

"Well, yes," says the man. "I'd stay, you know, if it weren't for him," indicating the lizard. "I told him he'd have to be quiet if he came. His kind of stuff won't do here. But he won't stop. So I'll just have to go home."

"Would you like me to make him quiet?" asks the angel.

"Of course I would," says the man.

"Then I will kill him," says the angel, stepping forward.

Then the man begins to panic at the thought of permanently losing the lizard, which he had, for years, grown accustomed to. There were the sweet fantasies that the creature whispered in his ear. But he is tired of carrying him around. He argues back and forth between the two beings, afraid to choose one path or the other. The reasons for not killing the lizard are many (I have taken a bit of editorial liberty to include some commentary from recalled personal experiences with my own kind of "lizard").

1. *He doesn't want to bother the spirit with killing it (God is too busy to worry about me and my problem).*

2. *It isn't presently bothering him because it went to sleep (I haven't felt much lust lately...maybe it is going away?)*

3. *He'll be able to get it under control himself through gradual process.*

4. *He doesn't feel well enough to go through with "the operation."*

5. *He'll go and get his doctor's opinion (back in hell), and come back later (let me study more and pray about this).*

6. *Finally, he asks why the spirit hasn't killed the lizard yet. If God wanted it gone, He could take it away at any time; this must be my own personal "thorn in the flesh!"*

The lizard has his innuendos and points to make as well (I have taken a few liberties here too):

1. *The angel can kill me, but he'll be killed as well.*

2. *Every other guy has the same issues…it is only natural…like an Irish temper, right?*

3. *The lizard promises to behave himself in the future, especially since you are so much smarter now than before.*

Finally, in anguish, the man asks the angel to kill the lizard, which he immediately reaches out and crushes. "Ow! That's done for me," gasps the man, reeling back. He thought it was the end of him because it hurt so much.

But then, gradually, something wonderful begins to happen. The man begins to be transfigured into a being of beauty and power….much larger in size, yet still the same man. The joy of freedom fills his heart. When he looks over to the carcass of his old wicked friend and companion, he sees that it also has begun to transform. Wonderfully, it grows and changes into a mighty white horse, rippling with muscle, with a golden tail and mane. And he instinctively knew he was the new master of the magnificent beast.

Leaping confidently upon its bare back, they gallop away across the green plains, scaling majestic heights like a fiery comet, into the everlasting presence of eternity.

At the end of this chapter is an opportunity to see God **crush** the lizard of lust in your life. When I was finally fed up of being led by the lizard and faced my fallenness in total confession and surrender, I was still afraid of what life would be like without the old companion. It was not until I was desperate enough to go beyond confession to God and opened up…and stayed open…with a few trusted guys, that I found the freedom I had so longed for.

The secret, as so well revealed by Lewis' analogy, is that your very weakness, now mastered, will release a mighty multiplication of speed and strength to your walk with God.

War's a team sport

Mike was recently a divorced man and, in fact, his failed marriage was a key factor in him coming to faith in Jesus as his personal Savior and Lord. After he learned that his addiction to pornography was a sin, he enrolled into a Christ-centered, sexual addiction class, and he became an active participant in his small group, which held each other accountable to walk in sexual purity.

Mike and his friend Daniel, who led another small group in the same class, gradually developed a close friendship. As the details of his divorce were finalized a year later, Mike met and fell in love with Barbara, who was a single mom and a relatively new Christian as well.. As the relationship grew and got more serious, as happens in many romances, they became more intimate and eventually began having sex. Yet Mike was still leading a small group in their church's sexual purity class, helping guys get free from porn or other debilitating sexual habits. When Daniel discovered this, he knew that he had to risk the relationship by confronting him.

The two men had a private dinner together and chit-chatted for about twenty-five minutes and then Daniel asked him how he and Barbara were doing. A little later, he was able to navigate over to the big question, *"Are you guys having sex?"* He said they were, and he said it as if he was embarrassed, yet without any real understanding of how it might compromise their future together. We all have heard the logic, *"How can two people move to the next level in their relationship without first discovering if they are sexually compatible?"*

The conversation finished with them both concluding that Mike should step down from leading his small men's group while he spent some time praying over what to do. His heart was to align his behavior with the Word of God. Happily, Barbara was reading the Bible on her own...and she began feeling the need to cool off the physical aspect of their relationship as well. Mike and Barbara soon began to walk in celibate love, became engaged, and are now married.

The enemy has so seeded our world with the values and spirit of multitudes of Baals and Asherahs that we often don't realize how he has set up our world to disable us. Our environment has been contrived to buffet our resolve, confuse our thinking and sap our strength. This is why we need to drink of His living water, daily...why we must ingest His Word and surround ourselves with the strength of trusted warriors who share the values of the Kingdom of Heaven. Mike needed a Daniel in his life and Daniel needed the courage to lovingly call Mike on his behavior. Alone, the world system piles on with our carnal nature and will eventually dominate our ways of thinking, demand our resources and ultimate obedience. Eventually, we end up passing these worldly values on to our children.

Satan's strategy for capturing Christian men, and diverting entire families out of alignment with God's Word, has been very successful. Abundant "pornification" attempts to pollute every stream of holiness. "Gentlemen's" Clubs have multiplied and hotels discretely leave movie titles off their receipts so spouses and bosses remain in the dark of what is done in the dark. *We are losing this war*. A big part of the reason is because most of us have been playing defense alone. An *attitude* of "defense only" will make both you and me a loser in the end.

> The reason we are losing the spiritual war is because most men are playing defense alone.

Most guys I know wake up each day wanting to please God. They are subconsciously hoping and praying to yield as little territory to darkness as possible...that their day would not be the day...*or the hour*, to fall or have their breath taken away by lust. "*If this spiritual battle would only stop!*," said one overwhelmed young man, as we talked over breakfast. I told him it won't, but that there is *hope for sustained victory*. He must realize he is in a war and that playing defense leads only to gradual attrition. Most men I know who are otherwise devoted to Christ will confess that they venture out into the workplace without being "suited-up." We will wander out into a crowded mall in the summer with, spiritually speaking, wearing a t-shirt and shorts.

Let him who wants peace prepare for war. -- Vegetius A.D. 4th Century

In the chapters ahead, we will focus on getting suited up and learn how to utilize each component of weaponry with skills taught in God's Word. For now, statistically, most of you have your hands shackled in sexual sin. The three dimensions of warfare strike often upon unarmored men who may not even be aware that these threats exist. The deceiving "angel of light" is so well-disguised, so alluring...and has so infiltrated your private camp, and men camping solo are oblivious to its seduction. Like the proverbial frog in the kettle, the water is boiling and the solitary man is getting poached.

It is all about the seed

Sexuality was created by God as a blessing to enjoy with your bride, to express your love, and to assure that the human race would continue through children. **God knew** that it would be a huge challenge for men to overcome and direct these passions in a healthy way, taking an incredible fabric of character, self-denial, and strength, and would increase his confidence as a warrior.

Understand that *God is angry* about how many of his redeemed sons' lives are squandered through our succumbing to lust. His jealousy for you and me is neither selfish nor childish, but rooted in His deep love for us, combined with a passion to see His sons walk free from these limiting and binding influences. Seeking validation through sexual conquest, whether in fantasy or reality, is a direct rejection of who He has made us to be. And He *hates* to see you being held captive by *anything*.

We have been given, through Jesus' resurrecting power, and by our name being written in the Lamb's book of life, the highest possible level of power and value in all eternity...just short of being equal to God Himself. He is fashioning us to be His Bride!

Then I heard a loud voice in heaven say: "Now have come the salvation and the power and the kingdom of our God, and the authority of his Christ. For the accuser of our brothers, who accuses them before our God day and night, has been hurled

down. They overcame him by the blood of the Lamb and by the word of their testimony; they did not love their lives so much as to shrink from death. Therefore rejoice, you heavens and you who dwell in them!

Revelation 12:10-12

For those who have believed in and have been washed with that saving fountain, the Blood of Christ, they were able to overcome "by the word of their testimony." Paul exhorted us to "*Preach the word; be instant in season, out of season; reprove, rebuke, exhort with all long suffering and doctrine.*" [6]

In the Bible, the word "seed" is used 280 times. In Old Testament writings, there is a distinct focus on the "seed" of man, and success was often measured *not* by the kind of wagon you had or the square footage of your hut, but by the quantity of your sons and daughters....and how large your tribe of grandchildren was. In other words, success was measured by your personal fruitfulness.

The "seed" of Abraham was Isaac, the son of promise, and all of us who followed in his faith. In Hebrew, seed was the word *zehrah,* and it was used interchangeably for the verb "to plant," seed, children, sperm, and as a general reference word to describe future familial generations. It also was the word used by God himself when he promised an inheritance to the many generations of the future.

On the dark side, there was also the curse that the sins of the fathers would be passed on through their seed for four generations,[7] and so it was assumed that sin and the predisposition to sinning would pass along through the seed as well. As is true today, consequences for disobedience and rebellion against God spanned generations.

In the New Testament, the most common word used for seed is the Greek word *sperma.* One of my favorite stories told by Jesus was the Parable of the Sower[8]. In this story, seed was dispersed by the skilled Sower on four different kinds of soils, all of whom related to the seed differently. The seed, per Jesus' interpretation to His disciples, stood for the Word of God sown into men's hearts by God, the Sower.

In one of his letters to the church in Corinth, Paul exhorts the believers towards giving, also using the Sower analogy. He further uses the seed allegory for reaping a fruitful harvest of souls through the extension of preaching the Word of God and the ministry of the church to one another. In addition, most of the miraculous operations of the spiritual gifts given to believers by the Holy Spirit were conveyed through *speaking*. John writes in his first letter that a believer cannot continue to habitually sin because the "seed" of God is in him.[9]

You may want to know where I am going with all of this. This is important. The way Satan has orchestrated our world is for the *primary* purpose of *shutting off the life-giving stream of the spoken seed of Spirit-breathed words from men*. He has attacked our loins so to speak…the seed of our posterity…in order to keep us ashamed so that we are mute. Satan has designed sexual sin as his primary strategy to make men geldings in the Kingdom of God. Your spiritual posterity, which flows from your mouth as a living seed, is "cut off."

> If God has put His seed…His Word in you… If He has called us to be sower's of His message and speakers of new life to others, does it not makes sense that this is where the enemy would strategically work to prevent us from speaking these words…these seeds of life?

Think about it…how often have you or I *not* prayed the way we needed to pray? How often have we not been able to speak words of life and encouragement to someone who needed it? How many times did I fail to sense the flow of the Holy Spirit in me because I was living in the hall of shame? I still today lament that most of my most vigorous years were stolen from me by the thief who had broken in…like the Midianite horde… and neutered the inherent power God had placed in my heart and mouth for the advancement of His Kingdom. And how often have we been *muted* when around non-believers because days, or maybe hours before, we had compromised our souls in mental immorality? When we do speak, there is very little weight, conviction, or authority in our words because of our compromised hearts; for out of the abundance of the heart, the mouth speaks (Luke 6:45).

The enemy is angry and has an increased sense of urgency in these last days…and he is winning the war in our country because our mouths are gagged due to feelings of disqualification. Therefore, our wives, sons and daughters wither like vines without the fuel they need to follow Jesus.

Gideon first heard the prophet calling for repentance. God challenged him and gave him an *explicit prescription for freedom…to chop the goddess into pieces*. Once he finished, there would be no way to rebuild the idol because it would be consumed in the flames of Gideon's offering of worship. The Holy Spirit, the great liberator, is calling you to be free from the dungeons of sterility and to see God break through years of sinful habits so that you can wield the Sword of the Word of God and do mighty exploits in His Name.

I envision Gideon and his troop of ten helpers ascending to the detestable hillside equipped with axes, pikes and ropes. This was a "Special Ops" mission so they probably had a few swords as well, in case they were discovered. As they begin to tie the ropes to the idol of Baal, their memories of sacrificed sons or daughters, nieces and nephews, and maybe brothers and sisters now long gone, surely stirred in their breasts. By the time they moved to the female deity, I can see them in a *frenzy of destruction*, violently cutting the Asherah pole into pieces. Those fervent actions broke her grip upon their souls...on their wives (remembering how they had been with other men in the rituals before the idol) and their children I can imagine that these guys were like Viking "Berserkers"...overcome with a zeal for justice and yet unhealed wounds in their soul as they dealt out retribution for the years of loss, guilt and shame!

We must capture this fury when we face a stronghold of Asherah in our lives.

Then, like Gideon, who brought ten men with him to destroy this stronghold, we should encircle ourselves with strong and trusting brothers who will stand with us, shields braced, to defend, and protect one another...and advance towards God's predestined plan for our lives. It's a team sport.

I look at the demonic spirit behind Asherah as *like a heinous virus*, seeking to gain a foothold on me and spread its DNA throughout my soul and my family....and generations of "seed" to come. Ultimately, it carries with it the programming to both consume us and make us a carrier to infect others that we love. Each time you kneel before this Asherah, the virus lays thin tendril of an invisible cord around you...and then seeks to extend "her" feelers into your next generation. One or two times the influence is easy to break, but over the months and years, it continues to lay down...row after row, line after line, year after year, until you realize that you are a prisoner.

Where do you start? First, you must acknowledge that you're responsible for your actions and that God is not happy with you being tied up in personal, repetitive, sexual sin. He *passionately* wants you free, and that is very sobering, but good news.

Some lizards are "reasoners", planting theologically false premises in the minds of some Christian leaders who then teach others. Like the man with the lizard on his shoulder, some pastors and theologians would rather *pretend* that there is no real threat of demonic oppression for believers. As in the Apostle Paul's day, various "theories" crept in to the mainstream church that may have seemed innocuous at first, but they were deadly traps of bondage, and Paul railed against them with all the force he could muster. Pretending that a Christian cannot be seriously encumbered by demonic influences is like declaring that the Emperor his no clothes...simply because you wish it to be so, doesn't make it so.

I believe that a Christian cannot be *possessed* by a demon, but he can be *oppressed* and harassed and sometimes even trapped by forces of darkness. The mighty freeing power of Jesus is needed here, as it was in the first century, to break the cords of repetitive sin once and for all.

Given the same amount of intelligence, timidity will do a thousand times more damage in war than audacity.

Carl von Klauswitz 1780-1831

As in the last chapter, we have some final business to do before we enter that phase of boot camp where we begin building ourselves up with the armor that God has prepared for us.

If you have not done so yet, I *am going to ask you to make an authentic connection with two other men.* Tell them your story. One at a time is ok if that helps. With 70% of Christian men admitting that they watch pornography once per month, or more, you are in a familiar crowd. They may admit to the same...or not, but the important thing is that they listen to you and accept you. If you get a lecture, drop the friend and find another.

Second, listen to the rest of the **Breaking Down Your Altars** CD...this time all of the way through.

Third, as you heard in the introduction of the CD, I am going to ask you to fast from breakfast and lunch all through the day until after you meet with your friends for prayer. If this is not possible due to diabetes or some other serious ailment, then fast for a week from television or coffee or some other activity that you value. Denying your stomach of food is good for you to do from time to time. You can tell your belly who is boss for a change! If it growls at 10 AM, tell it to "shut up!" It will. Set the date of your fast and then end the fast with a time of a special prayer of freedom with your two or three brothers.

Since Gideon was instructed to cut down the altar of Asherah into pieces for firewood, I have seen thousands of men find cleansing and freedom from sexual bondage by using their body, and in this case, their hands in a chopping fashion. It will help to symbolically invoke the violent breaking of the bonds of sin.

Prayer of Releasing

"My Lord Jesus. Thank you again for claiming my victory when you rose from the dead, and for the present power of your resurrection right now. Thank you that you also provide me with the mighty two-edged sword of Your Word, to break down and chop to pieces the stronghold of Asherah in my life!

I confess to you my sin of allowing sexual sin to influence and control me. Forgive me Lord and wash me as white as snow with your cleansing blood...from the crown of my head to the sole of my feet, I receive forgiveness and cleansing for all sin. Open my eyes to see the freedom that you have for me as your mighty warrior.

(You may say this privately to God)

I confess the following sexual sins in my life:

1.

2.

3.

And I repent of serving this idol. I forsake this behavior and renounce its influence in my life forever!

Now, in Jesus Name and in His power and authority over every high thing of darkness, and over the world spirit, **I break down** *the altars by name (begin intense clapping or chopping motion with your hand into your other open hands, as you destroy the lizard of lust).*

I cast it down, *far away from my mind. I tear down every philosophy, every argument, every habit, every influence, every website, every bondage, that these have in my life and through me in my family.*

Lord Jesus, **crush the Asherah lizard on my shoulder** *and turn my weakness into that mighty stallion to anoint my words with your love, boldness, and power! I offer myself on the altar to you now,*

It is vital to your success as a warrior that you also take a few minutes and call one or two of your "911" buddies. Tell them the name of the things you confessed and ask them to stand with you against them. We have almost completed the steps of boot camp, called Breaking Down to Build Up. In the next chapter, the warrior awakens, stronger than ever!

Make me pure, free, and holy in your sight. Holy Spirit, fill me with the newness of your spirit...making me totally devoted to your service. Heavenly Father, I come to you as a free man, Thank you for setting me free! Amen.

Table talk

1. Read Eccl 4:9- Does every man at this table fail sexually? Why?
2. What are the triggers that precede my falling? Why do we stay alone?
3. Why don't we call a trusted brother before we fall sexually? Who is your "911" relationship? What one brother can we commit to and call before we fall into sexual sin?

4. Make that commitment to call that man this week and ask him to be your "911." Hold each man accountable in the group to report on the assignment next time.

An exhortation to pastors and elders

If you are a pastor, like I was for 15 years, or an elder in a church, then consider yourself a marked target. If you are an American, you are probably at an additional high risk of standing alone, which means that you are even more at risk of accountability before God for every believer who will be hurt and could potentially fall away from God if you fail morally.

There are snipers in the woods with a contract to take you down. If you fall in battle, and we all do at times, don't let it be because you failed to man-up, by confessing your pride and casting down your fear! Connect with a couple of guys now and make sure that they know *you inside out.*

If your seminary told you that you cannot have close intimate friends in your congregation, *they are idiots.* When I pastored, I believed this crock of a lie and wound up bound and alone. My bishop was overseeing 225 churches so he was not able to help. My local pastor friends from other churches were my competition. When we had our annual and regional denominational conventions, we always had a good time, but the platform was for the super heroes with the best books and the highest numbers and everyone was posturing for success while privately, many marriages were in peril and many pastors were in pain.

No secret sins

Loners will lose. No friends? Ask God for two 911 brothers and then go make yourself friendly among some good men in your church. The Lord will handle the rest. And remember, this doesn't mean your best couple-friends for double dating fun. There needs to be guy-to-guy and gal-to-gal sharing of your inner battles and fears. Head disaster off at the pass now, because if you don't do this, you will be toast, one way or the other.

Chapter Seven:

Blowing Your Own Horn

Gideon had succeeded in his obedience...and his quest to destroy the worship of demons and restore the worship of Yahweh...but then things got deadly serious for everyone. Judges 6:33 says:

> *Now all the Midianites, Amalekites and other eastern peoples joined forces and crossed over the Jordan and camped in the Valley of Jezreel.*

Now the deed was done, and he and his core of 10 men who served him were somehow miraculously spared the angry crowd by the intercession of his father. Overnight he had earned yet another name, Jeruba'al, meaning "he who contends with Baal."

But this was just the beginning. Before the ashes of Asherah were cold, the report came to the villagers that the Midianites were assembled and about to yet again swoop down upon them, but this time they had

128

brought friends! Amalekites and other eastern tribes had joined in the raiding party.

The imagined fears of Israel…and of this village in particular, are now beginning to become real again. This was going to be the eighth year of pillaging…worse than ever before! The village has just lost their gods, and now, in disarray, Gideon hears word of this imminent threat to his people.

What would you do? My tendency would be to do what had worked before. Save the family. Cut and run. There was surely no dishonor in protecting them first, right? The option of fighting must have looked insane. There was no plan. They had few if any weapons. They had no combat training or experience. And there was a palpable, deep fear in the hearts of the men he knew….his included!

The call to leadership

Leadership is lifting a person's vision to higher sights, the raising of a person's performance to a higher standard, the building of a personality beyond its normal limitations.

-- Peter Drucker

It was two-thirty in the morning on a warm August evening, and my crew and I were half way through our shift. And it was a motley crew of young men…Bible college and seminary students called into the ministry, who had been forsaken, like me, to clean up the two city-block campus of what was **The Church on the Way**, in Van Nuys, California. Five years earlier I had attended my first Men's breakfast and now, after a fulfilling run of success in business, God had called me into Bible College…and this job.

Part of my inherited job description was to "supervise" these young men, and make sure the classrooms, offices and meeting rooms were all cleaned and set up for the events and functions of the next day. Did I mention the restrooms? Over 100 toilets and sinks waited for our "ministry" every night.

I can see their faces now …all good guys between the ages of 19 and 25. I was the old man at 30. We had begun our shift together at 10:30 P.M with prayer as usual. I then had to give out the specific jobs to the teams of two and three, who would then fan across the property armed with their evening tasks.

When I had started working with these men three months earlier, morale was at an all time low. My predecessor supervisor would meet with the men and assign them the duties and then retire to the office for most of the next eight hours. Once each shift, he would walk the property to make sure the guys were working.

When I first met the crew, I knew there was a problem. Their uniforms were disheveled, un-ironed, and often dirty from one or two previous shifts. Some wore their shirts out, others wore theirs tucked in. Some had brown belts, others black and still others used no belt at all. One guy used a rope.

Grooming was no better. Their low estate as a menial laborer had been offered to them, in part, as a method of "discipling"…so they could cut their ministerial teeth in humility. They looked like they had been sentenced to the below decks rowing galley on a Roman slave ship! I knew that change must occur, so I prayed for the first few weeks, seeking wisdom from God while I slowly got to know each man and understand the workflow requirements of the job.

I missed my wife and family in this dark season that spanned three years. These men missed their families as well. As I continued in prayer, I remembered what it had been like to suit up each day in my business suit and tie, and with a recently washed and organized company car. I would drive from customer to customer to sell my company's products. I represented The Parker Pen Company, arguably at that time, the greatest quality pen manufacturer in the world. We all were professional and had earned our customers' respect and loyalty over the past 70 years. When you are the best, you don't need to tout it…you don't need to posture or look bigger than you are.

I began to envision the finest *janitorial crew* in the world and determined that somehow, with God's help, this young rookie leader was going to lift the eyes of each of these men and inspire them to significance.

For starters, I instituted a new rule that no one could be on the clock, unless their uniform was ironed and clean. Torn shirts were discarded or recycled for repair. All would wear black belts and be well groomed. If these young men were going to be representing Jesus Christ as a Pastor in the years ahead, they needed to learn a spirit of excellence now, not later.

I also told them that we were no longer going to play small, but be men who served God and brought Him glory every time we knelt before a toilet, every time we swept and scraped chewing gum off the sidewalk and every time we changed a light bulb.

The effect was dramatic. Their attitude changed. Their posture was different, and their work became a beautiful offering of praise to God in those silent nights where only He saw. People who worked on the church during the day would see us at the beginning or end of our shifts and make comments. They could see the lifted heads and the enthusiasm.

We began to experience less sick days and we began to grow closer to one another. The perfunctory blessing at the beginning of the shift became real. Prayer requests began to include financial hardships, sick babies, and needs for help in their young marriages. Single men began to open up to their struggles with purity. We were in full-time ministry, serving Jesus right where He wanted us!

There were also fewer complaints of below standard work performance from the staff. Most of the comments from staff and pastors were positive. I did get into a bit of trouble from some of the 'Brass" later on, for inadvertently giving these men, who had been assigned to empty out sanitary napkin bins, vacuum acres of carpet, empty trash and scrub floors, *a sense of pride in their mission*. We actually believed what we were doing was as significant to God as the efforts of the worship team and Sunday preacher. The criticism was that someone relegated to this kind of role needs to be *"servantile,"* shuffling along in their humiliation as an outward sign of their humble state.

These young men *lifted their heads*, not in arrogance, but in their sense of *calling* and the *importance* of their mission before *God's* values and rewards system. See what James 1:9-10 has to say:

The brother in humble circumstances ought to take pride in his high position. But the one who is rich should take pride in his low position, because he will pass away like a wild flower.

Like it was in Jesus' day, too often religious leaders are looking for outward appearances. Maybe it is because they perceive themselves as higher in God's value hierarchy?

Much Christian leadership is exercised by people who do not know how to develop healthy, intimate relationships and have opted for power and control instead.

-- Henri Nouwen

Our prayers (and sometimes laments) were lifted to heaven while we kneeled over the commodes, and they were as clear in the ears of our Father as the most holy monk praying in solitude...or the senior pastor preaching his finest sermon! Imagine that.

Through these formative years, God had taken me through my own personal wilderness experience. When I came to this job, I had a history of ambition and accomplishment in sales. I earned the top money in my field and climbed the ladder to gaining top honors among my peers.

Now with a fresh call to the ministry before me, I thought it would be the same process: work hard, work smart, and pay your dues. A church of thousands, and a significant role as influencer in my community and among my pastor peers, awaited me! But after about two years, in the isolation of working a graveyard shift, God began to whisper a question to me in my heart of hearts; *"What if you had to do this for the rest of your life? Would you still love Me?"*

At first, I thought the voice was one from the bowels of Hell, trying to break me down with despair. I would throw my hopes, my records of success and my calling to ministry against these dark thoughts and attempt to drive them away. God had big things for me! But the thought persisted. Would I be able to live like this for the rest of my days? Was it possible that God had called me and purposefully brought me to this place to live in obscurity, serving him alone?

Then they came to the place of which God had told him. And Abraham built an altar there and placed the wood in order; and he bound Isaac his son and laid him on the altar, upon the wood. And Abraham stretched out his hand and took the knife to slay his son. But the Angel of the LORD called to him from heaven and said, "Abraham, Abraham!" So he said, "Here I am." And He said, "Do not lay your hand on the lad, or do anything to him;

for now I know that you fear God, since you have not withheld your son, your only son, from Me."

-- Genesis 22:9-12

I sat in the chair, stunned. Somehow, I had gotten on the radar and been called into the office of the man of God who founded and ran the church. And now, I was getting a pretty stern lecture…a lecture that was long overdue.

"You think that the road to success in ministry is like navigating from stepping stone to stepping stone, higher and higher; it is not like that with God," said my pastor and sometimes mentor. "The road to ministry is treacherous, like a switchback filled with holes, setbacks, and changes in directions."

He continued, "And God is not going to tell you how the story ends. Just because he stopped Abraham from plunging the knife into the heart of his son doesn't mean he will rescue you the way He did for him."

We know the end of Abraham's story, but only God knows the end of yours or mine. God had to kill my ambition, and he had to destroy my dream in order to accomplish His ambition in me. The knife came down that year and God gave me the grace and, yes, even the joy, to embrace a life of serving him as a janitor. It was enough.

> Our ambitions are not often inherently bad. Is there a personal ambition or dream (maybe even one that God gave you), that God is asking you to sacrifice like He asked of Abraham with his son?

When the enemy finally assembled their massive fighting force at Israel's borders (which we learn in Judges 7 is 135,000), the Lord moved with sovereignty upon Gideon, filling him with the Spirit of God.

Then the Spirit of the LORD came upon Gideon, and he blew a trumpet, summoning the Abiezrites to follow him. He sent messengers throughout Manasseh, calling them to arms, and also into Asher, Zebulun and Naphtali, so that they too went up to meet them.

-- Judges 6:34-35

133

Values alignment

God had a confidence that Gideon shared not only His agenda (winning the war ahead) but that he would act according to the *values* that they shared in common.

I risk two things with you by going for a few paragraphs into a short detour into behavioral science. One is that I could be accused as posing as a psychologist (which I am definitely *not*). The other is the risk of losing your interest. Bear with me though, because this is essential truth about God and how He slowly shapes us in such a way that our values begin to align with His.

For much of the last decade, it has been my occupation to coach and train corporate and government leaders. God desires that you and I should be ever-expanding in our leadership influence with others. But as with Gideon, God can only release your predestined leadership if He trusts that your core values are in alignment with His.

Values are root "operating systems" from which we lead our lives. Like deeply embedded and custom-coded software, they are the source of our attitudes, feelings, and ultimately our behaviors. Values can be defined as those ideals that guide or qualify personal conduct and interaction with others. They are that inner voice that operates in our human conscience that helps us distinguish what is right from what is wrong. Walking a Spirit filled life is much about allowing the values and heart of God to flow through you and to the degree that your values are reshaped into His values, then you and I can progressively take on God's nature.

This deep place where the code has been written into your soul, much of which happened in your earliest of years, is where the sharp, two-edged sword of Hebrews 4 surgically operates to sensitize us to our motives, and help us to identify the source of our emotions.

Even more important, your core values are the main arena in which the Holy Spirit operates. It is where He does His best work in us…to grow you and me into Christ's image.

*For as he (*a man*) thinks in his heart, so is he.*

-- Proverbs 23:7 NKJV
(parenthesis mine)

134

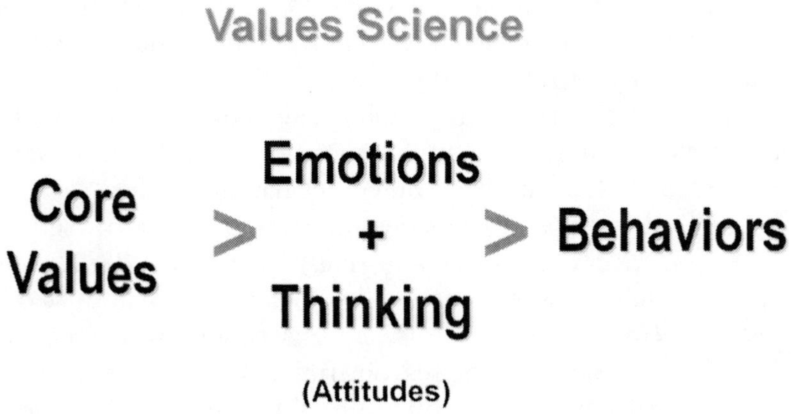

Values Science

$$\text{Core Values} \quad > \quad \substack{\textbf{Emotions} \\ + \\ \textbf{Thinking}} \quad > \quad \textbf{Behaviors}$$

(Attitudes)

Figure 6: Values Science asserts that all behaviors come from how you think and from your emotions. Thinking and emotions, which create our behavior, flow from your preset, core values[1]

At a time when most psychology was founded in theory postulated by Sigmund Freud, Robert S. Hartman, a Jew who converted to Christianity in his adult years, built his values theory and his definition of what is good versus what is evil, on a biblical viewpoint. Much of today's popular "Positive Psychology" has roots in the same conclusions Hartman presented in his many books and articles decades earlier.

We have discovered that there is a set of human strengths that are the most likely buffers against mental illness: courage, optimism, interpersonal skill, work ethic, hope, honesty, and perseverance. Much of the task of prevention will be to create a science of human strength whose mission will be to foster these virtues in young people.[2]

--Dr. Martin Seligman, Founder
Positive Psychology, 1988

Each person has built-in personal "core" values that include predetermined valuations of God, self, others, things, tasks, ideas/opinions and attitudes about your future and your role in the universe.

In addition, Hartman's work established and even measured these valuations through an assessment instrument[3] he developed over three decades of research. Each of these valuations has an attached *"bias."* Your bias towards God may be pessimistic/untrusting due to a low self esteem *("I am not valuable enough for Him to really care for me like He does for others"),* abandonment issues or faulty theological viewpoints (*"God is an angry, vitriolic God"*) of who He is and His nature. So our beliefs and internal positive or negative biases determine how we relate to work, stewardship (versus ownership), time, our future role in the world, and many other important factors.

You can begin to see, then, how vital our internal values are to shaping our destiny...and how they impact those around us.

One of my biggest values challenge is that of performance. The passion to win or the drive towards finishing a task has wormed its way to the top of my values hierarchy. When that happens, anything or anyone who interrupts my forward motion is a potential threat to my success, even if it is my young son, who wants to sit on my lap and tell me he loves me...or my wife, who wants to talk to me about her Bible study group that met that morning. Too often I will listen halfheartedly...or even brush them off for "later" (which rarely ever comes) so I can stay on task and achieve my goals.

But Hartman's Value Index captured the essence of the values from which Jesus operated:

136

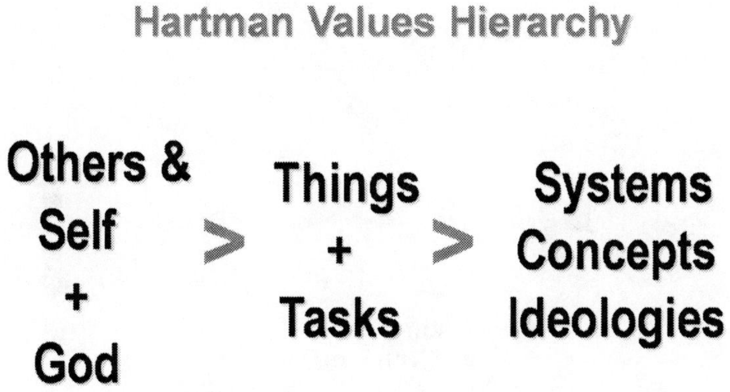

Hartman Values Hierarchy

Others &
Self
+
God
> Things
+
Tasks
> Systems
Concepts
Ideologies

Figure 7: Hartman's Value Theory

In Figure 7, we see this simple hierarchy as another important part of Value Science.

Hartman proposes that "Good" is the degree in which your comparative valuation occurs in this hierarchy; God, others and self are *always* more valuable than things and tasks, and these are *always* more valuable than ideas, concepts and dogma.

Therefore, if through his intensive interaction with God, Gideon's values had not come into alignment with God's values, God would not have been able to release His glorious power on the Midianite army, nor could He have even trusted Gideon to lift the horn to gather the army together.

The same is true of us as men. We are destined for the throne...to lead others in Jesus' name, but we must first embrace the lifestyle of a road-hardened, obedient disciple who has *learned* Christ's values.

Values Science

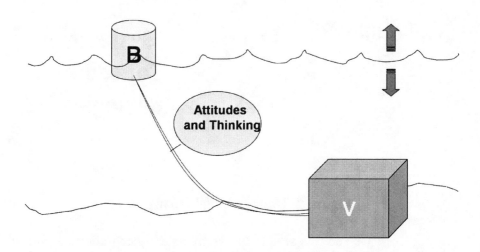

Figure 8: B=Behavior; V=Values. Tides and circumstances may change, but our attitudes and thinking are anchored to our values. Values change very slowly, but they are the root of all human behavior.

Jesus exemplified this when he violated the mores of his time and the Jewish legal prohibition of touching a leper. The leper, who might be compared to someone with a deadly contagious disease, was a person that Jesus loved. How could He not show that love without touching him? Another case was when Peter was confronted by Paul for hypocrisy (due to prioritizing religious ideology and dogma over loving and accepting his fellow Gentile brothers) because he was fearful of being ostracized by a group of legalists, he had shunned the Gentile Christians and segregated himself with those Jewish converts who viewed themselves as superior to those who were not Jews by birth.

When Peter came to Antioch, I opposed him to his face, because he was clearly in the wrong. Before certain men came from James, he used to eat with the Gentiles. But when they arrived, he *began to draw back and separate himself from the Gentiles **because he was afraid** of those who belonged to the circumcision group. The other Jews joined him in his hypocrisy, so that by their hypocrisy even Barnabas was led astray.*

-- Galatians 2:11-13 (bold is mine)

Picking up on my story of working as janitorial supervisor, a lesson God wanted to teach me was how to be a servant leader who put others in front of performance. Thomas was different from the other guys in my crew. He was twenty five, older than the others, and had just recently given his heart to Christ and was looking for direction. At the time he was saved, he was a pretty hard living, hard drinking, Hollywood stunt man. He was masculine, imposing, and muscular, with an aggressive and intimidating presence.

During the winter months he had worked twenty hour shifts for 6 to 8 weeks, nonstop, on an Alaskan crab boat in the freezing waters of the Bering Sea. This guy was tough! And the stories he would tell were not always edifying.

Scott, a twenty one year old newlywed, and Thomas would get into petty arguments from time-to-time. But they also seemed to be growing a good friendship. I thought that the match was a good one, so they were often linked up to work together as a team for their shifts.

Now it was two thirty in the morning (where I started the story) and I had noticed that Thomas had been particularly agitated earlier in the week. This night he seemed to have an attitude that was even more surly than usual. I left my crew to go and check on him and Scott and found him angrily shoving Scott against the outside stucco wall of the Prayer Chapel. The words that came out of his mouth were as inappropriate as his behavior. I felt a wave of panic, but I knew I had to intercede.

Stepping between the two of them, I was eye-to-eye with Thomas and forced him away from Scott. Now committed, I firmly told him to "*stand down.*" He made himself larger for a moment, glaring hatefully into my eyes. Then he faltered, and I released him. and he strode away. Relieved, I asked him to meet me in the office in twenty minutes after he had cooled down.

Scott was unsettled, but he calmed down and we discussed what had just transpired between the two of them. After a few minutes he went back to his shift. I went to find Thomas. When I found him sitting at the maintenance office we had a "heart-to-heart" together. I was tempted to get him back to work and to reprimand his unacceptable behavior. But this young, abrasive man was in a great deal of personal pain, and Jesus ministered to him that night mostly because I just listened. Eventually, he broke, and falling into my arms he wept deeply. He wept about his loneliness and he wept about his bondage, failing as a disciple of Christ. I felt a bit like a Priest, hearing a confession and then I remembered that Jesus had commanded us to forgive sins.[4] I lifted his head and looked into his eyes and said, "*I forgive you in the Name of Jesus.*" I could see him opening his heart to receive the absolution from Father-God, but there was no penance for Thomas, just a heartfelt hope and peace that can only come when you see how truly loving and accepting God is. Sometimes we can only see that aspect of God when it comes through someone else.

We all picked up the slack that night, extending our shift for a few minutes for the work time lost. It was so worth it.

A man who wants to lead the orchestra must turn his back on the crowd.

-- Max Lucado

As fathers, husbands and men at work, it is far too easy to recall our failures when it comes to getting values backwards. The child who gets slapped for spilling milk, the teenager who is yelled at for the messy room, the wife who burns the toast and then braces for that *look* that says, "*how could you be so stupid,*" from her husband. These all spring from *whacked values*. Jesus must teach us and *train* us in a more excellent way.

In necessariis unitas,
(In essentials unity,)
In dubiis libertas,
(In doubtful things liberty)
In omnibus autem caritas,
(But in all things love)

-- St. Augustine

There are so many things I have done, or have not done, as a man of influence, that did not have good endings as this one did. Leadership failures often result when we put tasks and things in front of people. Even worse is when we allow our own unique "flavor" of doctrine to divide us as believers. Looking down our noses at someone from a different tradition causes divisiveness between denominations. How are we to flourish in *isolation* from one another? If Paul was so grieved at Peter's self-segregation from Gentile believers, how much more is the Holy Spirit grieved today when Roman Catholics look down upon Presbyterians who then condescend to Baptists who then are seen as inferior by Charismatics (and Baptists think they are *all* weird)? Much of what separates us is fear of the unknown and a difference in style. Maybe that's why there are over 35,000 Christian denominations worldwide! What if the real doctrinal differences between us are simply tests from the Holy Spirit to see if we will overcome dogma with love? What if God made some doctrinal issues subject to differing interpretations on purpose?

Gideon was also thrust rather suddenly into the role of subversive leader, and I am amazed at the scope of his willingness to obey God. His trust in God was reciprocated by God placing His trust in Gideon. Obedience and a fearless faith were the main qualifications on his resume. Each "stepping stone" for him called out an ever increasing danger. Not only was his career on the line, but his life and the lives of everyone he cared for were as well.

Biblical leadership

One of my favorite warriors is Dr. Henry Blackaby. His **Experiencing God** series is transformative to hear or read. He continues today, in advanced years, to work full time to build up the Body of Christ worldwide.

In a recent conversation with Dr. Blackaby, I thanked him for not "retiring" yet and for how his tireless ministry of bringing his own unique and too infrequently heard perspectives to the church worldwide had made a deep impact in my life.

His response to me was, *"It is not a sacrifice, it is obedience to God…and the alternative to obedience is unthinkable."*

According to Blackaby, there are three illegitimate and five legitimate sources of influence[4]:

Illegitimate Influence:
1. Position

2. Power

3. Personality

Legitimate influence:
1. God's Authentication

2. Encounters with God

3. Character/Integrity (*aligned values*)

4. Successful Track Record

5. Preparation

Gideon had numbers 1 through 5 on the second list going for him (admittedly, his track record was rather short, but it was consistent). But before we follow Gideon as he gathers his army for battle, we must remember that we are in boot camp. One of the touchstones of boot camp is learning to follow and then learning to lead others. We can see this progressing in Gideon's life and it is no different for us.

We have already established that everyone reading this book is called to be a leader. Being called to war is simply a dynamic component of servant leadership. It is a part of the talent God has bestowed to *each one* of His children. What we do with it is up to us.

Scripture is peppered throughout with inspiring earthy leaders who rose to the next level by placing their faith in God. It is also spiced with the deep disappointments of what could have been in men who took the lower path.

Nehemiah is one of the few sterling leaders of latter Old Testament Jewish history. We see him stepping up into leadership when faced with staggering odds of seeking to rescue a fearful and helpless people who had been living behind broken down walls. In addition, they were surrounded by those in power who were threatening an imminent attack. Their leader Sanballat had just delivered a series of public trash talk and veiled threats:

I answered them (the enemy) by saying, "The God of heaven will give us success. We his servants will start rebuilding, but as for

*you, you have no share in Jerusalem or any claim or historic
right (posterity) to it. (parenthesis mine)*

--Nehemiah 2:20

And after the threats had escalated into a planned imminent military
assault, he inspired his people to redouble their efforts...and to be ready to
fight:

*After I looked things over, I stood up and said to the nobles, the
officials and the rest of the people, "Don't be afraid of them.
Remember the Lord, who is great and awesome, and fight for
your brothers, your sons and your daughters, your wives and
your homes.*

--Nehemiah 4:14

Read the book to find out what happened, but it is enough to point out
here that he moved them *to believe they could win*...and they did. The part
that is a challenge for you and me is that previously, Nehemiah was never
a governor, never a military man, and he was never really much of a leader
as far as we know. His previous career path was in the food and beverage
service industry...as the wine server who worked at the royal dining room
in Babylon!

Filled with the Spirit

This was now Gideon's moment of truth. Just days earlier God had
appeared to him and called him a mighty warrior who would defeat the
Midianites "as if they were one man." This is where the narrative says,
"Then the Spirit of the Lord came upon him." This was to be Gideon's
fourth encounter with God in the last few days. First, the angelic visitor
and conversation; second comes the miraculous combustion rising from
the rock of sacrifice; third, the appearance and directives God gave him in
his dream that same night; and fourth, he was filled with the Spirit of God.

There are many instances of men and women being filled with the
Spirit of God in both the Old and New Testament. Of particular note for
believers on this side of Calvary were the last commandments that Jesus
gave to his followers before He ascended into heaven.

143

Do not leave Jerusalem, but wait for the gift my Father promised, which you have heard me speak about. For John baptized with water, but in a few days you will be baptized with the Holy Spirit... you will receive power when the Holy Spirit comes on you; and you will be my witnesses in Jerusalem, and in all Judea and Samaria, and to the ends of the earth.

--Acts 1:4-8

Is this Baptism in the Holy Spirit for us today? John the Baptist's core prophesy of The Christ who would follow him was that as He was the One who baptizes with the Holy Spirit and with fire (Luke 3:16). In Jesus' teaching on how we should boldly ask His Father for good gifts, he says:

If you then, though you are evil, know how to give good gifts to your children, how much more will your Father in heaven give the Holy Spirit to those who ask him!

--Luke 11:13

Is the Spirit of the Lord that fell on David, Solomon, Gideon and the church in Acts 2:4 for His church today? Many Christian leaders are divided on this question. The entire argument seems to dissipate into the question of whether tongues are for today for every, or any, believer. Schisms of theological "opinions" cast shadows of suspicion and division in the Body of Christ. It must be sad and disappointing to God, who values our oneness so highly.

In the book, **The Leadership Secrets of Billy Graham**, Harold Myra writes the true story of a young man's encounter with the Holy Spirit:

As he found some success as an evangelist, he continually sought a greater connection and empowerment. During one of his earlier missions to the British Isles, he met a young Welsh Evangelist, Stephen Olford, who had spiritual qualities he had longed for. "He had a dynamic...and exhilaration about him that I wanted to capture," said Billy.

After hearing Olford preach on being filled with the Holy Spirit, Billy approached him and said, "You've spoken of something that

144

*I don't have. I want the fullness of the Holy Spirit in my life too."
Olford agreed to set aside two days ...the two would talk and
pray during the day, pausing long enough for Billy to preach at
night.*

*Quite frankly, Olford said later, "His preaching was very
ordinary." The crowd was small, passive to Billy's invitation,
and unresponsive. The next day, Olford continued the instruction,
telling Billy he "must be broken," like the apostle Paul, letting
God turn him inside out. "I gave him my testimony of how God
completely turned my life inside out—and as I talked, those
marvelous eyes glistened with tears, and he said, Stephen, I see
it. That's what I want...," and both men knelt and prayed on the
floor. "I can still hear Billy pouring out his heart in a prayer of
total dedication to the Lord," said Olford. "Finally, he (Billy)
said,' My heart is so flooded with the Holy Spirit!' and we went
from praying to praising...laughing and praising God, and Billy
was walking back and forth in the room saying, 'I have it! I'm
filled. This is a turning point in my life.'*

*That night, said Olford, "as Billy rose to speak, he was a man
absolutely anointed." Members of the audience came forward to
pray even before Billy gave an invitation. At the end of the
sermon, practically the entire crowd rushed forward.*

Dr. Billy Graham called Stephen Olford "the man who most
influenced my ministry."[5] Billy Graham yearned for all of what God had
for him and God met him right where he was as he sought Him with all of
his heart. He will do the same for you.

You can pause right now if you like, or set aside a time this evening to be alone to pray. Better yet, find a friend whom you know has already been baptized with the Holy Spirit and ask him to join you in prayer. This has nothing to do with changing churches or doctrine...only asking God for *all of Him*, His way. Do you remember how simple a thing it was to initially turn your life over to Jesus? But it was hard to surrender. It is the

Doubts and dogma aside, why wouldn't you want all of the power and all of the gifting and all of the grace of God operating in and overflowing in your life?

same with this. When you are ready, after a brief time of praise and thanksgiving, pray this prayer:

Lord Jesus. You told your followers to wait in Jerusalem to receive the powerful baptism of the Holy Spirit. I ask you now to give me all of what you have for me. Fill me to overflowing with the Holy Spirit. Hold nothing back. I surrender, yet again, to you. Thank you for the promise of the filling of the Spirit. I receive it now, by faith.

Begin to let praise and worship fill your thoughts and then speak those words. Let it flow into you and through you, back to God in worship!

No Turning Back

Now filled and empowered with the spirit, Gideon runs to find his *shofar*, or rams horn. As he does, he may have paused, realizing that he is about to cross a chasm of commitment that was a one way leap. Gideon never comes back to his old life as a simple farmer. In retrospect, it was a broader jump than any in recorded history since Moses lead Israel out of Egypt, backing them up against the Red Sea; further even than that shepherd boy David who would courageously take on the Philistine giant 250 years later. Gideon was about to muster an untested, unnumbered, unarmed army of browbeaten men and boys, to take on the biggest bully in Israel's history since Egypt. The Midianite army, which numbered at 135,000 "swordsmen" (Judges 8:10), did *not* include charioteers, camel riders ("*Their **camels** could no more be counted than the **sand** on the seashore*")[6], armor bearers, spearmen or archers.

Gideon, now freed from guilt by God's forgiveness that had come with the shedding of the blood of the sacrifices made days earlier, and freed from the grasp of bondage to Baal and Asherah, *commits*. Raising the horn to his lips, he breathes in and blows out a clear, long sound. This rallying call fell upon the weary ears of men and women and children throughout the land. It was the sound of hope…of rescue…and of a promised peace. And it would come through the violent gauntlet of war!

The definitive measure of a leader's success is if they moved their people from where they were to where God wanted them to be.[7]

Henry Blackaby

Gideon's next action, we are told, is to select runners to fan out *"throughout Manasseh, calling them to arms, and also into Asher, Zebulun and Naphtali."* Other tribes would later join this inexperienced makeshift army that assembled from these four tribes. But now with his loyal messengers gone, he has time to think.

Consider for a moment what Gideon might be thinking: *"Mighty warrior? Me? Oh my God, what have I done! I have sent the messengers to gather an army of farmers and tradesmen and they will be expecting me to lead them! How arrogant to think that God would use me for something as great as this? Who do I think I am anyway...some sort of a Deliverer? And the prophet God sent had not said anything about fighting, only that we should repent of our idol worship. How presumptive of me! I must entreat God once more to see if He will visit me again!"*

So Gideon musters up the nerve and says to God:

If (emphasis mine) you will save Israel by my hand as you have promised- look, I will place a wool fleece on the threshing floor. If there is dew only on the fleece and all the ground is dry, then I will know that you will save Israel by my hand, as you said." And that is what happened. Gideon rose early the next day; he squeezed the fleece and wrung out the dew—a bowlful of water. Then Gideon said to God, "Do not be angry with me. Let me make just one more request. Allow me one more test with the fleece. This time, make the fleece dry and the ground covered with dew." That night God did so. Only the fleece was dry; all the ground was covered with dew.

--Judges 6:36-40

Gideon had no right to impose a test on God. Yet he cuts a deal with God, and God meets him right where he was. Then Gideon, knowing he is now on shaky ground, asks for a second miracle! *"God do the same trick, but do it the opposite way this time,"* he pleaded. God met him again in his unbelief and in his fear. Our Lord did the same thing for Thomas some 1,300 years later.

Now Thomas (called Didymus), one of the Twelve, was not with the disciples when Jesus came. So the other disciples told him, "We have seen the Lord!" But he said to them, "Unless I see the nail marks in his hands and put my finger where the nails were, and put my hand into his side, I will not believe it." A week later his disciples were in the house again, and Thomas was with them. Though the doors were locked, Jesus came and stood among them and said, "Peace be with you!" Then he said to Thomas, "Put your finger here; see my hands. Reach out your hand and put it into my side. Stop doubting and believe." Thomas said to him, "My Lord and my God!"

--John 20:24-29

Many have been critical of "Doubting" Thomas for his unbelief. And yet this was the same one of the twelve who just a few chapters earlier had misinterpreted Jesus comment regarding Lazarus' death and had enthusiastically and courageously offered to go and die with Jesus and the rest of the Disciples![8] Why do we so often read shame or failure into these kinds of stories? There was no hint of accusation from Jesus with Thomas, and there was none with Gideon either. God met these men right where they were. He understood their broken dreams and he knew their hearts needed his presence in a special way. He will do the same for you and me. How gracious and patient a loving Father He is to us!

Ahead in our story, God, who met Gideon twice where he was, now raises the ante again, with two tests of His own.

Table Talk

1. What do you think are some of God's values? Are your values in alignment with God's?
2. You are called to lead. Where do you think you may have abdicated your leadership? How can it be reclaimed?
3. If the baptism of the Holy Spirit was given to New Testament believers, is this for us today as well?

DO NOT VENTURE FORTH ALONE!

Chapter Eight:

All Other Ground is Sinking Sand

Early in the morning, Jerub-Baal (that is, Gideon) and all his men camped at the spring of Harod. The camp of Midian was north of them in the valley near the hill of Moreh. The LORD said to Gideon, "You have too many men for me to deliver Midian into their hands. In order that Israel may not boast against me that her own strength has saved her, announce now to the people, 'Anyone who trembles with fear may turn back and leave Mount Gilead.'" So twenty-two thousand men left, while ten thousand remained.

--Judges 7:1-3

Men began to arrive with their things—satchels of food and skins of water for the road. Some brought with them staves and pitchforks; others carried swords, axes and knives. From every direction, they came…in pairs, by villages, fathers and young sons. Gideon looked out in hope and uncertainty. He saw that some these men had the mettle for a great fight against a multitude.

Fear. It is the bane of mankind. And it is a deal killer with God. He told Gideon to send the fearful home. Ask any general if there is *anything* more debilitating than fear. It afflicts every man. Two-thirds of these men who gathered were carriers of the fear virus. Many men I have known, when we begin to peel back the layers of pride, anger, posing, posturing and overachieving, are practiced, unconscious cowards.

God had set this as a part of his battle precepts centuries earlier as we read:

149

When you go to war against your enemies and see horses and chariots and an army greater than yours, do not be afraid of them, because the LORD your God, who brought you up out of Egypt, will be with you...Do not be fainthearted or afraid; do not be terrified or give way to panic before them. For the LORD your God is the one who goes with you to fight for you against your enemies to give you victory." The officers shall say to the army... "Is any man afraid or fainthearted? Let him go home so that his brothers will not become disheartened too."

--Deuteronomy 20:1-8

You already know from some of my stories that I have a childhood marked by an ingrained yellow streak. I probably would have welcomed the release to head back home. And why wouldn't I? I am a son of Adam, like you. We have learned how to substitute for the real thing. Spiteful criticism, often cloaked in words of prayerful "concern," replaces thoughtful discernment. Rage and intimidation (breeding more fear) is deployed instead of real quiet authority and the rare quality of spiritual weight earned in the years of being tested in battle and personal sacrifice. Some are free enough to enjoy the bravado of chest thumping hugs and back slapping (I confess that I *really* enjoy this sometimes), but we have long since silenced the voices of truth that tell us we are afraid. Some men apply the insulation of success or power. During seasons like the current one, where job security is an oxymoron, many have quietly withdrawn into the shadows, pretending to be somewhere else...or someone else.

The Affliction of Niceness

*You can say almost **anything** (in correction) to someone if they know you love them.*

--Darrell Roberts

"Niceness" (not to be confused with the spiritual fruit of kindness, gentleness and goodness) has overflowed into the aisles. Paid professionals are often times too risk averse knowing that conflict can endanger a church's stability. They often nominate men or women for subordinate leadership roles which won't ruffle the feathers of the leaders' direction or the established *status quo.* Love, in many churches, has become vapid as we sharpen our skills at beating around the bush. Patrick Lencioni said:

> *Church staffs are the most dysfunctional organizations of any I have worked with because they have such a high level of "grace" that they are unable to "speak the truth in love" to one another. Stress from work is higher among these good people than I see in the secular workforce because they're afraid to be direct with one another in the fear that they might offend or be branded as unaccepting.*[1]

Fear can dominate families as well. Mom tries to be nice by seeking to be a peacemaker at any cost while Dad sees that the shortest distance between two points is a good fight, or *vice-versa.* Collateral damage mounts up in confused, angry, and scared kids, and a loss of intimacy in the marriage. Dad is trying to "fix" the problem, fearful it will fester; mom is afraid that conflict will hurt her family members; and the children are afraid their folks will break up.

Peter, Thomas, and the rest of the disciples fled when the temple soldiers came to arrest Jesus. Yet each of them sought to best the other just hours earlier by declaring their irrevocable commitment to follow Jesus to death if needed[2].

We love heroes. Stories and movies that portray men as brave gain our admiration. Men like William Wallace in **Braveheart**, when his just rage ignites at the senseless murder of his young wife. His fire spread throughout the common, oppressed men of Scotland.

And we all despise cowards…or pity them. Cowards like the usurping Commodus in the movie **Gladiator,** the ambitious and murderous successor who set himself up as Caesar after suffocating his father. He was terrified of Maximus and had to drive a killing dagger into his back to disable him while prearranging what was supposed to look like a fair fight. We were thrilled when he was taken down.

Cowards like I was. There was nothing that curdled my blood like those moments when I looked inside to see at my core, a fearful man. I *believed* it was the way I was wired, but *it was not true.*

I think of how the young disciple Mark must have felt after he cut and ran after things heated up in the battlefield of Paul and Barnabas' first missionary journey. Here they were, a triad of brothers, pioneering the launch of Christianity to the world with signs and wonders! They did not know that their invasion would result in violent persecution. Paul and Barnabas *stayed*...they bore up under it and leaned into the darkness, driving the sled of the Kingdom of God down the throats of Hell...and raising it as they went! It just got *"too hot in the kitchen"* for Mark and he bolted.

As a Christian man, I thought I pretty much had it all together. But then I encountered the The Warrior series. The series asked me to look deeper; we learned to sustain each other at our table, becoming our own support group, helping to examine our fears and acknowledge where growth was needed. Now in the light of trusted friends, we were able to give over our fears to God and put on the armor as His warriors. Together we grew and became stronger and more selfless servants of God.

-Dave Tofanelli
Core 300 Squad Leader

You can imagine that Gideon was having difficulty dealing with the loss of seventy percent of his fighting force. He was probably working through the battle plan in his mind and rationalizing to himself that those who remained were focused and unafraid. He probably thought, *"Better to have these ten thousand than a bunch of men who will turn tail and cause a rout."* Judges 7:4-6 continues:

But the LORD said to Gideon, "There are still too many men. Take them down to the water, and I will sift them for you there. If I say, 'This one shall go with you,' he shall go; but if I say, 'This one shall not go with you,' he shall not go." So Gideon took the men down to the water. There the LORD told him, "Separate those who lap the water with their tongues like a dog from those who kneel down to drink." Three hundred men lapped with their hands to their mouths. All the rest got down on their knees to drink.

I like to distinguish a difference between the word brave and courage. Synonyms for brave include "bold," "intrepid," "daring," "heroic," and "fearless." In its origins, however, it more commonly meant boastful or bullying. The word's origin is the same as the Latin word *brabus* which also carries the root "barbaric." God saw the bravery of the ten thousand who remained. But he knew that real courage was needed and it was a higher condition of the heart and soul than mere bravery. Courage has its roots in the Latin word *core* and was modified over time by the French language to *coeur* which is the present term for "heart." Courage then means *"with heart,"* and though it may resemble bravery on the surface, it is quite different.

Bravery can act *rashly* in spite of what is really going on. They fear if they stop and think they will lose their nerve.

Courage sees, weighs the risk, and chooses to act out of duty or faith.

Bravery uses anger and adrenaline to mask, deny, or even ignore prudent fear.

Courage sees what is real, feels real fear, and then chooses to act courageously, overcoming the fear with action.

Bravery fights for the individual

Courage fights for *others*.

The Midianites and the Amalekites are just over the hill. The pressure of imminent attack is building. Gideon's feeble plans for leading an army of 32,000 were going down the tubes. Then God said there were *still too many men*! God did not reiterate that they must be culled down again in order for Israel not to be able to take credit for victory. 10,000 against 135,000 had taken care of that liability. There was a *deeper layer of qualification* God was seeking. With seven years of Midianite oppression fresh in the memories of these remaining men, they were angry and humiliated. These guys were ready for action...ready for revenge! But they were not all soldiers...nor were they disciplined or seasoned by experience. If fearful hearts have caused the defeat of untold armies, rashness must be a close second. Hurried tactics without disciplined strategy often brought devastation to an army.

Small beginnings

God was looking for a few good men, men who had courage and foresight to be prepared, watchful and alert to danger; men whose heads were lifted up, not carelessly looking down like a dog lapping water out of a puddle. These 300 men had all been, at some time in their life, *taken by surprise*. Burned. They probably had the scars to prove it. They had learned to *never allow an unguarded moment*. It was the way they drank when they were in the field at harvest time. It was how they secured their household before they fell asleep at night. They were men who knew they were in a war and who had lived in the real world of danger, knowing that the consequences of dropping their guard could kill them and those around them. These men had chosen to stay like the other men, but they were not merely brave, they were courageous. They carried the reality of cold, prudent fear in their hearts but had managed that fear with the complimentary warm blankets of faith and duty. Fear was there, yet they would not allow it to chill their bones. They had a *lifestyle of vigilance.*

> *Then he (Jesus) returned to his disciples and found them sleeping. "Could you men not keep watch with me for one hour?" he asked Peter. "Watch and pray so that you will not fall into temptation. The spirit is willing, but the body is weak.*

> --Matthew 26:40

> *Be on your guard; stand firm in the faith; be men of courage; be strong. Do everything in love.*

> --1 Corinthians 16:13-14

As I touched upon in the introduction of this book, a while back our church was in a crisis. Everyone was shaken deeply but at the onset of this crisis, the church leaders called all men to come together and pray on a Saturday morning. Forty men showed up. At the end of that meeting, a leader in our church took me aside and told me that I needed to find a few men who would sustain this prayer covering over the months ahead, at least until we found a new pastor. I sensed the rightness of his exhortation and accepted this challenge as from the Lord.

From then on, twice per month, all male members…465 men… were invited by email, the church bulletin and on the church website, to come together and pray for one hour. Over the next long year, between five and fifteen would come. *It was enough.*

Read what was written by Shakespeare when he memorialized in script how the English forces faced daunting odds against a much larger French army. The encounter would be later called **Battle of Agincourt** (1415). King Henry V had roamed *incognito* throughout the night from campfire to campfire to talk with his men. Exhausted, they clung to the slim hope of living through the day. It was pre-dawn when the army gathered before the French attack. They came to hear from their Captain and their King:

This story shall the good man teach his son;
And Crispin Crispian shall ne'er go by,
From this day to the ending of the world,
But we in it shall be remember'd;
We few, we happy few, we band of brothers
For he to-day that sheds his blood with me
Shall be my brother; be he ne'er so vile,
This day shall gentle his condition
And gentlemen in England now a-bed
Shall think themselves accursed they were not here,
And hold their manhoods cheap whiles any speaks
That fought with us upon Saint Crispin's day.

-- **Henry V**, William Shakespeare
1598 (emphasis mine);

God is not looking for a crowd

Jesus changed the world with twelve men and a few women. He was not into crowds because he knew they could not be trusted. Our American preoccupation with numbers may have its roots in the great commission (which is focused on making *disciples*) given to us by Christ, but I suspect that much of its DNA might be found in capitalism, where growth and increase are the gods of the day.

> *The act of praying is the very highest energy of which the human mind is capable; praying, that is, with the total concentration of the faculties. The great mass of worldly men and of learned men are absolutely incapable of prayer.*
>
> -- Samuel Taylor Coleridge

Can a small courageous group of praying believers significantly impact their community for Jesus? I believe the answer is yes because I have seen it happen. History bears witness as well. Every mighty move of God began in the heart of a common man or woman who then began to pray; men like William Bramwell, the prolific Methodist preacher. Sir Henry Havelock, the famous 19th century British General with his statue in Trafalgar square, always spent the first two hours of each day alone with God. If his military camp was struck at 6 A.M., he would rise at four. Reece was a Welshman who led a movement of believers to fight World War II on their knees with remarkable and miraculous success. These were not all balanced people, but maybe balance is overrated?

> *Again, I tell you that if two of you on earth agree about anything you ask for, it will be done for you by my Father in heaven. For where two or three come together in my name, there am I with them.*
>
> -- Matthew 18:19-20

Jesus said the mighty resources of heaven are released in the Kingdom when two agree about anything. Will you take Him at His Word? What will happen if no one around you steps up?

I was recently talking to a men's ministry leader of a church of over 10,000 active attendees. It was the "poster child" church of its denomination. Their pastor is a world-renowned, best-selling author and speaker. But he painfully shared with me that, although they claimed a men's group of 2,000, he could only trust a handful in a fight. And he was exhausted. He said to me,

*Our men are baby Christians...even after a man is a part of our church for over a decade, they are addicted to the milk of the Word. The prevalence of recurring, debilitating sin in their lives is so great that we have not found the key to discipling them because they **continue to deal with the** effects of their sin. Most of the men who get saved and baptized end up falling away over time. The best we have ever been able to do for them is triage.*

Compare the current state of many of our men in church today to one of the most powerful motivational speeches ever recorded...and given by a leader who could back it up:

You may say to yourselves, "These nations are stronger than we are. How can we drive them out?" But do not be afraid of them; remember well what the LORD your God did to Pharaoh and to all Egypt...for the LORD your God, who is among you, is a great and awesome God. The LORD your God will drive out those nations before you, little by little. You will not be allowed to eliminate them all at once...But the LORD your God will deliver them over to you, throwing them into great confusion until they are destroyed... No one will be able to stand up against you; you will destroy them.

> -- God, through the mouth of
> Moses
> Deuteronomy 7:17-24

Not, "you will accomplish a cease fire"...nor just, "you can win," but, "you will **destroy** them."

I believe the mission of this book is to find common men, those Gideons, who will *first* worship and pray. Then, after hearing from God, blow the horn and call extraordinary men together to become part of those that share a "300" attitude. Maybe *there are only two or three like-minded warriors to begin.* No matter. It began with a guy all alone. But his faithfulness was what was needed for God to change his family, his village, and his nation. Let's pick up in Judges 7:

Now the camp of Midian lay below him in the valley. During that night the LORD said to Gideon, "Get up, go down against the

157

*camp, because I am going to give it into your hands. If you are afraid to attack, go down to the camp with your servant Purah and listen to what they are saying. Afterward, you will be encouraged to attack the camp." So he and Purah his servant went down to the outposts of the camp. The Midianites... (were) thick as locusts. Their camels could no more be counted than the sand on the seashore. Gideon arrived just as a man was telling a friend his dream. "I had a dream,"... "A round loaf of barley bread came tumbling into the Midianite camp. It struck the tent with such force that the tent overturned and collapsed." His friend responded, "This can be nothing other than the sword of Gideon son of Joash, the Israelite. God has given the Midianites and the whole camp into his hands." When Gideon heard the dream and its interpretation, **he worshiped God** (bold is mine).*

--Judges 7:7-15

For the fourth time we see God intervene to encourage Gideon supernaturally. For the fourth time we see Gideon's *first response* being that of *worship*. This word *worship* has deep and profound meaning throughout scripture. It has deep meaning for you as well. The specific word used in this case is the common Hebrew word for worship, *shachah*. It means to *"bow down"* and is often used alongside *"to the earth"* or *"to the ground."*

Gideon's knee jerk reaction—now four times in a row—is to worship God. He bowed down first, *then* he rose as their leader and exhorted the men to get up! It did not matter that they were outnumbered 300 to 135,000. His faith had been tested and he had come out of this crucible as purified silver. In each successive test, God had increased the ante. And in each successive test, Gideon had risen to a new level of faith.

Exodus 17:10-13 tells us, when Joshua fought the Amalekites as Moses had commanded:

Aaron and Hur went to the top of the hill. As long as Moses held up his hands, the Israelites were winning, but whenever he lowered his hands, the Amalekites were winning. When Moses' hands grew tired, they took a stone and put it under him and he sat on it. Aaron and Hur held his hands up—one on one side, one

158

on the other—so that his hands remained steady till sunset. So Joshua overcame the Amalekite army with the sword.

The Israelites worked *together* to defeat the Amalekites and Gideon had probably heard the story of Moses on the hilltop and Joshua on the battlefield growing up as a boy. He knew that worship and total dependence upon God were directly linked to the strong currents that assured victory in the tumultuous tides of warfare.

What is the significance of worship for us today? Many of us have grown accustomed to referring to the part of a church service that involves singing and music as the *"worship."* How often have we left a church service and commented on whether the "worship" was good, great or mediocre? Our observations have to do with the dynamic of pre-rehearsed music with choirs and musicians working together to help lift the congregation into a deeper connection with God. As worshippers, we are seeking to penetrate this mundane world and lay aside our cares and enter into *"the presence of God."*

But this was different. One guy bowed to the ground with his God. Amazed, thankful and empowered, he rose as one of Israel's greatest leaders. I believe God is looking for men and women today to worship him this way, and I believe that He is looking to trust the humbled soul who fully grasps the discrepancy between the power and majesty of our Father in heaven, and our feeble ability to contribute to His purposes without His help.

Growing up in the Episcopal Church, we had "kneelers" in every pew in order for us to participate in the service of Common Prayer. It required times of sitting, standing and kneeling. My dad came to church a few times each year and, as a boy, I would watch him closely. I wanted to see how the greatest man on earth worshipped.

At the appropriate times when we were supposed to kneel, he used to kneel on *one knee*. I always thought it a bit strange, yet somehow I had believed that when I had grown up as a man, I would only need to bow one knee before God. When envisioning myself as a grown, strong man like my Dad and no longer a child, it made sense somehow. I would be more self-reliant, have a job, and be taking care of and protecting others. I would no longer be a "dependent" on two knees.

I can't tell you how many days I have lived with a posture of being partly bowed before God. I journeyed onward, one knee on the ground, but leaning most of my weight on the remaining leg…where my strength is. Maybe you can relate. Are you comfortable finding a quiet, private place where you can lay prostrate on your face before God? One friend of mine calls this "carpet time." Now please don't misunderstand me, body language alone does not mean anyone is truly worshipping God. Jesus taught the Samaritan woman when he met with her at the well in her village, that *"true worshipers will worship the Father in spirit and truth."*[3] God looks on the heart, but he has linked our heart to our body and our soul as well.

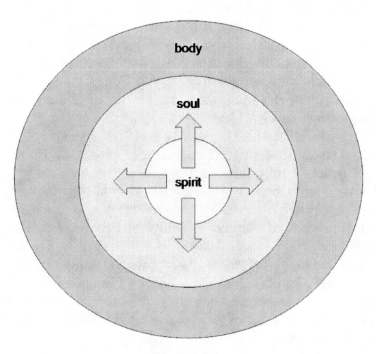

The Temple

Figure 9: Man is made up of three parts: body, soul and spirit - "May God himself, the God of peace, sanctify you through and through. May your whole **spirit**, **soul** and **body** be kept blameless at the coming of our Lord Jesus Christ."

-- 1 Thessalonians 5:23

After all, the entire person who has surrendered his heart to Christ is *His* Temple. The simple diagram (shown in Figure 9) shows the ongoing progress of the sanctification of the work of the Holy Spirit, who through being united with our spirit, is passionately and continually impressing the image of Christ into our soul which, in turn begins the cooperative commandeering of our body to worship, serve and love Him.

But ask yourself: Is it hard for you to lie down, or kneel, or put your forehead to the ground in *physical* obeisance to God? Is it hard for you to even kneel in submission to Him? Maybe it is time for you to do just that. Get back to ground zero…back to the earth where your roots are, and worship God in total abandon.

I knew a man once who struggled with this until he, alone in his private place, with no risk of interruption from a human soul, told God he felt "self-conscious" about laying on his face in worship and hoped he did not mind if he simply sat and prayed like usual. He told me that there came a curious, quiet question in response to his query. A soft, yet incredulous voice whispered in his mind, *"So, Robert, you are self-conscious because you are all alone with yourself? Are you afraid you might make fun of yourself?"* At this gentle rebuke, he laughed out loud at the ridiculousness of his resistance. Yielding, he succumbed to worship…a worship he had never experienced before.

One of the important barometers for spiritual health is whether worship and the vital presence of God, is increasing and/or broadening in your life as you grow in Christ.[5] Why is this? Because as you mature, your perspective of God…His grace, mercy, love and the magnitude of his power, should increase. If it has not, it may be a diagnostic that indicates you are disengaged or stuck in the whitewashed bleachers of life. Pray and ask God today to begin to renew your view of the reality of His magnificence. The larger your God, the deeper your worship.

Everyone who falls on that stone will be broken to pieces, but he on whom it falls will be crushed. (Jesus in referring to himself as the chief capstone rejected by the Teachers of the Law and Chief Priests of his day) (parentheses are mine)

--Luke 20:18

161

The core meaning of worship is derived from the Old English *weorthscipe* which was used for worthiness and respect. One of the Miriam-Webster dictionary definitions captures biblical worship as *"extravagant respect or admiration for, or devotion to, an object of esteem."*[4]

"Weorthscipe" later evolved to "worthship" as it transitioned in our language to its present form. It is my willing offering of obeisance of my calendar, my heart, my mind *and body* to God. All of these must lay prostrate, released from under my control and upon the earth from where I was formed. Total surrender is the only appropriate living sacrifice.

Talk is cheap, especially today when *great* sermonizing and writing can be picked up on the airwaves, Internet, bookstores or TV. Excellent biblical exposition with riveting stories and multiple camera angles can be found almost anywhere, anytime. I think we are at an all-time high in the quality of gifted speakers and teachers in America. However, if this is true, why do survey statistics report that we are growing weaker as Christians here in the US? We don't need any more great teaching. We need whole-hearted engagement. As it was with Gideon, engagement begins and is sustained by worship.

Finally, Gideon was ready. With confidence, he rose from the ground and,

> *He returned to the camp of Israel and called out, "Get up! The LORD has given the Midianite camp into **your** hands." (bold is mine)*

--Judges 7:15

William: Sons of Scotland, I am William Wallace.

Short soldier: William Wallace is 7 feet tall.

William: Yes, I've heard. Kills men by the hundreds, and if he were here he'd consume the English with fireballs from his eyes and bolts of lightning from his ass. I am William Wallace, and I see before me an army of my countrymen here in defiance of tyranny. You have come to fight as free men, and free men you are. What would you do without freedom? Will you fight?

Tall soldier: Fight against that? No, we will run, and we will live.

William: Ay, fight, and you may die, run and you'll live. At least a while. And dying in your beds many years from now, would you be willing to trade all the days from this day to that for one chance, just one chance to come back here and tell our enemies that they may take our lives, but they'll never take our freedom!

Hamish: Where are you going?

*William: I'm going to **pick a fight**.*

Hamish: Well, we didn't get dressed up for nothing.

From **Braveheart**, screenplay by Randall Wallace, Directed by Mel Gibson, 1995

Table talk:

1. Think about 2-3 movie action heroes. Were they brave or courageous? Why?

2. Share one of the things you are most afraid of with your Squad. What would be the worst case scenario if it came true? How can your brothers support you in being courageous as you face that fear?

3. What can you do this week to begin being that man who "infects" other men with a call into the arena?

Chapter Nine:

The 12 Strategies of Defensive Warfare

*He returned to the camp of Israel, and said, "Arise, for the LORD **has delivered** the camp of Midian into your hand." Then he divided the three hundred men into three companies, and he put a trumpet into every man's hand, with empty pitchers, and torches inside the pitchers. And he said to them, "**Look at me and do likewise;** watch, and when I come to the edge of the camp you shall do as I do: When I blow the trumpet, I and all who are with me, then you also blow the trumpets on every side of the whole camp, and say, 'The sword of the LORD and of Gideon!'"*

So Gideon and the hundred men who were with him came to the outpost of the camp at the beginning of the middle watch, just as they had posted the watch; and they blew the trumpets and broke the pitchers that were in their hands. Then the three companies blew the trumpets and broke the pitchers—they held the torches in their left hands and the trumpets in their right hands for blowing—and they cried, "The sword of the LORD and of Gideon!" And every man stood in his place all around the camp; and the whole army ran and cried out and fled. When the three hundred blew the trumpets, the LORD set every man's sword against his companion throughout the whole camp; and the army fled .... (bold is mine)

-- Judges 7:15b-22

After passing every test...after destroying every vestige of idolatry in his life and declaring his leadership, Gideon, now cleansed and filled with the Spirit, is ready to fight. After worshipping a fourth time, Gideon returns to his camp filled with faith that God has given him the victory.

Gideon declared that God "has delivered" them the victory. Past tense. The same is true for us. Gideon leveraged his knowledge of how God had delivered Israel in the past with God's contemporary words and workings in his life, and now his confidence had reached critical mass.

He was now the leader of 300 courageous and battle-ready men. They did not have his experiences of step-by-step obedience to God, but they saw the effect God had made in his life. You can sense authentic leadership when you see it.

Gideon had shared the story of God's visitation, of his costly sacrifice and the fire that erupted from the rock. They also learned, or may have even observed, his consistent response of worship. He had earned the new name Jeru-baal, freeing his village from spiritual bondage when he obediently took on the gods and destroyed them without incurring any personal harm. Then he showed courage and gave the people hope when he blew the trumpet for the first time, calling the armies of his nation together.

After the army assembled, Gideon wisely obeyed God's counsel and sent the fearful away and then exemplified obedient faith when he selected, through divine insight, 300 men out of the 10,000 who had remained after the first cut. Our scripture for this chapter brings us to where he approaches his men just after he returns as a behind-the-lines spy with radiant, faith-filled fervor and the certainty of victory!

Transformed before us, in the narrative of Judges 6 and 7, Gideon takes on an almost surreal glow as the culmination of God's interaction and spirit-endowed anointing transcends this once fearful farmer into something like one of the mighty mythological figures of ancient Greece, or the Nephilim[1] of old:

> *The **Nephilim** were on the earth in those days—and also afterward—when the sons of God went to the daughters of men and had children by them. They were the heroes of old, men of renown.*[2]

--Genesis 6:4

One of my favorite historical fiction authors, Stephen R. Lawhead, wrote a stirring and compelling three-book Celtic fantasy series called **The Song of Albion**. Once I read the first book of this series, I was hooked. Not unlike C.S. Lewis, many of his fantasy-fiction works have strong underlying biblical themes. The last book of this trilogy, **The Endless Knot,** describes a phenomenon called the "Battle *Awen*" as a special divine anointing that comes upon a warrior at special times of imminent danger.

This *awen* elevates a warrior's capabilities to a super-human dimension making him move with unstoppable speed and powerful, focused deadliness. The hero of the story, a once very common man named Lewis Gillies, who had been translated to a parallel barbaric world called Albion, became transformed into a tribal battle champion. In the first book, Lewis was divinely given a silver hand and a new, powerful body through a dark spiritual struggle similar to the event that transformed "Gandalf the Grey" into "Gandalf the White" (for you Tolkien fans).

The village in Albion is attacked by a massive ancient dragon that was wounded, but not beaten, and was in the process of retreating to fight another day. But then the Battle *Awen* came upon our hero:

> *The ground beneath my feet trembled and the earth lost all of its solidity. And I felt my spirit expand within me; I was seized and taken up as if I were no more than a leaf released from a branch and set sailing on a sudden gust of wind. My ears pounded with the blood rush; my vision hardened to a sharp narrow field: I saw only the winged serpent—scales gleaming blood red in the shivered light of our fire, grotesque wings stiffly beating, lifting that huge body to the freedom of the night sky. I saw the Red*

serpent of Oeth escaping; all else around me dimmed, receded, vanished...Oliathir's battle awen burned within me and I would not be held back. Power surged up in a mighty torrent. Like a feather in the flood. Lightly riding the currents, upheld by them, I became a part of the force flowing through me. The strength of the earth and sky...(landing on the serpent) I planted myself there, and raising my silver hand high, I smashed it down hard. The metal broke the skin and slipped under the ridge of bone at the base of the serpent's skull. I stabbed deep...cold silver...plunging...penetrating the red serpent's cold brain...Die! I shouted, my voice a loud carynx of battle. "Die![3]

Gideon had changed in a way that marked him for life. Many of you have read of men who have gone through this process in fiction and in real life. Men like Abraham, Joseph, Moses, and Daniel were frail at times, but faithful. Gideon's fire, however, was condensed and brilliant:

- **He had heard the prophet** and had taken it to heart
- **He was blessed and chosen** with a visitation from God
- **He made a bloody sacrifice** of great cost and great risk to himself and his family
- **He consistently responded to God with worship**
- **He was courageous**, risking his life to destroy idol worship in his village
- **He had become a legend** in his own village...and tribe, known as Jerub-baal
- **He stepped out as the leader**, and blew the trumpet of war
- **He showed wisdom** in selecting his fellow warriors
- **He led by example**, at the front of the lines and beyond

Now clearly, as a leader they can trust, he challenges them to "*Look at me*"... and do what I do. Gideon himself had become the vision of God's hope for deliverance, incarnate, and anointed with God's Holy Spirit because God's Word had captured his heart. He *was* victory. Now it was time for his team to suit up and take up the weapons of warfare and join Gideon as true "mighty men of valor."

So He poured out on him the heat of His anger, and in the fierceness of battle and it set him aflame all around, yet he did not recognize it

-- Isaiah 42:25 New American Standard Bible

What it must have been like to walk alongside Gideon in those days. We cannot know, but we know that the people tried to crown him as their king (Judges 8:22). We can also accurately guess that he had brought *mojo* to these 300 men...and to the thousands who joined in the battle later on. Their heads were lifted, and *nothing* was impossible. Little did they know the battle *awen* was about to fall on *them*.

Defensive warfare

The adage, "*An ounce of prevention is more valuable than a pound of cure*," applies in the dimension of living defensively in a constant state of alertness. The universal principles of warfare discussed in these next few pages are derived from the Word of God. They can be applied to our cache of defensive weaponry as a template that can help us avoid the cycle of defeat while reinforcing the cycle of victory.

I believe defensive, preventative warfare is a critical *biblical* principle as well, because of the many admonitions and wisdom found in scripture.

"To subjugate the enemy's army without doing battle is the highest of excellence."

-Sun Tzu, The Art of War

There is so much biblical guidance to assure our safety and strengthen our position that they cannot be dealt with adequately in several books, not to mention a chapter.

However, I would like to provide a partial list of those things I have discovered along my not so illustrious journey that might be fruitful ground for further individual or small group study. Let's look at 12 defensive strategies and tactics of the well-trained warrior:

1. Obedience

So Samuel said: "Has the LORD as great delight in burnt offerings and sacrifices, As in obeying the voice of the LORD? Behold, to obey is better than sacrifice, And to heed than the fat of rams. For rebellion is as the sin of witchcraft, and stubbornness is as iniquity and idolatry. Because you have rejected the word of the LORD, He also has rejected you from being king."

1 Samuel 15:22-23, New King James Bible

Obeying God and His Word are by far the best means to hold us firm in our Father's hand. Submitting to God goes beyond how *we behave.*

With my children I learned to discipline the **attitude** *before it became an action whenever possible...because an attitude will always become an action if left unchecked.*

-- Dr. Jack Hayford, lectures on child discipline

As we looked at Malachi's writings in Chapter 3 on how God will "rebuke the devourer" as we worship Him wholeheartedly, obedience provides a seal or umbrella of protection over a man and his family. As we steward the lives and resources we have been given *as entirely belonging to God,* He releases even more blessing to us. However, disobedience, or even an 'owners' attitude, can cause His hand of covering to be lifted from our lives.

2. The fear of the Lord

If you fear the LORD and serve and obey him and do not rebel against his commands, and if both you and the king who reigns over you follow the LORD your God-good! But if you do not obey the LORD, and if you rebel against his commands, his hand will be against you, as it was against your fathers.

--1 Samuel 12:14-15

The study of the rich vein of teaching regarding the fear of the Lord could easily be a series of contemporary books. Fearing (a deep and holy respect for) God combined with sincere love for God is oftentimes the core mental and emotional combination that motivates obedient thinking and behavior. The phrase the "Fear of the Lord," or some form of that phrase, is used over 90 times in scripture. The unique thing about it, however, is that it is almost always presented as a warning, exhortation, or a promise of God's protection and favor.

3. Watchfulness

Watch and pray so that you will not fall into temptation. The spirit is willing, but the body is weak.

-- Matthew 26:41

Gideon was told to select only the men who drank with their heads up...watching. We are instructed in scripture to be wary of certain kinds of people, evil spirit beings, and the carnal and philosophical mindsets of the world system. Watchfulness can prevent untold evil attacks in our lives.

4. Trusting God

Trust in the LORD with all your heart and lean not on your own understanding; in all your ways acknowledge him, and he will make your paths straight.

--Proverbs 3:5-6

We cannot manipulate or *test* God (although Gideon appears to have pulled it off twice with the fleeces!), but placing the full weight of your faith in our Father will create a compelling release of God's heavenly power and protection. It is Daniel in the lions' den...and David sprinting in descent into the arena of the valley to engage Goliath. And today, God still seeks for His children to step out of the boat and cast their cares upon Him in trusting abandon.

5. Confession

Therefore confess your sins to each other and pray for each other so that you may be healed. The prayer of a righteous man is powerful and effective.

--James 5:16

Many Christians are unthinkably horrified when a real sinner is suddenly discovered among the righteous. So we remain alone with our sin, living alone in our lies and hypocrisy...he who is alone with his sins is utterly alone.

-- Dietrich Bonhoeffer

We will cover the power of confession in a later chapter, but these quotations are self-evident. At the epicenter of the Core 300 movement is the *fearless commitment to authenticity*: *"What is said at the table, stays at the table."* A man who has the courage to adopt the lifestyle of sharing his scars, openly, with fellow colleagues, has a serious leg-up over men who continue to hide their inadequacies and sins.

Jesus taught that there will come a time in every man's life, sooner or later, when God will enable the full disclosure "from the rooftops" of that which was done in secret. Those who pray and serve in secret will be honored...those who secretly harbor sin in the private places of their souls will one day share in that open proclamation. It only makes prudent sense to prevent this level of public humiliation in the future by sharing within a circle of trusted brothers and use that knowledge to help hold yourself and others

Are you one of those guys who resist stopping and getting directions when you suspect you may be lost? Do you try to complete furniture assembly without reading the instructions? No? What does your spouse say about that? If you are...or if you find yourself on the wrong end of a limb with a saw too often, you are probably in even more need than most of asking God to identify for you a circle of 2-3 trusted advisors who seem to have figured things out among your Christian friends. Do it...it will save you and, more importantly, it will save your wife and children, a ton of grief and wasted years.

accountable. The light of confession will lighten your load. It also causes any demonic association with that sin to begin dissipate and lose its grip. Light always throws darkness into retreat!

6. Godly counsel

> *For lack of guidance a nation falls, but many advisers make victory sure.*
>
> --Proverbs 11:14

> *In the church at Antioch there were prophets and teachers: Barnabas, Simeon called Niger, Lucius of Cyrene, Manaen (who had been brought up with Herod the tetrarch) and Saul. While they were worshiping the Lord and fasting, the Holy Spirit said, "Set apart for me Barnabas and Saul for the work to which I have called them." So after they had fasted and prayed, they placed their hands on them and sent them off.*
>
> --Acts 13:1-3

Not only does seeking godly advice represent a kind of "threefold cord" that is not easily broken, but we have been given the principle of safety in the midst of seeking plurality of wise input and perspectives for key decisions in our life.

"Timing is everything" they say. We know from earlier writings that Paul felt called to the Gentiles *for years*. The Spirit inspired decision to send out Paul and Barnabas in Acts 13 was made by a group of leaders at the church in Antioch. The effect of the patient waiting, and the joint counsel of these prophets and teachers changed the world.

7. Marriage

This is as good a spot as any to segue into the skill of husbanding. Treating your wife with loving understanding will keep your prayers from being hindered at the throne of God, not to mention the many other peaceful benefits that come from loving treatment, including sexual fulfillment, which helps keep the enemy from gaining leverage for excessive temptation in both of your lives.[4] And, by loving her as Jesus

172

loves you, you will be surprised by the gradual response of her unfeigned admiration.

8. Praise and worship

He put a new song in my mouth, a hymn of praise to our God. Many will see and fear and put their trust in the LORD.

--Psalm 40:3

O Lord, open my lips, and my mouth will declare your praise.

--Psalm 51:15

Now I, Nebuchadnezzar, praise and exalt and glorify the King of heaven, because everything he does is right and all his ways are just. And those who walk in pride he is able to humble.

--Daniel 4:37

As mentioned earlier, Gideon built his unique relationship with God upon the foundation of his regular and devoted worship to God. Verbally praising, singing and/or even glorifying God with instruments or dance causes two things to occur:

1. God's habitation—His very presence, enters the place where you worship Him.[5]

2. God will release confusion and destruction upon enemy forces around us as we exalt His name out loud.[6]

You may think, "but Art, you don't understand, I am not charismatic or outspoken like that. My worship to God is private and holy. After all, God knows my heart." Is it quiet and holy or are you simply "mute" when it comes to verbal praise and worship?

Maybe it is that you have not tried it alone? It is true that not everyone is designed to be an extravert, but if you have jumped to your feet and raised high fives around you in excitement when your team scores a touchdown, maybe you need to own up to the need to blow out the dust from your "pipes," and get alone and boisterously read some of the more outspoken psalms of praise.[7]

I find it is true with most guys that we simply are not comfortable with the *vocabulary* of worship, but after reading the Psalms of praise out loud before Him a few times, outward expressions of praise will begin to roll off your tongue naturally. The blessings we lose and the loss of the energizing joy of the Lord we suffer when we fail to obey the scriptural exhortations to praise Him out loud, are too great for us not to employ this activity of defensive warfare.

9. Honoring your parents

"Honor your father and your mother, as the LORD your God has commanded you, so that you may live long and that it may go well with you in the land the LORD your God is giving you.

--Deuteronomy 5:16

Seem odd to put this "tactic" here? This is the *very first* commandment with an attached blessing. It releases God's blessing on you for both an extended life and personal wellness. As Kingdom men called to be "ground gainers," it is not a coincidence that God's blessing extends to the *"land the Lord your God is giving you."*

One of the best friends of my youth, John-Charles, had been instrumental in leading me to a saving encounter with Jesus. I observed his life taking a harmful turn when, at the age of 20, he announced to his parents that he was going to propose to his girlfriend. He recalled to me later that the look on their face said it all. Both of his parents together attempted to dissuade him…they knew she was not a good fit for him, and that he was not ready for this level of commitment. His dad even asked John to consider joining the Marines during the peak years of the Vietnam War!

I was reunited with John-Charles a few years ago and he shared with me how he regretted that his foolish heart did not heed his parents' warnings. "I should have known better," he said. He had other warnings along the way. He recalled that his fiancée had sensed that his parents did not approve, and so she persuaded him that they needed to *accelerate the date…* and they did. Now, almost four decades later, he is still attempting to unravel the pain caused to others, his two oldest daughters in particular…not to mention harm done to his own soul and that of his first wife, because he did not heed his parents.

But God, though He hates divorce, loves people as individuals. He is a redeemer and the champion of second chances. Some years later, after the marriage was dissolved, he met a wonderful woman of God. As he sensed a developing seriousness of his feeling for her, he set up a double date…with his parents. After their evening together, he called his mom. *"Well Momma, what do you think of her,"* he said. Her reply was immediate and priceless, *"Don't let this treasure get away, son…I think she is wonderful for you."*

Ten months later, they were married, and, in John-Charles' own words, "Other than the day I surrendered my heart to my Savior, and let His love and eternal forgiveness flood my heart, it has been the best and wisest decision of my life."

10. The pursuit of wisdom

My son, if you receive my words, and treasure my commands within you, so that you incline your ear to wisdom, and apply your heart to understanding; Yes, if you cry out for discernment, and lift up your voice for understanding, if you seek her as silver, and search for her as for hidden treasures; Then you will understand the fear of the LORD, and find the knowledge of God.

For the LORD gives wisdom; From His mouth come knowledge and understanding; He stores up sound wisdom for the upright; … is a shield to those who walk uprightly; He guards the paths of justice, and preserves the way of His saints.

-- Proverbs 2:1-8 New King James Version

Therefore, brethren, seek out from among you seven men of good reputation, full of the Holy Spirit and wisdom, whom we may appoint over this business;

-- Acts 6:3

This is a *lifestyle*. Reading through the book of Proverbs is a great place to begin to become wise. Heeding its warnings and embracing its principles will save you years of defeat, confusion, and heartache. It covers the secrets to a long life, business acumen, the agonies of sexual misconduct (along with how to spot and avoid a promiscuous suitor). It adds a crown of authority to your head and provides straight and unhindered pathways to walk in your life (Proverbs 4:5-12).

In addition, hiding the Word in the "sheath of your heart" and meditating on scripture is promised to help make us wise, preventing sinful actions and bad decision making (Psalm 119:11).

11. Understanding your enemy

Be sober, be vigilant; because your adversary the devil walks about like a roaring lion, seeking whom he may devour. Resist him, steadfast in the faith, knowing that the same sufferings are experienced by your brotherhood in the world.

--1 Peter 5:8

The enemy is a *person*, and he has a personality like a roaring, people-devouring lion. Examining the adversary of our souls, and his hierarchy of demonic forces, is never a pleasant task. But we must individually seek to understand his strategy and tactics in order to achieve success as a follower of Jesus. Let's look at a few false notions that have tried to creep into my thinking from time to time.

Firstly, we must accept that the devil is *real*. His demonic followers are real as well. He is the orchestrator of the three dimensions of evil that assails humanity every day.

Philosophies within and outside the church will seek to water down the active existence of evil beings at work around us, and minimize evil as "mysterious," calling it anything from a dark, indefinable force or simply psychologically explainable or "pathological" behaviors resulting from disturbed or deprived childhoods. Believing in these is actually a part of the deceiver's subtle strategies because his influence comes from *lies* and *slight of hand*.

Secondly, he is *old*, as are his cohorts. Since he was cursed by God in the garden, and then delivered a crushing wound upon his head by the resurrected Christ, his major operational tactic is subtlety and counterfeit. This imposter, masquerading as an "angel of light" has copied or

176

mimicked everything good about God and His gospel. An expert truth twister, he preys upon the fallen nature of man and leverages the combined dimensions of warfare to slowly erode confidence, faith, and clear thinking. There is no sphere he will not seek to pollute and corrupt.

Some of Satan's synthetic substitutes for godly characteristics are listed in the chart (Figure 10) below:

God	Satan
Truth	Partial Truth
Motivate	Manipulation
Love	Lust
Passion	Driven
Anger	Rage
Rest	Escape
Joy	Party Spirit
Distrusting someone	Unforgiveness
Courage	Bravado
Beautiful	Brazen
Wisdom	Craftiness
Inspire	Intimidate
Trust	Control
Forgiveness	Judgmental
Justice	Revenge
Giving	Possessive
Steward	Owner
Submission	Subversion
Upright	Twisted
Praise	Boast
Humility	Humiliation
Repentance	Workaround
Fear of God	Fear of Man
Poise	Arrogance
Brokenness	Bitterness
Childlike	Sophisticated
Discerning	Critical
Excellence	Winning

Figure 10

Marriage, a once solid institution has been torn apart by divorce, unfaithfulness, and financial stress by couples who fought to have it all.. For 30 plus years, mislead organizations like the ACLU have dealt out debilitating and sometimes *diabolically inspired* campaigns to redefine the ever-sliding slopes of morality and family values under the guise of human rights. Today, there are more slaves bought, sold and owned than at any time in history ...and the list of social, ethical and spiritual erosion goes on. It seeps into our houses like the black ooze of the angel of death that took the lives of the firstborn of Egypt long ago.

In addition, entertainment became an unwritten tenet in the Bill of Rights. If American Christians spent a tenth of the time each day in active prayer that we invest watching television or surfing the internet, we would see a significant change away from disintegration in our world. But what fun would that be?

Thirdly, he is the ultimate agent of *selfishness*. Time will tell how God will review our quality of stewardship of the wealth that each one of us casually allows to pass through our fingers to support our own insatiable want of more "stuff." Richard Stearns presents a riveting argument in his book **The Hole in Your Gospel**. His well crafted and documented message changed my paradigm of prosperity and is a *must read* for every North American Believer.

Some of the names used in scripture for Satan are[8]:

Adversary (1 Peter 5:8); The Devil (Ephesians 6:11) The Deceiver; The Wicked One (Matthew 13:19, 38); Beelzebub (Matt 10:25; 12:24); Liar, Father of lies (John 8:44); Murderer from the beginning (John 8:44); The Dragon (Isaiah 51:9); The Lion-Devourer (Malachi 3:11; I Peter 5:8); The Prince of this World (John 12:31); the Prince of the Power of the Air (Ephesians 2:2; 6:12); Lucifer (Isaiah 14:12); Angel of Light (2 Corinthians 11:14); The god of this World (2 Corinthians 4:4); The Accuser of the Brethren (Revelations 12:10); The Enemy (Matthew 13:39); The Serpent (Genesis 3:1); The Tempter (Matt 4:3).

There is *absolutely no light or redeem-ability in him,* nor is there anything redemptive in the three realms he orchestrates (CWD). *All* of what he has and does is fully corrupted. Here is what scripture tells us about the ancient foe:

They overcame him by the blood of the Lamb and by the word of their testimony; they did not love their lives so much as to shrink from death. Therefore rejoice, you heavens and you who dwell in them! But woe to the earth and the sea, because the devil has gone down to you! He is filled with fury, because he knows that his time is short." When the dragon saw that he had been hurled to the earth, **he pursued the woman** *who had given birth to the male child. (bold is mine)*

-- Revelation 12:11-13

And sir, you and I are the vanguard…the sentries…the warriors of the Bride (the "woman" in the previous scripture) called to drive the serpent far from our lives and from those we are called to protect. Who else will step up, if not you or me?

Man can be the enemy's agent. Joseph was betrayed by the jealousy of his brothers and then condemned to prison unjustly by a spurned woman when he acted honorably before his master Potipher's wife. Elijah fled in fear because of the price laid on his head by the evil Queen Jezebel. John the Baptist lost his head due to the connivings of an evil woman and her daughter. Jesus and many of those who followed after Him, suffered at the hands of evil men:

…many people saw the miraculous signs he was doing and believed in his name. **But Jesus would not entrust himself to them,** *for he knew all men. He did not need man's testimony about man, for he knew what was in a man.*

--John 2:23-24

Be on your guard against men; *they will hand you over to the local councils and flog you in their synagogues… All men will hate you because of me, but he who stands firm to the end will be saved… Do not be afraid of those who kill the body but cannot kill the soul. Rather, be afraid of the One (God) who can destroy both soul and body in hell. (parenthesis and bold is mine)*

-- Matthew 10:17-28

179

Paul also suffered at the hand of religious leaders and jealous men who stirred up the mob:

Beware lest anyone cheat you through philosophy and empty deceit, according to the tradition of men, according to the basic principles of the world, and not according to Christ.

-- Colossians 2:8

Most Christian men are oblivious to this warfare and wield their best energies towards advancing the cause of provision in their occupation of choice and bringing the comforts of the American Dream to their family. But as we discovered in Chapter 4, we wake each morning into a savage struggle of light against darkness, faith against fear and confidence against uncertainty. There is a strategic head who will patiently plot out your and my demise...and he has distinct plans for every member of your family and every member of your church.

As a consultant for many years, and while on the inside as a corporate officer, I have met and worked alongside organizational leaders of all types. After you pull back the layers, every organization shares a similar web of human flaws, and almost every corporate culture includes a daily morass of intrigue, hidden agendas, power plays and positioning. Like the grown-up playground, cowards and peacemakers are bullied by the ambitious and the stubborn dig their heels into slow progress out of fear or wounded egos.

Most of us would believe that Christian, mission-based organizations and churches, are more people-centric and share a "love" quality for their constituents more openly and sincerely than their secular counterparts, but even these cultures can be subject to the additional invisible and sometimes deceptive cloak of "doing work for God" and His highest purpose. I have to guard myself from a real tendency to overvalue, at times, my perception of the will of God. When I have crossed that line, it often resulted in making people around me feel like they were simply a means to an end.

My two oldest sons will both bear witness to the struggle they felt of needing to be extra good and maintain the appearance of being a strong, Christian family in the fishbowl of public ministry. They both continue to bear the scars from feelings of personal failure that resulted from my unrealistic expectations. It is no secret that many times pastors' kids get pretty "jacked up" from feeling they are on display every day. Spouses can often feel powerless, wanting and needing more attention from their Christian partner but unable to openly compete against the obvious priority of the "mission of God."

Five years after I left my fellow janitors in Van Nuys, California, I was serving as the new men's ministries director as well as the pastor to a group of 75 college and career aged "twenty somethings" at a church of 1,800 Sunday attendees in northern San Diego.

I had developed a close friendship with Allen, a man in his mid-forties, who was in a similar position at another church close by. He was breaking back into part-time ministry after a year-long season of rest and rehabilitation following a half decade spent in the field leading a church start-up in northern Ohio.

The college group I was serving was thriving and it was an exciting season in my life. But now, after some twelve months of developing a close friendship together, Allen sat across from me at Denny's over a cup of coffee. His heart had been shattered.

Allen's assignment was to lead men's ministry in his (larger) church and it was beginning to take shape as something special. When he took over men's ministries, it was pretty much on "life support," with occasional breakfast events that drew a hundred or so guys twice per year. God had put a message on his heart to call many of the 1,100 men in this church into engagement as a servant leader in their homes, workplaces, and in the church.

With all volunteers, he planned and executed a "Hunters Harvest" fall dinner event that drew over 350 men. I was invited too, and helped out a bit with the food because I knew two guys who were avid hunters and who had freezers filled with wild delicacies. They were willing to donate some of their cache of game.

Allen then hired a vendor who specialized in roasting wild pig over 24 hours in a barbeque spit, and who also was willing to grill the other wild game we had appropriated. The spread was incredible…including venison, wild turkey, duck, bear, and of course, the pig.

We had an awesome time together in worship, feasting, and fellowship as this great company of men gathered to break bread together. Allen's senior pastor and Dave, the executive administrator attended with what seemed to be glowing satisfaction. In the three hour evening event, Allen spoke for about fifteen minutes, much of which was an introduction to the guest speaker. But he did have time to lay out a powerful vision for the men that called them to step up as disciples and to be agents of God used to transform their families and community.

Allen continued telling me his story: *"That next week, the men were on fire with enthusiasm. For weeks afterwards,"* he continued, *"they seemed to walk with a new sense of energy and purpose whenever the church family gathered together. They wanted to know 'What's next?' So I found a group of men who volunteered to help me with the 'heavy lifting' of planning and bringing a high-impact, winter retreat for the men."*

Allen said that that winter retreat (where he brought three challenging messages) saw the release of God's presence and power in the men's lives, and they began to see men set free from years of habitual sin and fear. As he shared with me, he openly confessed that there were areas where the Holy Spirit had called him to repent as well. He showed me his scars…and I reciprocated. I had grown to love and trust the authenticity of this servant of God.

After the men returned, Allen shared how the feeling in the church lobby that next Sunday was different as many men came together in warm embraces. Wives and kids were introduced and camaraderie was apparent to any casual observer.

The next month he met together with his team of servant leaders, he told them that he felt a sense of warning from the Holy Spirit. Satan was not happy when men bonded together in truth. He hated when men begin to pray together and see the Kingdom of God extended through their lives to their sons, daughters, and wives. He said to them, "Guys, I believe that the enemy is going to attack this work because he is ticked off that men like you are stepping up to the next level." I can imagine that all eyes were fixed on him as he continued, *"And, I think that the attack will come from within our church, not from the outside."*

It was a month later that Allen first sensed the change from Dave, the church's executive administrator…and from the Senior Pastor as well. In addition, his right and left hand guys, the two men who labored closely with him, his "Tontos," seemed to act differently towards him. He told me that he could not put his finger on it but, *"I had an uncomfortable feeling that something was wrong…and that somehow, I was in trouble."*

As the plot unfolded, it read not unlike any story of corporate intrigue. Allen had learned that the Executive Pastor, Dave, was juggling money every week to make payroll. The church was not only overstaffed, but the economy had taken a turn for the worse and, as the Senior Pastor was getting on in his early sixties, he was working less and less. A rash of increased layoffs in the community had disturbed the congregation as well.

Fear often operates subtlety, changing the lenses through which we view the world. Like the fabled "frog in the kettle," Dave was afraid for his job, and the job of his pastor. Providentially, God had raised Allen as a leader and he, along with the men around him, were catalyzing others into ministry. The net effect was the release *of a great source of latent power in the church.* This is often a dream come true for any priest, minister, or elder board. Ironically, this men's movement was also bringing a higher call to obedient and sacrificial giving to the church.

Instead, Allen, a gifted and inspiring leader, got on Dave's radar as one who Dave believed was insidiously inserting himself as a potential *wolf among sheep.* Too many people were talking about Allen and how his ministry had changed their lives. Staff members and women in the church were talking as well. The ultimate fear was the possibility that Allen might be able to somehow leverage his newfound followership to start a new church close by. This would spell disaster for the struggling church.

Based on that false belief, Allen was believed to represent a very real threat to the already fragile state of the church. The insinuation in Dave's mind was really the voice of the *accuser of our brothers*[9], using his age old trick of getting one man or woman of influence, to sow seeds of discord among others.

These six things the LORD hates, Yes, seven are an abomination to Him: A false witness who speaks lies, And one who sows discord among brethren.

--Proverbs 6:16-19 NKJV

Dave never talked to Allen according to the clear directives of Matthew 18. He simply executed a plan to remove Allen's influence through criticism and innuendo. A whisper here and an innuendo there caused a silent withdrawal of the support for Allen's work. The critical comments took root as well within the hearts of the two men closest to Allen. Believing the lie, the conspirators were able to effectively stop the flow of God's dynamic movement through Gods chosen leader and, in the end, the church suffered.

Secretive meetings happened behind closed doors with the elders and denominational leadership, and Allen was "nicely" recommended to take pastoral leadership in a small church two hours away, and encouraged to fulfill his calling.

Through this men's movement, the Holy Spirit engaged a few common men (not unlike Gideon) as disciples in the arena. But by returning to status quo, the new ground gained in the lives of many of these men was slowly given back to hostile forces. Fresh, soon to be fruitful gardens, returned to weed patches. Many would settle for mediocrity again and exchange their role as God's warrior, for the unfortunate norm of nominal American Christianity. Men who were willing to join others for the adventure of a lifetime in the arena, returned to the stands.

Let's return to our cup of coffee. Allen's heart was broken for several reasons:

1. He was *hurt* because of being falsely accused. His only personal ambition was to impact his sphere of service to lift men to a higher call and freedom in Christ.

2. He was *saddened* that men who were stepping up as godly husbands, fathers and leaders, might lose the ground they had gained. He had loved these men.

3. He was *harmed*...talked about in private meetings behind his back. *"I was tried, judged, and sentenced,"* he said, *"...and I was hurt and angry."* Enshackled by their judgment, he wanted to imprison them to God's justice as well.

4. He confessed to me that he did have to take a *hard look inside* to see if God was displeased with him for any reason. He prayed the prayer of David in Psalm 139:

"Search me, O God, and know my heart; test me and know my anxious thoughts. See if there is any offensive way in me, and lead me in the way everlasting."

According to Allen's own account, there were areas of pride that had begun to sprout in his heart from which he needed to self-examine and repent. As the story unfolded and I understood the measure of his pain, we wept together in the parking lot before we parted. I was both humbled and changed by this Saint's story, and grateful that it had not happened to me.

Some years later, we caught up at a pastor's seminar. He told me that the hardest lesson God wanted to teach him was how to forgive and release these leaders...and his two close friends...and move forward. How could he trust church authority again? Why hadn't God been big enough to overcome the petty lies planted in this administrator's thoughts and allowed his mind to be bent towards false accusation?

> God cannot forgive us if we retain judgment or unforgiveness against another person. Think about someone who has harmed or hurt you. Look inside your heart and see if there is anyone you may not have forgiven yet. Choose to forgive them, and more importantly, make forgiveness an automatic lifestyle. You won't "feel" the forgiveness right away, but every day, speak your words of forgiveness before the Lord. It will diminish and finally fade into an unremarkable memory.

In addition, he found that his new ministry assignment was in God's *perfect timing*...if he had stayed on at the first church, he and his wife would have missed the window God had opened for them.

You may have had a similar experience. Maybe it has happened to your more than once. Workplace or family betrayals...or from friends or fellow churchmen are tough to forgive. Jesus warned us that this would happen. Then it happened to Him. Yet, He was unwavering in the ascent to Calvary. Just prior to breathing his last, he looked up to heaven and asked his heavenly Father to forgive those who so abused him because they did no know what they were doing.[10] As it says in Hebrews, Jesus learned obedience *by* the very experiences of suffering that His Father allowed to bring into His life[11].

Isaiah tells us Christ was *"despised and rejected by men."* He also had to bear the foreknowledge that each of his key followers would abandon

Him after He was arrested. The wounds suffered by this combined with Judas' betrayal, and Peter's denial must have cut deeper than the deepest lashes He received. – and added sorrowful weight to the cross He bore.

For me, one of the greatest battles I have had to face and embrace as a man is the scourge of being betrayed or abandoned by a close Christian brother, sister, or business colleague. How we respond to being misunderstood or being critically judged makes all the difference to our heavenly Father. Will I love? Forgive? Must I relinquish fully into the hands of Him who sees all and knows all and makes all things right in the end? I must, or take the downward road to prideful bitterness and ultimately, risk a shipwrecked soul.

12. Remembering our mission

Let us fix our eyes on Jesus, the author and perfector of our faith, who for the joy set before him endured the cross, scorning its shame, and sat down at the right hand of the throne of God...In your struggle against sin, you have not yet resisted to the point of shedding your blood...Endure hardship as discipline; God is treating you as sons. For what son is not disciplined by his father?...God disciplines us for our good, that we may share in his holiness. No discipline seems pleasant at the time, but painful. Later on, however, it produces a harvest of righteousness and peace for those who have been trained by it.

Hebrews 12:2-13 (partial)

As we discussed in chapter five, God's image is being forged in us that we might be made ready and gain the experiences needed to sit by Christ's side as the Bride in the new age yet to come. Reflecting on this helps me stay focused on the great cosmological plan of the Infinite One who loves me. Enduring the cross was surely the most brutal trial of suffering and sacrifice ever endured, but Jesus held a certain joy before Him as He endured the ordeal. It was the knowledge that the gift of His life would enable the saving of countless souls and usher in the new epoch of the Kingdom of God. We are then enlisted today in the mission of the gospel in preparation as the chosen Bride, the Church, ruling with Him in eternity.

Getting strategic

> The
> Mountaintop.
> Down on the battle
> field, everything is
> smoke and confusion. It is
> hard to tell friend from foe,
> to see who is winning, to foresee
> the enemy's next move. The general
> must climb high above the fray, to the
> mountaintop, where everything becomes
> clearer and more in focus. There he can see
> beyond the battlefield ---to the movements of
> reserves, to the enemy camp, to the battles future shape.
> Only from the mountaintop can the general direct the war.

-- Robert Green[12]

We call this perspective in business the "big picture" or the "30,000 foot view." Scripture advises us through prophetic writings to take that long view. If history was a football game, we *must* be aware that in these last times, we have passed the 2 minute warning in the fourth quarter. In reality there may only be seconds remaining on the clock. Here is where immeasurable hours of practice and discipline,...married to sacrificial conditioning will determine the ultimate reward of each of us. Huddled up with our eyes on Jesus, what do you see when you gaze into His eyes? What does He see in yours...the certainty and confidence of personal victory? What of others (your family and your 911 brothers) that His providence has brought to this final huddle? Will you inspire them, fight for them, and execute your final assignment? Or will you wilt under the scorching heat of pressure?

Table talk

1. Which of the strategies of war do you need to work on the most?

2. Think about a recent event in your life where things "hit the fan," or you or a family member were seriously hurt by others or adverse circumstances. Share the story briefly with your Squad. With some of the strategies discussed thus far, how might you have seen God help bring about a different outcome?

3. How does taking the "long view" change your perspective on being a disciple of Christ today? What does it do to you priorities? How does it impact your stewardship of time and money?

Core conditioning

Sit down with your spouse or best friend and talk about heaven together. Search the scriptures by typing in 'heaven' as a key word search at www.biblepathway.com. Imagine what the two of you might be doing in the next age. Think on other believer-loved ones that have gone on and being with them…and think on those whom you wish to thank and meet. Think on meeting and touching Jesus for the first time.

Chapter Ten:

Dressed For Success--Body Armor

Therefore put on the full armor of God, so that when the day of evil comes, you may be able to stand your ground, and after you have done everything, to stand. Stand firm then, with the belt of truth buckled around your waist, with the breastplate of righteousness in place, and with your feet fitted with the readiness that comes from the gospel of peace.

-- Ephesians 6:13-15

The armor of God

Most guys I know have been fascinated with battle gear, weapons, and the activities that take place before, during, and after a battle. I am clearly in that category as well. But we need to ask the question, why spiritual armor? What was Paul getting at when he used this metaphor of equipping ourselves for battle?

To answer this, we need to go back to where it all started...in the Garden of Eden. Adam and Eve were made in God's image and were naked and unashamed. After they sinned, their eyes were both opened to their sin, and they covered up from shame before each other, and then hid from God. Man has been hiding ever since.

189

This vulnerability…this nakedness is our *natural* condition. God not only understands that we are unprotected; He designed us that way intentionally. Adam and Eve felt compelled to "put on" the covering of leaves to buffer their sense of exposure. Many people I have gotten to know have built up some pretty elaborate, cover-up mechanisms.

A Christian psychotherapist Brian Lee, who experienced The Warrior course at his church, recently shared with me some insights on how common idolatry impacts human experience:

Because we were all born naked, we learn to "cover up" to protect ourselves as we grow through the stages of life. After a while, some of these coverings evolve into armor to protect us from being hurt, or to satisfy felt needs that we have. This "armor" then, matures into full blown idols in our life, which we cling to for support, affirmation, or temporary pleasure.

Paul teaches that we each must **first** "put off" or remove (by our own act of will) these sinful mechanisms:

- The works of darkness - Romans 13:12

- Anger, rage, malice, slander, and filthy language, lying. - Colossians 3:8

- The old man – Ephesians 4:22, Colossians 3:9

After we have put off the old nature, *then* we can put on something new. This is an illustration similar to what we experienced in previous chapters as we tore down the altar of Baal(s) and destroyed the Asherah. For many of us, these became substitute idols that we "put on" to cover our vulnerability and nakedness.

In other passages, like Ephesians 6:10, Paul exhorts us that we should "put on" various traits, garments or attitudes. The phrase means the same today, but in the original language "put on" is specifically designated for clothing. "Get dressed" could be another way we would use it in today's vocabulary. In any case, it is *intentional* and involves you and me *purposefully selecting* a garment, attitude, weapon, or accessory (shoes, belt, helmet) and then putting it on. Other examples where we are told to "put on" are:

- The armor of light - Romans 13:12
- Christ as a covering – Romans 13:14, Galatians 3:27
- Incorruption and immortality - 1 Corinthians 15:13
- Our heavenly dwelling (our new body) - 2 Corinthians 5:2-3
- The new man (is righteousness and true holiness in God) Ephesians 4:24
- Compassion, kindness, humility, gentleness and patience - Colossians 3:12
- Over all these virtues (from verse 12), put on love - Colossians 3:14

Guys today are fairly familiar with much of the vocabulary, actions, and missions of our armed forces. The same is true for local uniformed law enforcement and fire fighters. Paul was no different...except he had first hand experience with Roman soldiers, and was knowledgeable about their habits. Scripture shows that sometimes he was protected by them, and at other times, they held him captive. He overheard their conversations and he probably saw them drill and exercise together. Thus, he most probably had observed both their offensive and defensive training in "full gear."

We can only imagine the moment his insight intersected with the revelation of the Holy Spirit, and while observing soldiers in training, linked together the rich imagery of how the components of the armor worn by these men (men who trained to conquer and sustain the great *Pax Romana*) were allegorical to the battle armor God had prescribed for the children of God.

After we have put off the old nature, then we can put on something new.

As a student of scripture, Paul would know that God himself was described often as our shield (24 times in Psalms alone). The "sword of God" (Numbers 22, Deuteronomy 28, 33, Joshua 5:13, Ezekiel 11:8, 30:25) had plentiful applications in scripture as well. He also understood that God Himself was the *only* Savior...the source of all that is holy and righteous. God even describes *Himself* as wearing the breastplate of righteousness and a helmet of salvation...all wrapped in a cloak of zeal (Isaiah 59:7).

The purpose and design of the armor was not for peacekeeping, but to equip men for conquest of new lands, to engage and fight to win the day, and to seize new hostile territory. Their mission was to extend their Emperor's domain. Once the land was seized, a military peace was established, which paved the way for the ever expanding occupation of the kingdom of Rome. So it is true with us.

An overview of the Roman army

Gaius Marius, an experienced Roman officer, was an elected proconsul in Rome in 107 B.C. He is credited with revolutionizing the Roman Army which paved the way for the expansion of the Roman Empire. He standardized equipment and developed common uniforms and weaponry throughout the Roman military, and then introduced year round drilling and skills training. Marius is also credited with organizing the army into strategic fighting units of legions, cohorts, and centuries. They were organized as follows:

> Balance is key to all of our lives. A 10-month old baby boy begins to stand, holding on to Daddy's hand with a tiny-fingered vice grip, attempting to rise to his full twenty-nine inches in height. The rest of life is about finding that balance...to walk and then run.

The legion contained about 6,000 men of whom 5,200 were actual soldiers. Each legion consisted of ten cohorts of six "centuries" each, and each century contained 80 men. The century was divided again into eight man units, or squads, called a *contubernia*. The century led by a centurion officer fought as a unit, marched as a unit, and camped as a unit. The soldiers and officers, who frequented the pages of the Gospels and other New Testament writings, were trained rigorously to peak physical condition and discipline, unmatched in the ancient world.

The armor

The body armor of the Roman foot soldier was designed for mobility and protection. Garments were worn both under (tunic, leggings) and over (cloak, poncho) the armor, based upon the climate. What we are accustomed to seeing in history book pictures and on the big screen (and the cover of this book) is the summer or warm weather uniform style.

For our understanding, we will focus on those components that were referred to in scriptural passages. A deeper dive into the details behind the daily life of the soldier and all of the varieties of weapons, clothing, and armor is readily available on the internet.

The belt of truth

The belt, or girdle, was in reality, several components including the loin cloth, put on first (equivalent to a rather bulky jock strap); a tunic, which covered the shoulders and torso down to the knees; and then a very unique war belt.

This belt or *cingulum* included a heavy leather skirt that was cut into strips and studded with stamped plates of tin or bronze to protect the front of the lower belly, groin, and upper legs. The dagger, or *pugio*, with its sheath, was suspended from the *cingulum*…usually on the left side of the body. To say that this girdle assembly represented the "core" of every soldier is an understatement.

We will examine the sword in the next chapter and although it was laced to the side of the belt, it had its own shoulder harness for support and was put on separately over the breastplate.

Truth is the name Paul gives to the belt. Earlier in Ephesians, he identifies truth as being found *"in Jesus.*[1]*"* Many of us know the phrases uttered by Jesus: *"If you hold to my teaching, you are really my disciples. Then you will know the truth, and the truth will set you free"* (John 8:31b-32); and, *"I am the way and the truth and the life. No one comes to the Father except through me"* (John 14:6).

In addition to declaring that He was the truth, Jesus talked about the present and future role of the Holy Spirit, calling Him *"the Spirit of truth."*[2] And later in Chapter 16:13, *"But when he, the Spirit of **truth**, comes, he will guide you into all **truth**. He will not speak on his own; he will speak only what he hears, and he will tell you what is yet to come."*

Lastly, when Jesus prays his intercessory prayer to the Father, He prays, *"My prayer is not that you take them out of the world but that you protect them from the evil one…Sanctify them by the truth; your word is truth."*[3]

Christ Jesus ⇒ Word of God ⇒ Holy Spirit ⇒ Truth ⇒ Our Sanctification

How do you and I apply truth to our day-to-day living? Truth, of course means truthfulness with yourself and others. In the context of the Word of God operating in our life, it means we look regularly into it each day, with an attitude that we will see ourselves more clearly due to the Word's light-giving, mirror-like qualities.

In reality, an open heart before Scripture (reading and studying), is in constant danger. You will see the thoughts and the intents of your heart as its seeker-sword probes your innermost parts. The man of courage, who knows that the scalpel of truth will have its way in their lives, knows that it is a part of the very armor that protects his soft underbelly. Yes, it can hurt, but it will never harm. Neglecting the Word of God will harm you profoundly, however.

What is the root meaning of the word "truth?" Interestingly, when John writes the words of Jesus, he chooses the Greek word *alētheia*, for truth. This word is used in other ancient Greek writings as a synonym for our word "reality." *Alētheia* was also used more esoterically as the "unbiased pursuit of the highest in excellence." In all probability, Paul's meaning held a richer and deeper meaning than our modern word (as in truth versus lie).

Combining the meaning of the word truth as it is used by both Jesus (in John's transliteration) and Paul in his writings, truth may be considered as a component of the very nature of God, and it has the power to clarify what is real, bringing total freedom to the one who possesses it. As we put on the belt of Truth, we put on Christ and the Holy Spirit and begin to see the Divine nature moving through us. When it moves through us in battle, we help bring God's freedom to others.

The phrase "gird up" or "gird on" often represents the action of a warrior preparing for battle. In the Old Testament (examples in I Samuel 25:13 and Psalm 45:3), this phrase is used with a sense of fear and expresses the need for unhindered or protective readiness and action. In the New Testament, the meaning is similar. Strong's[4] web commentary defines "gird up" as:

A metaphor derived from the practice of the Orientals, who in order to be unimpeded in their movements were accustomed, when starting a journey or engaging in any physical work, to bind their long flowing garments closely around their bodies and fastened them with a leather belt.

I was playing catch with Toni, using, of all things, *a tennis ball*. I was twelve and she was eleven and we had an emerging, mutual crush on each other. We were about 15 feet apart, and, being an idiot twelve year old with absolutely no skills in relating to the opposite sex, I wanted to show her how hard I could throw, so I fired the ball to her. Toni was quite the jock however, and she somehow managed to catch it. Then with a playful smile, she surprised me by firing a blazing fastball right back at me, which slipped beyond my attempt to catch it and made a direct hit on my pre-pubescent manhood. *SteeRRrriyyyeeeke*!! I went down…and again, it was over.

The loins are often thought of by most guys, as our *place of greatest vulnerability*…the one place where even a soft blow can bring us to our knees. We often joke about it. It is also one of the more common pratfalls for comedic TV….a part of "bathroom humor."

Here, scripture guides us to link our physical vulnerability to that of walking in a kind of holy fear…and the need to be protected so we can be prepared for battle with our enemy. Walking as a wary warrior requires us to gird up our mind in order to protect our most vulnerable area…our sexuality. If we are not on guard and girded up, sometimes even a tennis ball can take us down.

The other day I had already plowed well into my day and missed my devotional time. My early morning habit is to slowly read a chapter of the Bible and then go to my prayer rock to worship and pray for those I love and finally to pray for my day. I get the best ideas and reminders from the Holy Spirit when I do this and every day is different when I am faithful to put first things first. After my shower and dressing, I then place my Armor of God coin in my right pocket, visualizing myself putting on the components of the armor of God to help prepare me for whatever might assail me…or for whatever ministry or serving opportunity might come my way.

Around mid-morning, I received an email notification that someone new was "following me" on Twitter. I did not recognize the female's name but clicked through only to find a blank screen and another cryptic link. I was curious, but there was a voice inside that whispered ever so quietly, *"don't click through."*

I minimized the screen and went back to work. Later that morning, when I stumbled upon the page again, my curiosity got the better of me, and this time I clicked. The page was filled with pornographic images of very young women in various compromising postures. Embarrassing as it is to admit, I looked for a few moments, and the fire began to burn in my belly…then I closed the page and caught my breath. I had been caught with my loins un-girded and the polluting images in my mind took a while to wash away.

Strengthening your core

Part of what **Called to War** is about involves developing a group of "Core Men" in community. What is a Core Man? "Church speak" will often define the Core as that group of active members that revolve much of their life around a particular church, as both recipients of ministry and contributors to the life and mission of that particular church.

The root word comes from the Latin *cor,* meaning heart and from which we obtain the word "coeur" which is French for heart and the root for the English and French word courage. The word "Corps" (Latin for body), shares the same essence as core, and is often used today in reference to a fighting troop or body of soldiers or for Americans, the US Marines. The lowest common denominator for military unit leadership is commonly called the "Corporal" which has its origin as the squad leader or overseer of the Corps unit.

Of course, the word "core" has modern applications as well. Two meanings seem to resonate with the overall meaning of what it means to be a "core man." The first meaning is the name given to the center of a fruit, like an apple. This is often discarded when the fruit is eaten. However, this is where the seeds are. As we develop the core together, expect that there will be seeds planted in your heart which will germinate and bear fruit. The fruit of the spirit from your life is then sown and germinates in the hearts of others.

The potential for all of your future generations also abides in these core seeds. How we as men steward our abilities, make decisions, and invest in our children and those around us is the essence of our legacy. It can determine the direction of many generations to come.

As I sojourn deeper into middle age, I am asking myself more frequently,

> *What will be the enduring legacy that will be left to your children's children? How can I at this late stage unknot the binding scars upon my older sons that have been inflicted upon their souls because of my actions and failures?*

If you are at all like me, this question poses both pain and promise. Pain for too often missing the mark for my five sons and for those I have had the privilege to be called "mentor." And promise for that good seed which I have sown...and for that which I intend to sow for the remaining years God gives me here on earth.

At a recent introduction to a Core 300 session, a man in his early sixties came up to me with tears and shared his sad story. He said, "My two grown children sided with my ex-wife in the (recent) divorce...and I have lost them forever. The years of emasculating abuse hurled upon me by my "Ex" has turned their hearts away from me and we don't even speak any more."

We talked for a while and I sensed that God wanted to encourage this elder warrior with hope and vision. Hope that:

- It ain't over yet

- He's got fifteen to twenty five years left on earth to win them back

- He has a battle to fight...*but it is winnable*

He needed vision for seeing them back in his arms and seeing them eternally in the arms of Father God. Vision—as a grandfather, pouring his core, the seeds of life, into his grandchildren's young hearts. I prayed with him that God would show him a way of love, healing, and forgiveness for his kids.

A second common use of core appears in physical fitness. Your "core" consists of those lower back, hips, and gut muscle groups which become your foundation for strength, balance, endurance, and stability. This is why most fitness coaches and physical therapists recommend that we build out our core before moving to other muscle groups. This is where the first few weeks of military boot camps focus as well.

As a warrior, *you will only be as strong...or last as long, as your core allows.* Core strength for a man of God, then, is critical to victory and to being able to stand, take new ground, and protect your family and brothers in arms. Ultimately, your core serves as the springboard from which you are able to sustain your predestined life of service and ministry to others for God's glory.

A couple of years ago, my lower back "went out" for what seemed to be the umpteenth time. I went to my twenty-year long ritual of Advil, ice, alternated with heat or the whirlpool. Occasionally I would get to my stash of prescription pain killers if movement was too painful. You may criticize me for my self-doctoring, but it is what it is...and it usually worked in a few days.

But this time it did not get better. I had just hit the magic age "50," and was also spending more time at my desk. The 80 minute commute to downtown Los Angles was not helping either. I called a well respected orthopedic center, asked for a low back specialist, and made an appointment...telling the receptionist that I was in a great deal of pain and needed to see a doctor *as soon as possible.*

When I arrived a week later, my assigned physician and I hit it off right away. We began talking about the college sports teams he had been working with. Then we swapped old football stories for a few minutes as he began to examine me. At this point, I could not find a comfortable position for sitting or standing, and was using a cane to walk. It felt like the center of my body was slipping sideways...first to the left, and then to the right. He sent me to Radiology and I went back to the waiting room.

After the nurse summoned me to his office, he gave me the diagnosis. He confirmed that my lower back had severe degenerative arthritis. I already knew about the arthritis, but the word "severe" was new. Then what he said next hit me like a hammer, *"You have the low back of an eighty year old woman."*

After I caught my breath, he showed me the film. It did not look good. *"Art,"* he said, *"your back infrastructure is too weak to support your weight and your core has weakened as well. I see two possibilities. One, if you continue with your life as you know it, you will be wheelchair bound within five years.*" The image of spending decades unable to walk felt like a death sentence.

Then he looked at me with that Father Knows Best/Marcus Welby M.D. look and said, "*However, you can beat this thing and live a somewhat normal life, if you will lose some weight, and adopt a daily regime of exercising your core abdominal and lower back muscles.*"

I had never heard "core" used before when referring to the center of your body. I have learned since that it is the critical *seat of strength and balance*, and not only was having a strong core vital to athletic performance, but it was vital for everyday living.

He assigned me to a first rate physical therapy center where they had to teach me, over a period of weeks, how to begin to strengthen my core muscles. Patiently they guided, corrected, and aided me, as I learned new ways to exercise. My therapist, Carol, even went to the gym with me to observe my typical workout. I had adapted the old circuit routine I used in college only to discover that I was doing certain drills that *weakened* my core and destabilized my back!

Some of my old routines were okay to continue, and over the next two months, they added some new ones. In the process I learned a whole new way of moving. In addition, my therapist introduced me to the exercise ball. I had felt it was something *only women used*; in fact, my wife had one of these balls (a pink one) and used it to workout daily to a DVD.

Once I learned how to ride that puppy, I discovered that I was dead wrong about it being only for females.

It takes guts to hear the truth and guts to apply it. If you don't do the crunches, don't expect to have the fortitude to see the truth about your life (and God's bright hope for your future). Do the crunches.

To put on the Girdle of Truth is to put on God Himself.

I gained a new level of respect for my wife, and quickly noticed that she could do stuff on the ball that I couldn't even envision trying!

This sucker *burned my gut...and my low back,* when I used it...and the torturous exercises that have been devised with this colorful overgrown beach ball felt like they had their origins from the prince of darkness himself! But the alternative of continuing to deteriorate was not an option. I began to listen and learn as if my life depended on it. Although I still struggle with lower back pain, building my core strength has made it possible for me today to enjoy a normal standard of physical performance.

The point of this lengthy dissertation on core is this: How effective would it be for us to engage in deadly swordplay with one hand on a cane for balance...or from a wheelchair? Many Christian men today walk vertically compromised in their faith because they have not girded up their loins with the truth that they must embrace the basic disciplines of being a follower of Jesus in order to fight the good fight.

Gospel shoes

Paul knew that Roman soldiers wore special sandals to protect their feet. These were called *caligae*. The *caligae* were well-ventilated, strong leather sandals with leather straps. They had iron hob-nails protruding through the sole for extra grip and hard-wearing.[5]

Jesus came preaching the "gospel of the Kingdom" and Paul thinks of these military shoes as the foundation of what is needed to *take* redemptive ground. It entailed that we gain ground through bringing the good news that the King has come...and is coming again. However, the foot of God and of man has deep allegorical applications in scripture that go beyond simply bringing the message of salvation. It is the symbol of dominion.

The first instance of dominion we have appears in a conversation that took place just as the Trinity was about to create man in Genesis 1:26:

Walking your turf

You probably have a place you live called home. It has some kind of boundary, lot lines, outside walls or borders. Praying as you go, walk the entire perimeter of your yard or apartment asking God to take those steps of spiritual dominion and stewardship with you. Establish his Kingdom authority in every purposeful step you take. As you go, build a canopy or tent of prayer and praise over your home asking for God's covering and protection of you and your family. Try this approach as well where you work (and spend probably 70% of your time). Take the territory of God there as well as His agent of light and love.

Then God said, "Let us make man in our image, in our likeness,
*and let them **rule** over the fish of the sea and the birds of the air,*
*over the livestock, **over all the earth**...God blessed them and said*
to them, "Be fruitful and increase in number; fill the earth and
***subdue it. Rule over** the fish of the sea and the birds of the air*
and over every living creature that moves on the ground."

Then we see Adam *walking* with God in the cool of the day. Adam had
taken his leadership (literally his dominion) over only a specific garden
that God created and gave him. Each step within that garden was the step
of a king in training. He had dominion, but it was only a shadow of what
God had expressed in verse 26. His destiny was to rule, or have dominion,
"over all the earth." He never fulfilled his destiny because he failed in the
garden.

Abraham, similarly, was given a land of promise to him and his
descendants through God's personal promise. This dominion remains to
this day. However, he received the dimensions of his inheritance, the
Divine Deed of Trust, and the right to rule over the Promised Land, only
after he obeyed God's directive to walk the length and width of the land.

This illustration of taking possession of new territory by a man, who
really had no right to settle in this country other than God's directive, is
what God calls you and me to do as men. Paul's sandals of the gospel
brought peace and reconciliation between God and man. He had
experienced the Roman conquest of new territories firsthand and wanted
us to follow a similar *spiritual* pathway that Rome followed in the
physical realm. Their kingdom expanded with each marching step. The
territory they conquered was colonized and then held together by the
government of the *Pax Romana.*

As we take possession by faith of what God has for us, the warrior's
cleated shoes are not only designed to hold your ground, but gain new
ground as well. It may initially mean gaining control of your temper or the
discipline of controlling roaming eyes. Later on, it could expand to
coming alongside another man to lift him up after a fall and strengthen
him. Or it may be forgiving your wife and sacrificing a regular time to
simply listen to her for an hour. The ground you gain with her could
restore the trust needed for her to extend the gift of her esteem that you
need for experiencing deeper intimacy.

Paul exhorted Christ's followers in Ephesus regarding the tensions between believers, Jews and Pagans in the city;

Put on the whole armor of God that you may be able to stand against the wiles of the devil. For we do not wrestle against flesh and blood, but against principalities, against powers, against the rulers of the darkness of this age, against spiritual hosts of wickedness in the heavenly places. Therefore, take up the whole armor of God that you may be able to withstand in the evil day, and having done all, to stand.

--Ephesians 6:11-13 New King James Bible

And again, in his letter to the church in Corinth, Paul was defending the reasons for his authority versus opposing voices in the city, and, even among some naysayers in the church. His leadership was under attack. He argued that his power was not due to physical or intellectual strength, but from a spiritual authority that God had entrusted to him; the source of the resistance he faced was invisible and entailed spiritual powers arrayed against him. He had intentionally walked in Kingdom dominion over much of the Roman Empire and Christ's kingdom followed his steps.

The breastplate of righteousness

After donning the girdle and lacing up his shoes, the soldier would then strap on his body armor. We have often seen the breastplate as a single piece of armor that had the shape of built-in pectoral and abdominal muscles in statues and movie scenes. However, this "muscles" version was only used in real life for parades; it was impractical for real fighting and thus was worn on occasion by Caesar's or non-combat politicians.

It is unlikely that Paul *ever even saw* the muscles version. The breastplate that Paul envisioned when he wrote of the armor of God was called "*lorica laminata*" and was the core protection of the common centurion-led, foot soldier.

The gospel shoes are the feet and message of our King, Jesus Christ and in their wake is the Pax Deo.[6]

Figure 11 shows how it was made of many horizontal metal (iron) plates layered over each other and tied together by internal straps made of animal skin. The armor itself consisted of broad ferrous iron strips ("girth hoops") fastened to the strips that were arranged horizontally on the body. They surrounded the torso in two halves, being fastened at the sides to protect the front and back.

The subject of God's imputed righteousness in scripture is worth its own book. It is not definable in a single idea, but represents layers of truth regarding the reality of God's provision for us as well as the effect that wearing the breastplates brings (integrity, for example) to the seasoned soldier of God. Each of these components of righteousness should be studied in their own right because they are all critical for our being able to stand tall in God's armor. When we understand the full dimension of our God-given righteousness, we become protected from the accusations by the enemy of our souls, our own self-voice prone to harmful criticism...or by people who would speak on the enemy's behalf.

The multi-faceted components of righteousness are symbolized by the *lorica's* interlocking plates:

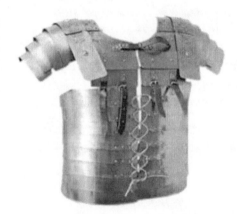

- The attitude of repentance
- Forgiveness of sins
- Covered by the Blood of Jesus
- No shame - declared "not guilty"
- Holiness
- No condemnation
- Good works
- Reckoned dead...alive in Christ
- Of one purpose "straightness"
- Confidence in God's high esteem
- Daily cleansing
- The Spirit of Adoption

Figure 11: The Roman Breastplate or "lorica laminate"

REMARKS AT JSCOPE 2000, JANUARY 27, 2000
By General Charles C. Krulak, USMC (Retired)

Integrity, as we know it today, stands for soundness of principle and character – uprightness-honesty. Yet there is more. Integrity is also an ideal. A goal to strive for. And for a man or woman to "walk in their integrity" is to require constant discipline and usage. The word integrity itself is a martial word that comes to us from an ancient Roman army. Tradition during the time of the twelve Caesars, the Roman army would conduct morning inspections. As the inspecting Centurion would come in front of each Legionnaire, the soldier would strike with his right fist the armor breastplate that covered his heart. As the soldier struck his armor, he would shout "INTEGRITAS," which in Latin means material wholeness, completeness, and entirety. Satisfied that the armor was sound and that the soldier beneath it was protected, he would move on to the next man.

At about the same time, the Praetorians or imperial bodyguard were ascending into power and influence. They no longer had to shout "integritas" to signify that their armor was sound. Instead, as they struck their breastplate, they would shout "Hail Caesar," to signify that their heart belonged to the imperial personage – not to their unit – not to an institution – not to a code of ideals. They armored themselves to serve the cause of a single man.

By 383 AD, the social decline that infected the Republic and the corrupted Praetorian Guard had its effects upon the Legion. As a 4th Century Roman general wrote, "When, because of negligence and laziness, parade ground drills were abandoned, the customary armor began to feel heavy since the soldiers rarely, if ever, wore it. Therefore, they first asked the Emperor to set aside the breastplates and mail. Then the helmets. So our soldiers fought the Goths without any protection for the heart and head and were often beaten by archers. They took their armor off, and when the armor came off, so too came off their integrity. It was only a matter of a few years until the legion rotted from within and was unable to hold the frontiers. The barbarians were at the gates.

"The integrity of the upright guides them, but the unfaithful are destroyed by their duplicity."

--Proverbs 11:3

The design of the breastplate was to protect the vital organs from sustaining a deadly wound. *It covers the heart* of the forgiven and forgiving man. To walk into battle without having forgiven all others who have harmed you is unwise. To engage the adversary, not knowing the confident clarity and refreshment of soul that comes with being cleansed with God's forgiveness, can disable the uncovered man because the accusations of the enemy are one his effective weapons.

Many of the battles we lose may have been waged in our hearts and souls for many years. We must therefore guard and test our hearts against men and that inner condition of unforgiveness which can put you on the "injured reserved" list before the battle ever begins.

The helmet of salvation

The Roman infantry wore an iron helmet that had a simple upside down bowl-like design with flexible cheek and ear coverings on either side of the head piece and a flared end to protect the back of the neck. At the crown was sometimes an acorn-shaped spike.

Its weight of 11-14 pounds was a serious issue for the new trainee and weeks of muscle had to be developed in training exercises in order for the neck and shoulders to become accustomed to the foreign, top heavy feeling it gave the soldier. Inside, although no complete remnants have been found, it must have had animal fleece or some quilted fabric underneath, which would have been necessary to add comfort, stability and avoid chafing against the skin, neck and hair.

One of the warriors of old made this statement: "The purpose of war is victory, and the purpose of victory is occupation." In the Kingdom, we add one more step to the process: The purpose of

205

occupation is expansion. It's important that we view life with the perspective of expansion and forward motion. It's not healthy to simply find a place you want to stay in and occupy. The moment you have found a leveling-off place is the moment you begin backsliding.

When your passion begins to decline, you already start to die. You were born to burn. When leaders don't have passion, it costs everyone who follows. Passion and the anointing run in parallel courses. A person with passion will take risks. You don't get it by coasting on yesterday's breakthrough. You were born for expansion.

-- From Occupation to
Expansion, by Bill Johnson

Prior to training or in response to the call to form up for battle, the helmet was then put on the soldier's head. It was vital to practice with fellow soldiers with their helmet on in order to be completely battle ready. Even sparring can be deadly and the warrior had to grow accustomed to the weight of his helmet...allowing his muscles and tendons to grow stronger, during sustained maneuvers and enemy engagement.

I have also found that many of my deepest wounds have come when a *fellow Christian* or loved family member inadvertently harms me...if I had not "put on" the Helmet of Salvation, their comment or disregard will rock my boat. It is important to always have the mindset of knowing *who* I am in Christ to stabilize and anchor me in the midst of even "friendly fire."

Christ's thought life

The helmet represents, among other things, a new viewpoint, attitude or perspective. The great Apostle exhorts us to meditate on the subject matters that are listed in the next verse:

Finally, brothers, whatever is true, whatever is noble, whatever is right, whatever is pure, whatever is lovely, whatever is admirable—if anything is excellent or praiseworthy—think about such things. Whatever you have learned or received or heard from me, or seen in me—put it into practice. And the God of peace will be with you.

-- Philippians 4:8-9

Self-humbling as an ongoing attitude

The distance Christ had to descend to go from being the exalted Son of God to become a baby boy, is the same distance man had fallen in his disobedience. Therefore Christ's colossal condescension was required to redeem the depth of our fallenness.

-- Anonymous

Both Old and New Testament writings universally concur that humility is a key attribute of the Saint. Jesus knew the reality that He was God. He understood that He was the fashioner and sustainer of the universe, and the hope of mankind. He had the constant worship and adoration of the most powerful created beings in all of creation. But He let it all go to submit to His Father's plan to become an anointed and Holy Spirit-infused male sperm cell as it fertilized the young egg in Mary's womb.

Let this mind be in you which was also in Christ Jesus, who... made Himself of no reputation, taking the form of a bondservant, and coming in the likeness of men...He humbled Himself and became obedient to the point of death, even the death of the cross.

-- Philippians 2:5-8
New King James Bible

This mindset is the best prescription for the sin of pride. Humility becomes ours willingly and intentionally when we put on the helmet of Salvation each and every day.

Christ's understanding of the ways of Satan

Jesus thoroughly understood the methods and techniques of Satan…he was clear on how the world system could try to play and persuade Him, and He was vigilant over his own human nature to give way to raw human emotions and their tendency towards carnality. The helmet represents *seeing life through the perspective of Christ* and gaining from His deep experience.

> *Therefore, the best warfare strategy is to attack the enemy's plans, next is to attack alliances, next is to attack the army, and the worst is to attack a walled city.*

-- Sun Tzu, The Art of War

When I get stuck in a track of thought or am so distracted that I shut out conversations around me, my wife claims that I must have spent too many years inside a football helmet! It makes me think of how a tackle football player's perspective changes once he dons the helmet. I remember the first time, at the age of 13, I put on that seven pound bright blue bowling ball! It was hard to keep my balance on my skinny neck. Everything looked different…and sounded different inside the helmet.

We were allowed to carry it to and from the practice field or to the stadium, but once the game or practice started, *it stayed on*. The player was not fully dressed until he, last of all, put his helmet on. In that subtle gesture of placing my fingers in the ear holes and pulling the helmet over my head and then strapping it snugly to my chin, I became more than a boy. I became a member of my squad…an Agoura Charger!

With the helmet came a sense of commonality with all of my teammates. We all heard things the same way and saw them the same way. We were armored to take head shots, as needed, and to deliver blows to our adversary with high impact. It made us hit harder and gave us the liberty to attack with the full force of our body.

It also made me be more alert. The sides of the helmet partially concealed my normal peripheral vision. The necessity of seeing around me was heightened and yet, like being a man putting on the Helmet of Salvation, there are good reasons for the warrior to stay focused….and to see this alien and captive world through a different lens....the lens of God's reality.

In other letters written by Paul to the church, he writes for them to put on the "helmet of salvation"[7] ...or asserts that "we have the mind of Christ"[8] available for us.

Paul saw that when a single recruit put on his armor, he became the force and authority of the Roman Empire wherever he went. He understood that the Christian man or woman putting on the shoes...girding on the belt...strapping on the breastplate and then, donning the helmet, was more than allegory...it *was putting on God himself.*

We get to embrace the reality that we are weak and vulnerable...naked before Him, and then we get to put on the only protection we will ever need. What was once just a common, everyday guy, hiding in the winepress of life, is now the dangerous vanguard of the Kingdom of God! The awesome thing is that God has chosen us to be enjoined by the Holy Spirit to conquer back this fallen planet by bringing many into the fold of our Father's family.

Table talk

1. How has the lack of being "armored up" caused you to lose ground as a Christian?

2. Share one application each at the table that most spoke to you about the Shield or the Helmet. How can your squad mates (or 911s) help you embrace that application for these next weeks?

3. Discuss how it is that the armor of God is actually God himself to you

Core conditioning

1. Write a short essay to share with your small group, spouse or best (Christian) friend that best describes how the putting on the girdle of truth and the shoes of the Kingdom are changing your life.

2. Read Isaiah 11-13 and then Revelation 19. What is God doing in these last days?

Chapter Eleven:

Total Annihilation

Before we return to our story in judges, we need to wrap up Paul's discourse on God's armor using the Roman model, and then we'll segue into lessons we might glean from Gideon and his 300 as they engage in the famous battle against the Midianites.

In addition to all this, take up the shield of faith, with which you can extinguish all the flaming arrows of the evil one. Take the helmet of salvation and the sword of the Spirit, which is the word of God. And pray in the Spirit on all occasions with all kinds of prayers and requests.

-- Ephesians 6: 16-17

The sword of the Spirit

The word "sword" is found in scripture 448 times and is one of the most common nouns in the Bible. To compare, the words "worship" and "praise" (all derivations) have 485 references *combined*! The first "named" sword we find in scripture is the "sword of the Lord" (13 times). The second named sword was the "sword of Gideon."[1] Others like the "sword of Goliath"[2] shared their name with their champion. The "sword of Saul"[3] and the "sword of Pharaoh,"[4] represented their royal authority and their army's ability to bring death and vengeance to their enemies. In most cases, the sword of a ruler was referred to as being directed by the hand of God Himself, but wielded on earth by those chosen as His instruments of justice.

Carried at the waist and supported by a shoulder harness-sheath, the Roman *gladius* was inserted into the sheath and supported by the belt after the breastplate was put on. Identified by Paul in Ephesians 6 as the Word of God, it is described in Hebrews 4 as being sharp with two edges, dividing between the soul and the spirit, and making known the thoughts and the intents of a man's heart.[5]

Legendary stories of swords of valiant warriors have been passed on for hundreds of generations. Swords wielded by legendary heroes had names, like Excalibur and Tanlladwyr[6] and mighty men of old like David's heroically won sword of Goliath. We have all been entranced while watching men be mystically blessed by monarchs when they received the noble touch of the sword upon each shoulder….to rise into a new, and higher, calling.

Even in modern times, at the end of every major war, the sword of the senior officer, symbolizing the power of the vanquished enemy, is surrendered to the victor.

We first see the sword in Genesis wielded by cherubim to prevent Adam and Eve from returning to the Garden:

After he drove the man out, he placed on the east side of the Garden of Eden cherubim and a flaming sword flashing back and forth to guard the way to the tree of life.[7]

-- Genesis 3:24

John describes Jesus, the returning King, as having a flaming two-edged sword coming out of his mouth. Thus, for the Christian warrior, the sword is not named for the one who carried it into battle (as was in the case of Gideon), but as an extension of God Himself. Like the sword of

Gideon, we wield the sword of the living God in the Name of His Son, who has *fully* empowered us as His instruments of justice and deliverance, here on earth! Other aspects of the Word of God used in scripture include the mirror, food, health, death and the imminent return of the King. Let's take a look at some of these attributes of the word.

The mirror

Mirrors have been in use for thousands of years. They have commonly had a very private purpose: to reveal the truthful image of its owner. The mirror is for you, and as you gaze into the Word of God, holding the sword of the Spirit, you will see *reality* more clearly. You will also see yourself....look deeply and you will see your selfishness, small mindedness, pride and fear.

> *Do not merely listen to the word, and so deceive yourselves. Do what it says. Anyone who listens to the word but does not do what it says is like a man who looks at his face in a mirror and, after looking at himself, goes away and immediately forgets what he looks like.*

> -- James 1:22-24

On a more positive note, it is also where we discover our divine identity as a ransomed child of God, highly valued and precious in His eyes. We learn how God places us in Christ and empowers us with the Holy Spirit, delivers us from evil, and mentors us in right living.

> *Now we see but a poor reflection as in a mirror; then we shall see face to face. Now I know in part; then I shall know fully, even as I am fully known.*

> -- 1 Corinthians 13:12

One interpretation of Paul's description of seeing a "poor reflection as in a mirror" could be that God allows us to see a *little of the truth about ourselves at a time*. One of the highest paid Executive Coaches in the world, best selling author and psychologist, Marshall Goldsmith, writes about an exercise he has done for thousands of corporate leaders based on their ability to focus on one area of personal growth at a time:

*I teach my clients now to pick the **one behavior** pattern for personal change that will make the biggest difference, and to focus on that. If we pick the right area to change and actually do so, it will almost always influence other aspects of our relationships with people. (bold is mine)*

Marshall Goldsmith's Blog,
January 11, 2010

Any Christian who has embraced growing in Christ intuitively subscribes to the experience of the Lord showing him a "growth area" that we did not see before. It happens through many of God's agencies of communication: people, a sermon, a song or a time of prayer. Mostly, for me, it happens while reading and meditating on the Bible.

Goldsmith happened upon a biblical principle and applied it to workplace behavior. For us, we know that the Holy Spirit often will quicken to our minds one area where we need to confess, repent, and walk in newness of life. We see unclearly because for us to see clearly every area we need to change would overwhelm us! We see a "poor reflection" out of God's mercy and His understanding of our weak frame, but it is still truth and we need to "do what it says."

Field rations

From the fruit of his mouth, a man's stomach is filled; with the harvest from his lips, he is satisfied. The tongue has the power of life and death, and those who love it will eat its fruit.

-- Proverbs 18:20-22

You may have the heard the story about the old Alaskan blacksmith in Anchorage in the late 1890s who had two massive work dogs. During the day they would haul loads of iron around his shop and then into town once a week to deliver his orders, pulling a flatbed wooden sled.

One of the dogs, a blend of Husky and Wolf, was pure white with blue eyes. The other was a Mastiff mix and was mostly black. Most Saturday nights, he would go to town for the weekly dog fights and many times place a bet on both his white dog and his black dog. Sometimes the wager was for them to win…others it was for them to lose, but the pattern was different each time.

One Monday morning, the charcoal man arrived to make his weekly delivery of fuel for the smith, but this time, instead of exchanging the coal for the Blacksmith's money and leaving, he had to ask a question that had been bothering him for weeks. He had been to most of the dog fights and saw the old man's dogs win and lose, but it bugged him that the old man always seemed to win the bet…whether his dog won or lost the match.

"How do you always seem to know whether your dog is going to win or lose," he asked.

"Well I'll tell you if you swear to never tell another soul," said the old man. *"Agreed,"* said the man, his curiosity rising, *"and here's my hand on it."* And they shook. The big smith broke a thin smile and cocked his head to the left and said, *"You see, they are both great fighters, but whichever one I feed that week, usually wins."*

The story illustrates a powerful yet simple truth: *"Man does not live on **bread alone**, but on every word that comes from the mouth of God"* (Matthew 4:4). If you feed your spirit with *daily* portions of the Word of God and commune with Jesus Christ, the living Bread of Life, you will win most of your spiritual battles. Starve the warrior…lose the battle. Starve him long enough and you'll lose the war.

The "two-edged" sword for healing and death

Ephesians, Hebrews, and Revelations, all written by different authors, reveal to us a unique quality of the sword of God. It is still sharp and still cuts, but it is seen as more of an instrument of healing, cleansing, or for nurturing and strength.

In the Old Testament, the sharpened edge of God's sword, or the sword of those he used, were usually for the purpose of executing judgment to their adversaries. Sometimes the "adversary" was even Israel or specific tribes of Israel. These were mostly times of discipline or scourging of his people for disobedience and idolatry. The design of the sword was for the purpose of bringing them to repentance and back into right relationship with Him.

214

1. The instrument of health

As God's Word, the sword often brings us cutting warnings. It exposes the visceral belly of our humanity in Hebrews 4:13;

Everything is uncovered and laid bare before the eyes of him to whom we must give account.

And it leads us towards contrition and humility. In 2 Timothy, Paul reminds his adopted son Timothy of the primacy and effective mission of God's Word

All scripture is given by inspiration of God, and is profitable for doctrine, for reproof, for correction, for instruction in righteousness. That the man of God may be perfect thoroughly furnished unto all good works (lit: enterprise or occupation).

-- 2 Timothy 3:16-17

God's inspired Word in our lives has a dual benefit, which is that we "may be *perfect*," (literally means well-fitted or complete), and it is profitable for equipping us for doing good works. Psalms 107, verse 20, conveys a softer aspect of the Word of God, informing us that God sends His Word to us for healing and wholeness.

2. The "bringer of death"

Let the saints rejoice in this honor and sing for joy on their beds. May the praise of God be in their mouths and a double-edged sword in their hands, to inflict vengeance on the nations and punishment on the peoples.

-- Psalm 149:5-7

Gideon's men lifted their battle cry: "*The sword of the Lord and of Gideon!*"[8] As we discussed in Chapter 5, unlike the physical enemies Gideon was called to overcome, we do not battle in the physical realm against flesh and blood, but instead our battle is "*against the powers of*

215

this dark world and against the spiritual forces of evil in the heavenly realms." (Ephesians 6:11-12)

The most common kind of miracle performed by Jesus was delivering men, woman, and children *from demonic bondage.* Even some of the physical sicknesses He healed were dealt with through exorcism. I find it easier and more comfortably "scientific" for me to believe in a recently named "disease," by someone with a doctorate degree, than it is to accept the dynamic operation of a demon, expressing itself through someone.

Today, most churches in America have purposely avoided the subject of the demonization of human beings, especially when it comes to believers. We have mostly bought into psychological diagnostics whenever bizarre or evil behavior is evident. Frankly, it scares most of us.

Can a Christian be demonized? Can believers be hindered, harassed, driven or oppressed by demonic entities that seem to have an attachment to the human soul? Most experienced Christian therapists and pastoral counselors will tell you yes. Scripture teaches us that we can be infested or besieged by demonic entities. In the case of Simon the Sorcerer, it was *clear* that he had been saved and baptized through faith in Jesus Christ. Yet, he had demonic issues that were directly confronted by Peter. Read what Peter says to Simon;

*Repent of this wickedness and pray to the Lord. Perhaps he will forgive you for having such a thought in your heart. For I see that you are **full of** bitterness and **captive** to sin. (bold is mine)*

-- Acts 8:22-23

The phrase "full of bitterness" means *into the gall of extreme wickedness.* "Captive to sin" means *bound and tied up in iniquity.*[9] Can a believer be demon **possessed**? No. If someone has confessed Jesus as Lord, then, through His saving blood he has been bought with a price and sealed with the Holy Spirit.

Can a believer be demon **oppressed**? Absolutely! The true account below helps illustrate how bondage can cripple the walk of a Christian and how God can set us free.

I had known Kevin ever since he had come to our church and given his life to Christ and confessed Him as his Savior and Lord five years earlier.

He had a heart for our youth and a winsome way with teens. He sat there in my office on a sunny Saturday morning and told me of the darkest accounts from his boyhood. He was five years old and lived in a rural area just north of metropolitan Baton Rouge, Louisiana. The street he lived on had no lights and he often huddled alone with his mom in bed at night listening to the cicada's hum and other night sounds. He felt safe in her arms. Little did he know that she drew comfort and strength in his cuddling embrace as well.

Their home was small, only three rooms, and Kevin could barely recall the last time he and mother were not alone together. He had the faint memory of someone he thought was his Daddy...or maybe it was just an angry man who had slept under their roof some distant time ago.

They had finished supper together as usual, the sun setting about an hour earlier. "Time for bed, Pumpkin," she said, and off he went to brush his teeth and put on his summer pajamas. He was in the back room when he heard the loud crash against the front door.

As Kevin entered the narrow hallway off to the side of the main room, he saw a dark haired man burst into the small living room, hungry eyes seeking for something, *someone*. His mommy! Brandishing a knife with a blade over ten inches long, the man yelled at her and then backhanded the terrified woman, who fell backwards into the tiny kitchen, her petite frame tumbling against the cabinets. Kevin huddled in the darkened hallway, stilled by the terror that had frozen the air in his chest.

The man began to threaten his mommy with the knife, yelling at her to take off her dress. The combination of his mother's sobbing mixed with the terror and shame on her face set his feet to action and the boy charged with all of his might into the back legs of the man. He turned and with the hand that held the knife swung a closed fist across Kevin's skull, sending him 5 feet across the room where he rolled up against the couch. Stunned and eyes blurred, the boy moved in and out of consciousness as the intruder violently raped his mother several yards away.

He tried to rise to help a few times but his legs would not work. The few minutes that transpired seemed like an eternity, and he could not shut out the screams of his mother mingled with the guttural groans of this monster.

Even after the silence came, for many years later in the solitude of darkness, the ravaging sounds of violence echoed in his mind. And that night an evil violence *entered* into him.

As he finished the story, his breathing had clearly accelerated and, now as he wept openly, tears of unhealed pain dampened his shirt. In a previous time together, Kevin had told me about personal acts of violence he had taken against others and himself over the past fifteen years, mostly before he was saved, but now I began to understand the origin of his injury and source of his rage.

I saw in my mind an image of a *heinous demonic spirit*...a "Strongman"...hidden deep within the soul of this young man. It had entered into Kevin that night, long ago, and as a pre-teen it influenced Kevin into choosing the darker side of martial arts to develop strength and a sense of invulnerability. Soon the evil spirit, who had taken residence in his wound, had begun to express itself as Kevin developed his own version of a black-clad, Ninja-like character. In his early teens, he began to hide in bushes or drop down from trees at night, to attack unsuspecting children or teens, beating them with a Samurai-like stick, kicking and terrorizing them. These attacks made him feel strong and it fed the beast within, who always demanded more.

Afterwards, he would hate what he had done, despising himself. At several points he had come to the verge of suicide... planning on using his long-bladed knife on himself, but God loved this young man and had sent people at different times to intervene at these moments of crisis until he could be set free.

Now that day, I knew it was his time. He had been reading the Bible frequently during that week, filling his mind with truth and the strength of the Word of God. All day prior and through the morning, he had fasted and prayed, preparing himself for our time of prayer together. I had joined him in his fast...believing that God would heal Kevin. Now God waited for me to bring the sword of the Lord against the powerful demon that had nested deep within this young man. I began to pray with him.

At first, Kevin began to agree in prayer with me, *"Yes Lord, we bind the power of this Strongman sprit and break its control over my life, in Jesus' Name...."* Then, after a short time, I remember his bloodshot eyes shot open wide, filled with hatred towards me. In a different voice, deeper and hateful, he commanded me to stop praying, *"Or I will kill you!"*

Frankly, this was getting pretty weird (and scary) for me at this point. I felt afraid and wished the two of us were not alone in the building! I do not recommend that you ever engage in the ministry of exorcism or deliverance unless two or three others are standing with you in faith. In fact, Kevin was a Black Belt...and pretty big. But I knew that the Name of Jesus was more powerful than any demon trying to vie for control in my friend, and I continued to pray with the rising authority of the Holy Spirit, wielding the mighty Word of God, and then *commanded* the Strongman to leave Kevin's body in Jesus' Name.

Kevin began to growl. His white knuckled hands firmly gripped the arms of the chair he was sitting in, and I continued to pray forcefully and in Jesus' authority. After what seemed like a long time of contending in authoritative prayer, his head suddenly snapped back and out of his mouth came a sound...unearthly and demonic, a loud scream followed by a long *"NOOOOO!"*

Closing his eyes, the young man's entire body relaxed in his chair. After several seconds, he opened his eyes, and I could see that Kevin was back! God had broken the power of the evil spirit and driven it out of his life! He began praising God and telling me how much "lighter" he felt. We worshipped God together for the freeing power of His Word.

Kevin told me later that all he could remember during the time of prayer was that he wanted to kill me, but that his hands were somehow chained to the arms of the chair and he could not budge! We serve a mighty Lord and must learn, as men, to wield the sword of the Lord as His warrior, and according to Jesus' definition of the Gospel, to see men and women set free from the prisons of Hell and the torment that binds them. If not you, then who will?

Strong's concordance identifies the word "spirit" as the Greek word *pneuma*, and defines it as an essence possessed with the power of knowing, desiring, deciding and acting. The warrior who deftly wields the living sword of the Holy Spirit, gains decisive advantage in battle...in discerning the enemy's intentions, and the nature of the spirit. As Jesus dealt confidently and succinctly with demons ranging from one who caused an 18-year menstrual infirmity in the woman who touched his garment, to the hosts of legion that jointly controlled the Gadarene

Demoniac, he was non-plussed when demons expressed or appealed to him.

The story below is a warning to anyone who is attracted to this kind of ministry…and to help balance the story about Kevin. Whatever you do, *don't mess with the ministry of deliverance lightly!*

> *Then some of the itinerant Jewish exorcists took it upon themselves to call the name of the Lord Jesus over those who had evil spirits, saying, "We exorcise ("command" in the NIV) you by the Jesus whom Paul preaches." Also there were seven sons of Sceva, a Jewish chief priest, who did so. And the evil spirit answered and said, "Jesus I know, and Paul I know; but **who are you?**" Then the man in whom the evil spirit was leaped on them, overpowered them, and prevailed against them, so that they fled out of that house naked and wounded. (bold is mine)*

> -- Acts 19:13-17 (NKJV)

Paul was a guy like you or me. But the realm of darkness *feared* him. Read the book of Acts and you will see vivid demonstrations of power recorded by Luke. The early church leaders never sought out demonic confrontation and neither should we, but when the moment was right, the Holy Spirit gave them discernment and direction to move in boldness and power in the Name of Jesus. They strove in confidence to see light pierce the darkness and, like a laser, cut through the chains of Hell that held people bound.

James wrote that all personalities and principalities of darkness are terrified by the Name of Jesus: *"You believe that there is one God. You do well. Even the demons believe —and tremble (James 2:19 NKJV)!"* The word for "tremble" here is the word which, when transliterated into Latin, is the verb *horreo*, the root of horrified. It denotes a freezing in their steps, unable to respond or breathe due to paralyzing fear.

In Jesus' ministry accounts, we see how the demons begged him not to torment them before their time[10]…and how they immediately did as he commanded. We, who have been redeemed by His loving, amazing grace, are told in scripture that we are "in Christ" and seated with Him in heaven with all of His enemies under His (and thus, our) feet. All the authority of

Jesus has been conveyed to us, who are in Him. Christ in you is not only the hope of glory,[11] but the certainty of victory over the beings of unseen darkness that operate around us. The Kingdom of the Light *dominates* the kingdom of the dark.

> *The Lord will go forth like a warrior,*
> *He will rouse His zeal like a man of war.*
> *He will utter a shout, yes He will raise a war cry*
> *He will prevail against His enemies.*
>
> -- Isaiah 42:13 New American
Standard Bible

God, who made an open display over all demonic powers when he raised Christ from the dead, "triumphing *over* them,"[12] has the full expectation that we, as members of His Bride in training, will not default on what He has placed in us when we surrendered to Christ and were adopted by the Father.[13] We became joint heirs in His triumph as sons and daughters of God, and were enjoined to His gospel mission of loving and walking like Jesus, doing *greater* works[14] than He did, while He was on earth.

The return of the King

As we draw towards the end of this chapter, it is health to my soul to remember the writing of John on the final pages of Revelation:

> *I saw heaven standing open and there before me was a white horse, whose rider is called Faithful and True. With justice he judges and makes war. His eyes are like blazing fire, and on his head are many crowns. He has a name written on him that no one knows but he himself. He is dressed in a robe dipped in blood, and his name is the Word of God. The armies of heaven were following him, riding on white horses and dressed in fine linen, white and clean. Out of his mouth comes a sharp sword with which to strike down the nations. "He will rule them with an iron scepter." He treads the winepress of the fury of the wrath of God*

Almighty. On his robe and on his thigh he has this name written: KING OF KINGS AND LORD OF LORDS.

-- Revelation 19: 11-16

Jesus returns on a white steed with his army and out of His mouth comes a sharp sword. Could it be that Jesus is preparing us in this hour to be made ready for His return? Read the whole of Revelations Chapter 19...you will see that *WE* are the army He returns with, following the Son of God on white horses![15] Maybe, as we continue to glory in the awe of the cross and celebrate His resurrection, we should also be kneeling in awe and fear of the very real majesty and soon to come King of Kings!

It is amazing what being a part of The Warrior course has done to change my life. Learning to wear the armor of God every day sets you apart and prepares you to take on the curve balls life throws at you. The armor has helped protect me from the anger, lust, jealousy, and greed that used to have control in my life.

-- David Lippman,
Utility Executive and Core
Warrior

The shield of faith

In harmony with the other components of the armor of God, we must first see that the shield is not built, created, or sustained by *our* faith. It is simply us trusting in *His faithfulness.* When we put our trust and confidence in Him, that trust he transforms into our shield of faith. The truth that God himself is our shield is repeated many times in scripture, 27 times, to be exact.

*You give me **your** shield of victory, and your right hand sustains me; you stoop down to make me great. (bold is mine)*

--Psalm 18:35

Our *trust* in His protection and ability to quench every fiery dart of the enemy grows, however, as we engage and listen to the Word of God.

"Faith comes from hearing the message, and the message is heard through the word of Christ."

-- Romans 10:17

The shield of our faith and the sword of the Word of God mutually compliment and work together in the life of the armored warrior to gain Kingdom ground and secure victory in battle.

Many people, mostly young believers or non-Christians, have said to me over the years: *"Oh, I wish I had your faith, but I just don't."* But the greatest expression of faith Jesus ever commented on was in His experience with the centurion and his dying servant. Read what the officer sent in a message to Jesus in Luke, 7: 7-9:

> Could it be that Jesus is preparing us in this hour to be made ready for His

I did not even consider myself worthy to come to you. But say the word, and my servant will be healed. For I myself am a man under authority, with soldiers under me. I tell this one, "Go," and he goes; and that one, "Come," and he comes. I say to my servant, "Do this," and he does it. When Jesus heard this, he was amazed at him, and turning to the crowd following him, he said, "I tell you, I have not found such great faith even in Israel."

The greatest faith was found in a Gentile who understood Jesus' *faithfulness* and the *power of his Word*. He knew this because he understood that because he was submitted in the Roman hierarchy, *he had been delegated authority to have his every command obeyed.* The same is true for us, except the relationship we have to one another is not hierarchical, but familial, made up of brothers and sisters in Christ.

Like the centurion who answered directly to his cohort commander, I know that I am accountable to Jesus. On earth however, I am also accountable to the Body of Christ and commanded to submit to other believers *in love*. The church includes my wife and even, at times, my children (God does have a unique and often humorous way of speaking to us through them doesn't He?). It also includes my trusted 911 brothers and my church leaders.

But God composed the body...that there should be no schism in the body, but that the members should have the same care for one another. And if one member suffers, all the members suffer with it; or if one member is honored, all the members rejoice with it.

-- I Corinthians 12:24-26

We err too often, I think, in using the world's corporate business or political hierarchical model when it comes to the organic church of Jesus Christ. The order of the human body, as an illustration artfully used by Paul in 1 Corinthians 12 through 13, is a *pretty flat organization.* A healthy rational person will nurture it and listen to...and heed...the warnings of pain or fatigue, heat or cold, that every part communicates to command central (the Head, which is Christ). The dynamic that the world is looking for is not *uber*-command and control or hyper-organization...it is looking for authentic love. And they are looking for real *connection* and *community* where they can be accepted, enjoined and valued.

The Vision of the Battering-Phalanx

This graphic vision came to me in a time of prayer for rescue from satanic onslaught against my family and me during the writing of this book. It came as a group of men gathered around me in intercessory prayer[16] to stand with us. We experienced miraculous and sudden driving off of the attack of Hell due to the effective and fervent prayers of the men and their wives:

I was wearing the full armor of God, riding alone on a journey to a faraway, darkened land. Like a Don Quixote, I saw in the distance my destination...an ominous fortress of stone that grew larger as I approached. Walls of slate grey rose fifty feet tall and twenty feet thick, surrounding the Keep. Bronze gates just as high, reinforced with iron, were closed at my path. This was the place I knew God had called me to go...but, forgetting the Mighty King whom I served, I trembled inside.

Then, as if brought to me by the wind, rising from the dungeons below, I heard the groans of men from my homeland...and the

224

haunting rattle of chains. I could almost feel the yearning of their hearts for freedom, and I felt too their despair of ever being rescued.

Bent upon doing something for my countrymen, I spurred my charger down the hardened pathway that led to the massive gates of the castle. Reigning in as I approached, I dismounted and hastened to the portcullis. With a newfound determination, I began leveling blows upon the gates with my shield and sword, commanding them to yield in the Name of the King, and I cried out to anyone who might hear inside the walls, to set my brethren free!

For a short while, nothing happened...and then, from up above, I heard a voice on the upper wall to my left. "Halloo man-child! It's only the fool who comes to these gates alone, and expects to live." Several others joined in with heckling laughter.

The next thing I heard was the "thwang" of a bow! The sound was immediately followed by an arrow, tipped in pitch and aflame, which struck the ground near my boot. It was followed by another, and I raised my shield just in time to quench several more as they began to find their mark. I was now pinned to the ground...alone in my zeal and foolishness. At that moment, I began to fear...and offered a desperate prayer for deliverance.

It was then that I first heard the sound of a distant horn. Not the brazen blast of the enemy, but the pure, beautiful wind of the horn of Gideon...the horn that only could come from my country. The rain of arrows ceased and I then heard gravelly commands, barking out the mustering to arms from within the gates.

Looking to the source of the horn, I gazed over to the hillside behind me to see the rise of scores...no, hundreds of armed men. As some of the men came into focus, I could see fierceness in their countenance; hard faces, set like flints. Then I heard the horn sound a second time, and a troop of foot soldiers arranged in a formation that looked like a living spear came charging down the path that I had just taken. A battle cry rose from their throats and it was mixed with the anthem song of praises to our King.

They had formed a phalanx of about a score of men in each of three rows; two on the outside and another score in between, wielding a large armored battering ram. Sixty men moving with a single purpose. I had seen this ram before and remembered that on the one side of the ram were carved the words "THE PRAYERS OF THE SAINTS," and on the other, "THE VENGEANCE OF OUR LORD."

I saw some of the men raise their shields over the men carrying the ram and others lifting theirs, interlocked now, on both sides.

In moments, it seemed, the men were over me, covering me so I might rise with them and, then together, with the Name of our King on our lips, we assaulted the gate. The booming sound was deafening, and the ground shook. We rained blow after blow. Some began to tire with me, but we continued on. Then, after what must have been the hundredth blow, there was an impossible shuddering...a high pitched screech of metal tearing away from metal, and the gates began to give way...

So thus, with this vital vision of communal shield-bearing, we come to the end of our boot camp journey. Assembled together in parade formation, you are just about ready to receive your Core 300 Armor of God coin[17] as a token of being armored to the teeth in God Himself, un-entangled in the things of this world.

This next and final chapter will talk a bit on what life is like in God's army and how, as was true for every Roman Legionnaire, your shield and mine *must lock together* with others close to us. Being connected as a community of warriors is the *only way* for us to win this spiritual war as individuals on earth. I think you sense that the battle is already enjoined around you...and the imminent return of the King may be weeks or even hours away. Until then, we must "occupy" *together*. There is no other way.

Table talk

1. How many ways can you think of to protect yourself, your family and your 911 with your shield?

2. Why do you think Gideon totally annihilated every Midianite on earth? How does this apply to your "Game Face?"

Core conditioning

Call your 911 today and catch up...let him know about a *current* challenge you may be facing in your marriage or at work. If you have procrastinated finding *at least one* 911 brother, ask God to bring a guy to mind right now and *then pursue him*. Maybe he needs a copy of this book to "get it." Don't delay!

Chapter Twelve

To Know Me is to Love Me

Scars and tattoos

The first time I saw the film **Die Hard** I became a Bruce Willis fan. In one movie, he transcended from a wise-guy TV heartthrob in **Moonlighting**, to a whole new kind of big box office action hero. I was glad to learn that Arnold Schwarzenegger and Sylvester Stallone had turned down the role before Willis was selected. His humanity made him not just funny, but *believably heroic*. We could see ourselves in the character of John McLane and we loved him too.

There were a number of scenes where McLane, a displaced and divorced New York Cop, was in a white tank top and you could see a scar on his right shoulder. Willis' bio says the scar (which was real) was the result of surgical complications from broken arm when he was 17. He was barefooted for half the movie and he ran around on broken glass! Men saw his scars and believed they could be like him.[1]

Mel Gibson's role as Detective Martin Riggs in the **Lethal Weapon** series showed him dislocating his shoulder and then relocating it back in place on more than one occasion. One time, in Lethal Weapon 2, Riggs escapes from a straight-jacket by dislocating his shoulder. In the dialogue that followed, his partner, Detective Murtaugh (played by Danny Glover) said:

Murtaugh: How do you do that man?

Riggs: Well, I dislocated my shoulder one time and now I can do it whenever I want.

Murtaugh: ...man, doesn't that hurt?

Riggs: Yes it does, but not as much as when I put it back in!

How we love these mixed up, scarred, and sometimes even psychotic heroes. Inside, we cheer them on, because they have shown us their humanity. But they are still fundamentally *good men.*

Scars are real, often the result of life's unplanned and unexpected turns. They are the result of times when we, as men, failed and fell...or when someone else took us out...capsized and blindsided by life. Scars come from surgeries, accidents and, sometimes, even adventures.

Jesus is the ultimate example of a man with scars. As a tradesman in carpentry for almost 20 years before he launched into a second career, he assuredly had many work-related scars suffered by errant hammer blows, flying splinters and chisel cuts. But it was later, at the age of thirty three, that he was mercilessly beaten, scourged, mocked...He bore our sins and diseases, and millennia of human suffering, in his broken body. By doing so, The Son of God built the bridge between God and man...and more, redeemed us as fellow sons and daughters, through the sacrificial blood that flowed out of his wounds.

Based on his post resurrection interaction with Thomas, many believe Jesus still bears the scars of the crucified criminal to this day, as He sits on His throne in Heaven in his resurrected body. Does he still have a flayed back, with scarred temples where the mocking crown of thorns dug in, and holes in his hands, side, and feet? The prophet Isaiah writes:

He was wounded for our transgressions, he was bruised for our iniquities: the chastisement of our peace was upon him; and with his stripes we are healed.

-- Isaiah 53:5

It may be difficult to see Him that way now, but for me, it is a reminder of the depth of His love, and to be authentic and unashamed before him and others.

Tattoos are planned markings inscribed into the skin by an artist. They show an image of whatever the customer or artist chooses. "Tattoos," as I mean them in this chapter, are allegorical for the common Christian "symbols," religious language, behaviors, with their approved list of rules, with which many men and women walk around today. These often habitual and unconscious behaviors are similar to the "Holy Posers" of Jesus day. Like "Hodads" who can't surf, or the black and silver Raiders fan who can't play ball, they are lonely and isolated...hiding in their facade of godliness, macho, or success, but are too terrified to venture out into real openness.

> It has always been true, but now, in our hyper-pornified, time-pressurized world, no one can sustain a victorious walk alone with God.

I will never be able to share close friendship with a man who displays his tattoos, yet never shows me his scars. I don't mind a few tattoos unless that's all the game he's got. I must love him, *but I can never trust him to have my back in a rumble.* If I don't know where he is weak...or truly strong, how can I trust him to come along side of me when I stumble in my weakness? And stumble I surely will.

I have adapted Gary Smalley's list of five levels of communication[2] below:

1. **CLICHES** - Typical, routine; "How are you?" "Fine." "Having a good day?" "Yes."

2. **FACTS** - Information/Statistics about the weather, the office, friends, the news, or sports, etc.

230

3. **OPINIONS** - Includes concerns, values, expectations, and personal goals, theological, social or political opinions. Due to differences of perspectives, biases (we all have them) and values between two people, this is typically the level at which we run into the first "wall of conflict."

4. **FEELINGS** - You both feel safe to share your deeper emotions and begin to truly listen and empathize with the other person, trying on their shoes for the first time. This is where real *koinonia* or Christian fellowship, begins

5. **NEEDS** - The deepest level of communication and intimacy where you both feel completely safe to reveal your unique needs and points of pain with each other. David, whose soul was knit together with his friend Jonathan[3], claimed that his love for Jonathan exceed even that of the love of a man for a women[4]. That is this fifth kind of communication...a oneness of heart...and it is the most fulfilling relationship one human can have with another.

Wounds and infections

A serious incision or laceration is a scar in the making. It is recent and still painful, but, with proper care, nature's course will rejuvenate the tissue and the pain will go away. It leaves behind a unique scar...and sometimes an interesting story. This flaw on our skin becomes a reminder to us and a story we might tell our children or friends. Sometimes the story might be told in good humor, but at other times, it is a warning. I think much of the camaraderie and commonality that we as men share together are around scarring incidents and the real life lessons that come with them. This is why we love and trust heroes with scars.

> People who lie to others, over time, will become a victim of self-delusion. In a similar way, those who cover up with others will eventually be unable to discern what is true in their own lives. They fall prey to the Father of lies.

Maybe you don't have many scars on your body, but I am sure, if you are over twenty, you probably have some scars in your soul. Scars caused by disobedience to God, or authorities in our lives; wounds inflicted by an absentee or abusive parent; scars of naiveté or foolishness; scars of shame of what we have welcomed and entertained in our mind or body; or scars from amputated dreams or relationships. However, when the wounds don't heal right, they can become *infected*. Many men today work hard to "armor up" and shield over, to cover their scars or infected wounds so others cannot see.

Wounds unhealed can slowly fester in the heart. For some who remain in the church, it may turn into judgmentalism and hypocrisy. Others may be more honest and simply drift away, fatigued from carrying the life-draining weight of pretense. When we first meet Gideon, he was cynical when the Angel first met him and he must have struggled with his own wounded soul. He wanted to know "Where was God when we needed Him? Why has He forsaken us?"[5]

Men often expend a great deal of energy hiding their wounds from God (how silly), others, and themselves. Jesus and the prophets often referred to those with a dull heart, hearing or vision. People who begin with covering up (a form of lying) with others will eventually be unable to discern what is true in their own lives. They fall prey to the Father of lies and become self deluded. The world is full of these kinds of people.

We do it as well through self-justification, comparing ourselves to another man or by blaming someone else. *"If only God…,"* or, *"If only my Dad…,"* or "if the elders would get their act together and straighten out the pastor," etc. With the cloak of pride to cover their shame and a sense of deserved rejection by their Creator, men go to church and go to work and put on a good show, but they are not healed.

True healing cannot begin until you:

1. *Man up*. It takes courage to welcome the sword of healing truth into the wound. The wound may look hideous to you but *God sees the future of the healed scar in your present state*

2. Bring your wound or infection openly in confession to God your Father. Ask for and receive His grace, cleansing, and the healing of the Holy Spirit.[6]

3. Intentionally find a few guys with whom you can show your scars…and then learn how to share any wounds that may still be hurting you deeply.

This is where God met Gideon in his hiding place. Like Gideon, God is calling us on a mission which must have its origins in the healing waters of confession.

The principle of confession

James gives us the principle of confession, which men need to embrace in order for us to be whole, healed men. Some men cannot even show themselves to God...He is so perfect after all. We avoid standing still for any length of time, fearful of being overtaken by introspective truth. You may have learned from your earthly father that openness is not safe or maybe even the *concept* of father is too painful for you. If this is so, begin with building trust with a close friend...someone who has willingly shown you his scars.

> *Confess your faults one to another, and pray one for another, that ye may be healed. The effectual fervent prayer of a righteous man availeth much.*
>
> -- James 5:16 (KJV)

The word for "healed" in this verse is a rich one. Per **Strong's Concordance**[7], it means to cure and to *make* whole...and to *free someone* from errors and sins; to bring about (one's) salvation.

If I have seen one of your scars...and am aware of any current wounds in your life, we can then, together, pray fervently and effectively for your healing! You can trust me that I won't judge you because you have been made aware of my scars and wounds as well. If all I see is your religious Tattoos and a "nice" friendly Sunday morning demeanor, I can only assume you are either doing well, or are a hypocrite. If I conclude you are truly doing that well, it can cause me to feel like, *"What's wrong with me?"..."I'm not doing near as well as that guy seems to be doing."* My temptation is then to try to also look good to you, and, by doing so, deepen my nest of hiding.

Now I am not advocating walking in a posture of dour joylessness, constantly "flashing" guys around you with "naked truths" about your soul! I am advocating for walking in a demeanor and lifestyle of *authenticity*. If you are truly wounded, or under a personal attack of CWD, you need the support of other men to get well or to bear up under the attack and win the battle. However, I have also known a few chronic "takers," whiners who, year after year, drain the energy out of people around them...always needy and never gaining traction. This condition may require some psychological expertise or pastoral counseling...or the loving but firm ministry of correction.

We are called to be men who edify and build up others, but part of the joy of fellowship is the *hope* that comes to a brother when he sees that you struggle as he does. The fortress of isolation and hiding crumbles at our feet when we discover that we are not alone...and that in a lifestyle of intentional, but discretionary, openness, we can gain the footholds of true freedom.

> If all I see are your religious Tattoos and a "nice," friendly, Sunday morning demeanor, I can only assume you are either doing well, or are a hypocrite.

Our Roman Catholic brethren had it right all along. *Confession is cathartic.* Unfortunately for most of us, there will come a time in every life...sooner or later...when God will enable the full disclosure "from the rooftops" of those things which were done in secret by you and me. It only makes sense that I might prevent this level of public humiliation (either now or in Heaven) by sharing my "secret stuff" openly with God and with a few close friends. It is a much smaller audience!

Unconfessed wounds can create a kind of "soul infection" that can set in very slowly. Like a cancer, it can take decades of hiding for a soul infection to become lethal, but the spread of toxicity can wreak devastation in your family, work, and ministry along the way.

When we moved to our third home in 1958, and our first house in Long Island, New York, my Dad and I were exploring the new and empty house before the moving truck arrived. We were down in the basement and we separated. In a dark corner behind the furnace, I discovered a treasure cache...a WWII infantry uniform, including faded green khaki shirts and trousers, boots, a woven canvas belt with canteen, and an army helmet. The thing that caught my eye was laying underneath the belt and canteen....a machete in its canvas sheath! My Dad gave it all to me to play with, *except* for the machete.

Four years later, I had forgotten that stipulation (after all I *was* ten at that point) and my friend Peter and I were out in the woods of Heckscher State Park, **playing** "Chicken" with the broad seventeen inch blade. The game was like this: I would stand with my feet a shoulder width apart, and Peter would face me about four feet away, the same way. The game was to see how close we could throw the blade in a one-handed, overhead arc, at the other persons' boot, *without hitting them.*

There were two ways to lose the game. If you moved during the throw (you, as in being the target), you were a chicken. However if you hit the target's foot (as in cutting off a toe), you lost as well. That day, I won, when my throw speared the earth within an inch of Peter's foot. His turn was next, but his throw actually sliced into the edge of my boot sole by about a half inch.

Elated at winning, it was getting dark and was time to get home, so I wiped off the blade and, holding the canvas sheath with my knees, quickly slipped it back into its sheath. But I pressed too hard with my knees, and the blade jammed half-way in. The momentum of my thrust carried my hands downward, sliding off the black handle. My clenched right hand slid across the sharpened blade, and my two middle fingers were sliced to the bone.

Blood was everywhere. But then I remembered that I was not supposed to be playing with the machete! I knew I'd be in big trouble if I got caught with the blade, so hurrying home, I pressed hard on the wounds to try to stop the bleeding.

After I returned the machete to where my dad kept it, I did the best I could for the next few weeks, hiding my injury from my parents with a Mega-band Aid field dressing, and regular dousings of mercurochrome. Every day my mind was racked with the fear of getting "lockjaw (Tetanus)[8]" from an infection. For weeks, it hovered over me like a dark cloud. Eventually the fingers healed, and my jaw never locked up, but today almost fifty years later, I have an angular scar across those fingers.

We do the similar things with those around us. We do something stupid that we know we should not have done...at a place where we should not have been, and our reaction is to cover up and act all normal. We hope no one will see it, yet we know that over time the wound may not heal...it might become *infected.* Worse yet, an unchecked infection, un-cleansed and exposed to healing oxygen and light, can go underground and become toxic to our entire system.

Any military unit worth is weight will be subject to regularly scheduled inspections by their superior officers ...oftentimes without warning. Accountability as a warrior in the Kingdom is the lifestyle of providing a *voluntary* inspection of your soul before another couple of guys that you trust.

The environment we have intentionally sought to create and sustain in **The Warrior** series is that *all things are possible at your table.* James tells us to *confess*...not under duress or command, but as a gift of trust to another. The Greek meaning of the word used here for "confess" is also a wonderful and multidimensional verb. It means: *To acknowledge openly and joyfully to celebrate, give praise to; to profess that one will do something, to promise.*

And what are we confessing? We confess our **sins** (meaning faults; where we have fallen beside the way; missed the intended target; a deviation from truth).

Soul scars are wounds that you have suffered but have been healed by forgiveness and time...and by God's grace-empowered Word, working in and through you. They are confessed wounds to both God and man. *Abba* Father knows the stories behind every memory of pain, and He loves and believes in you as His son. We must remember that when Jesus reached out and touched the leper with compassion and healing, *He saw him as clean.* In this, He demonstrated how God feels towards us and our condition, loving us with our scars, wounds, and infections. He wants His designed purpose for you to *emerge*, and His dreams for you to be fulfilled. However, they cannot unless others help you...unless others, such as your 911 brothers, also become your Confessors.

> Accountability as a warrior in the Kingdom is the lifestyle of providing a voluntary inspection of your soul before another couple of guys that you trust.

Love wounds

*Faithful are the **wounds** of a friend*   -- Proverbs 27:6

The core of authentic fellowship for me is when we blend good and fun experiences and conversation, with contemporary stories of the ongoing work (scalpel) of the living Word in our hearts. When I hear about how God is challenging a brother in his life, it encourages me...and I am inclined to trust him more.

> *The primary role we have as leaders is to help people remove the barriers they have in their lives that are preventing them from becoming the dream God dreamed when He made them.*

-- Wayne Cordeiro[9]

Most guys long for fellowship but don't have a clue how to get real and stay that way over the long haul. Lots of guys who have earned their stripes with **Promise Keepers**, or with several men's retreats under their belts, will think they are practicing true openness because they experienced it with some men in their past. Yet this must be an ongoing, *disciplined conditioning* of the soul...not something you used to do. Some men I know just like to *talk* about "accountability groups," being "real men" together and transparency, but don't walk in it.

I was having coffee with my friend Max, who at the time was the Director of Spiritual Formation and Adult Discipleship at a large church, and we were deep in conversation about this very subject. We had agreed about the importance about having 911 relationships[10] and he had told me about a mentor in his past and his more recent journey with a "Spiritual Director" who had helped him grow in Christ. I felt pretty intimidated by this mature man...he had a Masters in Psychology, ten years experience as a Christian therapist and was a key pastoral leader in his church. But, against my natural instincts, I felt impressed by the Holy Spirit to ask him a question; "Max, who are you accountable to right now...who is your 911?" He blanched, obviously embarrassed, and said, "No one right now Art." After a few uncomfortable moments of silence, he ventured, "I guess I need to fix that, huh?" I gently agreed with him...for his own safety...and for those for whom he was accountable as a shepherd in God's flock.

The problem, of course, is sin...and none of us is invulnerable. And, the greater your level of responsibility, the more people will be too afraid to tell you the truth. It is totally up to you to find and maintain your 911s in your life. The more your influence expands, the more complex life will become and the breadth of your 911s you should expand accordingly.

My unique ability to hide entire sectors of my life into separate compartments still defies understanding! This is so true for most men that we often are not consciously aware of the hidden compartments ourselves. The critical mass that occurs (often on the Saturday night of the men's retreat) when cabin-mates finally do open up, is difficult to sustain. We go down the mountain into our separate lives...back to our previous environment and don't reconnect with the guys on the retreat. Time erodes the intimacy gained together in a matter of a few days, and no one is there to lead or cultivate a way to remain at that depth of openness. In fact, most guys feel a bit sheepish about how they may have carried on...crying...even blubbering out their failures and isolation...and their desperate need for brotherly love. It is far too easy to return to back slapping and smiling with each other on Sunday mornings.

> The greater your level of responsibility, the more people will be too afraid to tell you the truth. It is totally up to you to find and maintain your 911s in your life.

God will not allow us to win the fight simply by having a vertical relationship with Him alone, while we walk isolated from others on the horizontal sphere of earthly relationships. It has always been true, but now, in our pornified, pressurized world, *no one can sustain a victorious walk alone with God.*

We are designed and commanded to be *interdependent in an intentional & organic way.* That is why scripture uses the analogy of the church's individual members as integrated body parts. *This analogy is not primarily about spiritual gifts...or about finding fulfillment in ministry, it is about **connection**.* This is why it is a common strategy of the enemy to leverage the three dimensions of war against us *as individuals* to keep us isolated away from other men. In this state, we become easy pickings.

Any time a man hides from others, and becomes solitary, psychological illness will gradually develop in his soul. All addictions and obsessions then, are substitutes for the Divine presence in our lives

-- Brian Lee

Because we were all born naked, we learn to "cover up" to protect ourselves as we grow through the stages of life. After a while, some of these coverings become armor to protect us from being hurt, or to satisfy felt needs that we have. This counterfeit "armor" becomes an idol in our life, to which we cling for support, affirmation, or temporary pleasure. **God provides** *His* armor to cover our natural vulnerabilities (nakedness) and to give us both protection and strength.

The code: "no man left behind"

The US Army Rangers are known for first using and embracing the "No man left behind" (NMLB) code, but today many military units from many countries, particularly "Special Ops," forswear the commitment to each other represented in this motto. Men will risk more in a battle mission if they know their comrades will not leave them behind.

Over the last forty years I have observed *hundreds* of men that I have known who have fallen away from God. The Apostle Paul often grieved and bemoaned the reality of those who had suffered shipwreck of their soul. Very few have I ever attempted to bring back. However, I am learning a new way.

> *What do you think? If a man owns a hundred sheep, and one of them wanders away, will he not leave the ninety-nine on the hills and go to look for the one that wandered off? And if he finds it, I tell you the truth, he is happier about that one sheep than about the ninety-nine that did not wander off."*

> -- Matthew 18:11-13

The Core 300 movement was founded, in part, to train men to live this code. Almost any good man, in the right (or should I say, *wrong*) situation, under circumstances of severe duress, or even casual inattentiveness, can get taken down or stray away from the flock. We already know that almost half of the marriages in churches today have failed. We know that a high percentage of Christian men are bound by pornography. We are all prone to try to go it alone, hiding in the wine press of life. When it comes to falling or failing, there is one universal truth; **none of these people set out or intended to fail.**

Jesus taught the story about the shepherd who owned a hundred sheep. This means he *counted his sheep*, and finding only ninety-nine present, he left the flock and sought for the one that was lost *until He found it*. His motto was "*No sheep left behind!*" This story is powerful in the lessons it teaches.

One lesson not often considered is that the shepherd had the *habit of counting the sheep*. How would you know if a guy in your church stopped attending? If he is in a small group, his absence would probably be noticed, but in a large church, there is usually no way to tell that he is gone. Even if we see a man go MIA, it is rare that other men will go find him and bring him back. We weren't trained that way. This is not only the role of shepherds...but the role of warriors as well. **Note when a man is absent and love him enough to go find him.**

As Jude exhorted the church:

Be merciful to those who doubt; snatch others from the fire and save them; to others show mercy, mixed with fear—hating even the clothing stained by corrupted flesh.

--Jude 1:22-23

Some people are just evil

It is easy to feel this way about historical figures like Adolph Hitler and Nero...even the guy who mouths expletives and flips you off on the highway because of some slight in your driving etiquette. But what about when people you know, even family members, act out what appears to be *evil* behavior?

The armor of God does not insulate your heart from being broken...no more than it did for Jesus or the authors of the New Testament, who spoke or wrote openly of their grief over the hard-heartedness and "lostness" of their beloved Israel. The very nature of bowels of mercy...and the girdle of truth causes us to feel the very feelings that God has towards others.

In your journey into the life of a warrior, you may find that some new "enemies" rise up against you. Your wife, who may have been praying for you to change for years, may now be *fearful* of that very change and how it might disrupt the way things have always been. Even your pastor may become intimidated with a rising up of men in the church to serve and extend the Kingdom. Men on the move; they are an awesome force!

For me, the pain of loving my enemies and choosing to not retaliate or defend myself when falsely accused is the hardest and most excruciating part of being a disciple of Jesus Christ. God has, and will continue, to use the evil actions of others to complete you as a man because, as was true with Paul, we cannot fully know Christ without sharing in His sufferings[11]. Embracing this level of pain will eventually yield the "*peaceable fruit of righteousness*" and enable a man to transcend to a new level as a noble, yet humble, servant of the Most High.

Legacy

In some of His final sayings to the Twelve, Jesus promised them peace but, "*In this world you will have trouble.*" We must not move away from battle, nor pretend there is no war. Far too much is at stake. The peace of God often awaits us at the other end of victory. This is a victory He has already achieved for us, yet, one in which we must enjoin *with Him*…and our brothers, by faith. The end of the verse comes full circle; "*But take heart* (*be of good cheer* (NKJV)*! I have overcome the world.*"

It is the greatest war of all human history…and it wages still. Will you be Gideon with me to claim your legacy as a husband…as a father…grandfather? As a **man?**

> *Thus Midian was subdued before the Israelites and **did not raise its head again**. During Gideon's lifetime, the land enjoyed peace forty years.*
>
> Judges 8:28 (bold is mine)

As I close this book, this is my personal "Legacy Prayer:"

> *Abba, Father. May my life bring You and Your Son glory. I pray that the sowing of years of imperfect husbanding, fathering, and ministry will reap a harvest, if your Son tarries, into many generations of Kingdom impact. Somehow turn the fragments of my incomplete and fragmented humanity into the power and beauty of Your Love.*

Bring my wife into the fullness of Your vision for her life, filled with joy. Take hold of the hearts of my five sons and make them Yours. Let Your blessings echo into our grandchildren, and great grandchildren not yet born. Strip away the memories and hurtful impact of my many sinful acts which were not of You, and detracted from the beauty of Your wholeness. Water and multiply the good seed, including the words in this book, with Your Spirit, to call many men into the arena so others may live. May my final years be ones of obedient faithfulness...fully eclipsing my former years. Use them to bring forth an abundant harvest until your Son returns in His might and glory. Amen

Table talk

1. At your table (or with your family), share a memory of a scar from your past where you disobeyed God. What lessons do the memories of these scars teach you today?

2. Discuss together how your table can deepen your fellowship and openness. What are you prepared to let go of today to help release openness in your group? Be specific and make a plan.

Core conditioning

Write a prayer of legacy in your journal. Make your first entry a Legacy Prayer, for "He who has begun a good work in you will complete it until the day of Jesus Christ."[12]

Epilogue

What's Next?

We have experienced a real spiritual boot camp together and embraced the reality that men, by a large margin, are the key pivot point through which God has chosen to extend His kingdom. We followed Gideon in his own private sojourn along the way and discovered that we have much in common. All of his flaws and weaknesses…his heart that seeks to obey God…and God's requirement to be completely stripped "naked" before Him. God has shed His light on every hidden altar of idolatry and every known bondage to sexual sin. Like us, Gideon's winepress was symbolic of the armor of his making…a beaten down self-view that screened him away from his fears, and his spirit-filled destiny as a warrior-leader.

American freedom is precious and bought with the blood of our military. Most of us merely inherited liberty…earned on battlefields by our forefathers. However, freedom must be vigilantly maintained by high cost strategic, and tactical military forces. For you and your Christian community it is the same. Freedom found in Jesus' Name through his

243

death and resurrection, must be *vigilantly* guarded like a mother bear guards her cubs.

> *You must make your opponent acknowledge defeat from the bottom of his heart.*

> -- Miyomoto Musashi
> (1584-1645)

Out of the stands...

We began our chronicle together with some stretch goals:

- **Learn and understand** the nature of **the unseen war** that you have been born into and *how to win that war*

- **Experience spiritual "boot camp"** and discover your mission as a mighty warrior.

- **Humbly, but surely step into leadership in your home,** lovingly leading your wife and children

- **Learn authenticity** and to find real protection, as you bond with and "lock shields" with other men.

- **Be freed** from debilitating sin and the influence of dark spiritual forces, and walk as an unfettered, free man

Into the arena...

Now we look towards what is *next*. History teaches us that routing an enemy does not equal total annihilation, nor is it the same as new-ground taking occupation.

"Occupy til I come" -- Luke 19:13 King James Bible

Jesus was teaching the parable about the money that was entrusted under the charge of ten servants by a nobleman who had to go away to another country to "receive his kingdom." Each of the servants received one *mina*. The master left them with these words; "Occupy till I come."

After a long absence, the nobleman returned and the servants were audited for the return on investment per the *mina* each had received. The first had seen it leveraged tenfold and after receiving the praise of "well done," he was given a dominion over ten cities. The second servant had multiplied the investment five-hundred percent to five *minas* and he received the same commendation and received five cities to govern.

The third servant returned the single *mina*, stating that he knew the master was a "hard man" and that he just wanted to return what he had been given. He received an extremely harsh rebuke and was dispossessed of all that he had.

This word "occupy," employed by Luke, has the common marketplace meaning of "continue on doing business," "merchandise" or, "continue transacting" until I return. Although this is a book fundamentally about warfare, we all understand the process of how, after a victory in war, an unconditional surrender is negotiated and, after peace is declared, occupation begins. We also understand that occupation is hard work, costly, and even perilous. We all watched Sadaam Hussein's statue fall as Baghdad submitted to the invasion of U.S. and allied troops. Then we saw hundreds of billions of dollars, and many thousands of lives spent, in our efforts to "occupy" Iraq to begin transitioning to self-governance.

What does it mean for and you and me as individual members of the church, to "do merchandise?" What is the "business" of the church that we are called to perpetuate until He returns? This is a critical component of the message of the Gospel that Jesus declared at the outset of His ministry when he read from the book of Isaiah:

> *The Spirit of the Lord is upon me, because he hath anointed me to preach the gospel to the poor; he hath sent me to heal the brokenhearted, to preach deliverance to the captives, and recovering of sight to the blind, to set at liberty them that are bruised, To preach the acceptable year of the Lord.*

-- Luke 4:18-19

The *arena is defined* by our Master in this verse, yet this is not just a peaceful, passive place of a mercy-full ministry, helping the needy. We are *not* a great white hospital ship upon which the wounded are carried in stretchers to recuperate in a tranquil, sanitized environment. *Pax Deo*[1]

245

must first be established in our own lives and then in our homes (where we cut our teeth in warfare and servant leadership). Then *we must go to the oppressed*...through the caissons of Hades...into the ICUs of shattered hearts and into the dungeons of darkness, securing the deliverance of enchained captives.

In his book, **The Hole in Our Gospel**, Richard Stearns, the President of World Vision, equates the American church to the church of Laodicea. Jesus, self-identified as one who *"has the sharp, double-edged sword,"* with *"eyes...like blazing fire"* and as *"the ruler of God's creation."* described this church as being in danger of impoverished dissipation:

> *Because you are lukewarm—neither hot nor cold—I am about to spit you out of my mouth. You say, "I am rich; I have acquired wealth and do not need a thing." But you do not realize that you are wretched, pitiful, poor, blind and naked....those whom I love I rebuke and discipline. So be earnest, and repent.*
>
> -- Revelation 3:15

Was this lukewarm water akin to warm tap water we might accidentally drink (and spit out) today? No! In biblical times drinking water needed to be boiled or fresh flowing from a cold spring or well. As is common in many third world countries, standing (or lukewarm) water would be dangerous to drink because it was infected and infested with polluting microbes. So Jesus' revulsion was that this church's wealth and worldliness had polluted the spring of living water!

No wonder no one is lining up for a drink in most American churches!

Stearns' prophetic exhortation to us is to get engaged in good works and to go beyond the four walls of our local church, showing real love and compassion to others in need. In addition, it is a call to sacrificially redistribute more of the wealth of the West to impoverished sick and famished peoples across the globe. Finally, it is clearly a word for pastors and elders to model this sacrifice and then lead their congregations to transcend the often myopic sustenance of church program to a dynamic expansion of the Kingdom of the Son of God.

Called to War attempts to go beyond exchanging a social gospel for church programs, though this is truly a critical component of us loving the world in Jesus' name and a requisite to earning the right to influence.

Historically we should remember that a social gospel alone, without the power and dynamic presence of the Kingdom of God, leads to disastrous attrition of faith in the faithful. Entire denominations have lost their fire and passion for God by turning their heads too far away from the necessity of coupling acts of charity with the dynamic of the Holy Spirit as he expressed Himself through the early church. Once fervent movements marked by the miraculous have descended into the cold cellar of humanistic relativism and the mythologizing of the Scriptures.

Do we need a solid kick in the pants to get into the arena to minister in Jesus' name to others? *Absolutely!* Have we turned away from real global pain and suffering in this world as we invested in advancing our quest for the *"American Dream?" Guilty as charged.*

> *Here I am! I stand at the door and knock. If anyone hears my voice and opens the door, I will come in and eat with him, and he with me. To him who overcomes, I will give the right to sit with me on my throne, just as I overcame and sat down with my Father on his throne.*

> --Revelation 3:20

But the warning of Jesus in this passage is that we have become "lukewarm," neither hot *nor* cold. Jesus prescribes the cure to unpalatable "lukewarmness" with the urgent call (*"Here I am!"*) to open the door *and to dine with Him,* and He with us (v. 20). We must contend for and maintain a critical tension between passionate love for and fellowship with God and the compassionate actions of love towards others.

Our Lord's command to *"be earnest (hurry now),"* and *"repent,"* combined with the promise of fellowship (*"I will come in and eat with him"*) is followed by the challenge to *overcome.* The outcome of this prophecy to the Laodecean church is *experiential victory* over carnality, worldliness and the realm of our adversary. This is the unguent required to heal the putrid condition of "lukewarmness," and to stir us to action based not only on Spirit-led compassion, but also energized by presence and His *power.*

> *For God has not given us a spirit of fear, but of **power** and of **love** and of a sound mind.*

247

-- 2 Timothy 1:7

We don't battle *physical* poverty and hunger, but rather we battle with the *Prince* of Poverty and the evil *spirit* of Famine that operates behind these travesties. Disease is not our adversary but the *spirit* of *infirmity* that is behind the escalating global plagues.

> *From that day on, half of my men did the work, while the other half was equipped with spears, shields, bows, and armor. The officers posted themselves behind all the people of Judah who were building the wall. Those who carried materials did their* **work with one hand** *and held a* **weapon in the other***, and each of the* **builders wore his sword** *at his side as he worked.*

-- Nehemiah 4:16-18a
(bold is mine)

The principle illustrated here is that the *work* of the Kingdom, which has practical requirements, daily, sacrificial "sweat-equity," is married to the *warfare* of the Kingdom.

Stearns is right. Like those who rebuilt the broken down walls of Jerusalem, we bring restoration with a tool of service in the one hand…but victory and protection are secured because in the other hand we must wield a sword against the root causes. The forces that break down the walls of communities and individuals are spiritual in nature.

Never venture forth alone

Yet, *we cannot keep that ground*, nor take new ground, without the duality of walking in the fullness of the Holy Spirit and the active locking of shields with close brothers in Christ with whom we walk in authentic fellowship and mutual prayer.

I was about to leave for a consulting trip for a client who had offices in Chicago and I would be there for three days. I was traveling alone, so I called Mark, a dear friend, and one of my 911 buddies. I told him where I would be, asking him to pray for me while away. We do this for each other…and, as you'll see, it is *"the next best thing to being there."*

That next day, after a full day of business in the "Windy City," training and coaching a couple of sales leaders and a senior executive, I went back to the hotel, did a short stint at the gym, and then went out to dinner alone. I like food. I particularly like a good steak and, as you may be aware, Chicago is renowned for their chophouses.

I don't mind being alone. I actually find it refreshing and somewhat contemplative on occasion to not have to converse, but to just sit and think and enjoy the ambiance of a good restaurant in a distant city. After I ate my fill, it was about 8:30 P.M. I was feeling pretty good…the day had gone well, and I felt that I had given my best for my client. And I was tired. Frankly, I don't recall having a single spiritual thought in my head for much of the afternoon and evening.

I returned to the hotel and entered the elevator to get to my room. Just as I was approaching my door, I was about to access my room key when my cell phone rang. *"Hey Art, this is Mark. How did your day go?"* His voice immediately brought me out of my reverie and shifted my awareness from neutral to drive. *"Mark, thanks so much for calling. You won't believe what I was just doing…"* and then we talked about our day.

Mark's call, which I had empowered and entrusted him to make as my 911, was just as good as his being there. His call also meant he would ask me when I returned if I had walked worthy of my Lord. I will never know what may have transpired in my room after I had entered that night. I had no *plans* of sinning by watching porn. But I was in *neutral*. I was not "armored up," vigilantly aware of the ever-present danger of entering a lonely room in a faraway place. God had taught me the principle of traveling accountability, and *He* had stirred Mark to call at just that moment…but at a moment when I had my shield down.

Wealthy Christians or senior ministers with budgets that allow for them to travel with a co-worker, spouse, or close family member can't relate to most folks where that solution is not practical. I recently heard a national celebrity-pastor say, *"I always travel with someone so I am protected from false accusation…or from doing something stupid."* I am happy for him, but for the rest of us mortals who don't have the resources to bring a partner along, this is a practical way to help insure that you walk in integrity when traveling alone.

My moment of victory was secured because God used the *horizontal* "on earth" relationship of loving trust I had built with Mark to strengthen me and keep me safe. After our brief chat, I simply got ready for bed, read the Bible, and went into a deep and restful sleep.

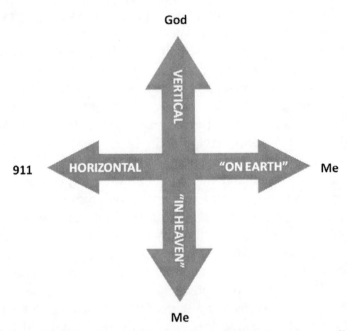

Figure 12 – God's two-dimensional design for us to walk in sustainable Kingdom victory mandates that we connect directly to Him *and* walk directly connected to others "on earth." This is how His will can be done *in* and *through* us.

Starting a Core movement where you live

Inviting a few other men to join you on a journey through this book as a small group study, may be the best way for you to seed the hearts of men close to you. In turn, these men will begin to yearn and pray for their church and social network to call men to be transformed and get *"out of the stands and into the arena."*

This book, along with the partner curriculum (Master Trainer Manual, Squad Leader Manual and Warrior Field Manual), can provide anywhere from a ten to twenty week group journey through boot camp…and can culminate with each man earning his **Core 300 Armor of God** coin.

This simple, but beautiful, talisman representing God's armor...carried daily in a pocket or wallet, has spawned thousands of stories as a reminder of our confidence in the strength of God's armor.

The seeding of prayer

For men, patience must be the byword for any who have a passion to see a sustainable, quality move of the Holy Spirit upon the men at your church. Leaders must understand that the cycles of sowing and reaping take many months. In addition, it is not uncommon for men of vision to see the long view...ten years or more of growing men into maturity in Christ. Our initial vision at our church was for 300 Core men in three years. Men, who like Gideon's men, are wary warriors and seasoned servant-leaders.

An initial group study can develop into *men who pray* for God to move upon the men of their church and for their church leadership to hear the trumpet of Gideon. At our church, ten men saw the vision of 300 men called to war and service and began experiencing a prayer burden which preceded and fueled four critical components of success:

1. It released the Holy Spirit to work in the hearts of leaders and men in the Congregation. It accentuated and focused the prayers of the women...building their faith that God was about to move.

2. It brought clarity of vision and birthed a Spirit-led planning process, which in the spirit of submission, called the church leadership to join into the vision of the powerful release of men in the arena.

3. It forged a loving solidarity between the core men who shared the burden. They learned to fight for one another and their families, side by side, and love one another deeply. (NOTE: *This is a critical component because* once Satan discovers the movement of men rising to their destiny as warriors, he will attack the unity of this core with false accusations, divisiveness and pride).

4. Using ***military imagery*** for the classes, and Table ("Squad") with a trained Squad Leader position helps bind men together in a common cause.

Leadership consists of reliable *Squad Leaders* for each table and a *Core Instructor* (who can teach from the **Master Trainer Manual** and support materials). However, **the Senior Pastor or Priest is often the best one to lead off in the teaching role**. At a minimum his endorsement and participation are critical to the success of this movement. Whether or not the pastor embraces the power of his being the key example of "a man" in the congregation, it remains a reality nonetheless.

"Eighty percent of success is showing up" --Woody Allen

The power of women

Although this book is written to men, it is as much for women as men. The war and armor are NOT gender specific!

I have sought openly the counsel and input of strong men and women of God throughout the writing process. I was talking the other day with Madeline, a good friend, who goes to a church across town. She serves there as a leader of a growing women's ministry. As I brought her up-to-date with the Core 300 movement, sharing what God had been doing, she became very excited. *"Are the men ready?"* I asked. *"Yes they are,"* Madeline said, and then as her eyes filled with tears, she continued, *"The women of our church have been praying for our men for over twelve months and we are hungry for men to rise up and lead."*

We have explored how *engaging men* is strategic to God's plan for His church and catalytic for the release of Kingdom power. In many churches today, women's ministry has thrived for many years. Our church sees about 700-800 women congregate weekly on campus for various Bible studies and fellowship groups. Yet until a couple of years ago, *the men never gathered*.

What would happen if women's groups across the country would seize upon these materials for a season and begin to pray in their armor? Women have always played critical roles in revivals. A key barrier to

Kingdom breakthrough is that many of your men are like Gideon…alone, hiding and feeling shamefully disqualified.

If you are a woman reading this book, maybe God is stirring you to take this into your small group…or to your Bible study gathering? I believe God can catalyze the *prayer power* of the woman to see God call men into the arena. I tell you, with all the conviction I can muster, that all Heaven will break loose as a result!

The launch

After a necessary initial season of prayer, and when your church is ready, it is best to kickoff the new series with a men's breakfast or some other high profile event. *Food is always a good draw.* We have developed "field tested" and proven materials and resources which are described in the beginning of our Appendix and can be found and ordered on our website (www.core300.org).

The sequel

After the men in your group or church have been through this boot camp, they will be equipped to be tested in their armor…and ultimately released into ministry. There are two more proven and sequential twenty week courses being programmed into follow-on books and curricula. They follow **The Warrior** course in sequence and build upon each other to provide a transformative discipleship and leadership development experience for men:

- **The Battle-Priest** – (two 10-week segments) Trains men as called and anointed priests of their home, church, workplace and community and then releases them as men of service and warfare to extend God's Kingdom where they live. These are the authentic knights and community story-tellers entrusted with serving the Divine "sacraments" to the next generation

- **The Shepherd-King** – (two 10-week segments) is a *mandate calling* to servant leadership…to mentor others…to be men who can self-refresh and nurture for ongoing spirit gifted service to the

Body of Christ and beyond. These are the trans-generational bridge builders and the passers of the baton.

Coming in 2011 - Be looking for Art Hobba's next Core 300 series book:

"The Battle-Priest: Bowed in Surrender...Swept-up into Victory!"

Curriculum

Deepen both your teaching and growth experience with the full launch kit, Master Trainer notes, leadership and field Manuals...includes paired media!

Go to www.core300.org to order

Master Trainer Manual and Start-up Kit	Complete leadership resource: Squad Leader Training Guide; study and lecture guidebook and a complete end-to-end process guide for preparing, launching and leading two ten-week sessions of The Warrior course at your church, ministry or campus discipleship group. Includes Presentation Power Point for all Sessions; Fourth session audio CD "Tearing Down the Altars", 2 Core 300 Armor of God Coins.
Warrior Field Manual	Student Curriculum includes ten, two-part, lessons of interactive teaching and study notes in parallel with both the Squad Leader and Master Teacher Manuals.
Squad Leader Manual	Complete Squad Leader resource, and study guidebook for training as a Squad Leader (3 sessions). Includes the Warrior Field Manual which moves in parallel with the Master Teacher Manual.

Core 300 is s registered California **501c3 non profit teaching organization**
www.core300.org

Appendix

Bible study

www.biblegateway.com - rapid search of verses and key words in multiple versions of the Bible

http://www.biblestudytools.com - *New Site* loaded with information. General and pastoral Bible Study tools including major commentaries...now all online.

www.eliyah.com/lexicon.html - also rapid search of verses and key words in multiple versions of the Bible, but a great word study tool for Strong's Concordance, Vine's and commentaries

Foundations for Pentecostal Theology, Guy Duffield and Nathaniel Van Cleave, LIFE Bible College Press, 1983

Lectures in Systematic Theology, Henry Thiessen, Eerdmans Publishing, 1976

An Expository Dictionary of New Testament Words, W.E. Vine, Revell, 1966

Strong's Exhaustive Concordance of the Bible, James Strong, Royal Publishers

War and deliverance

www.masteringlife.org – is a web TV site that supports an expert training platform and provides a virtual community to help find ongoing freedom and healing from a variety of sexual issues that men frequently struggle with.

www.specialopschurch.com is a Church resource website and missions outreach organization to help them:
1) Provide for Sub-Saharan orphans in Africa (www.icaninfo.com)
2) Identify its primary mission in relationship to the Great Commission.
3) Help the church learn the strategies and tactics associated with fulfilling their primary mission.
4) Help train and implement the 9 principles of spiritual warfare to win the battles they are fighting www.specialopschurch.com

The Arena

www.globalmediaoutreach.org Global Media Outreach uses the latest emerging technologies through its 102 websites to give every person on earth multiple opportunities to know Jesus through broadcasting the gospel on the Internet, cell phones, smart phones, Internet Radio, and Internet Television, as well as social networking and church partnerships.

Contemplative resources and monasteries

Books

In the Name of Jesus: Reflections on Christian Leadership, by Henri Nouwen, Crossroad, 1992

Ordering Your Private World, Gordon MacDonald, Thomas Nelson, 1984

The Hole in Our Gospel, by Richard Stearns, Thomas Nelson, 2009

The Life You've Always Wanted, by John Ortberg, Zondervan, 2002

Private retreat centers and monasteries

The Immaculate Heart Center for Spiritual Renewal, (Transdenominational), 888 San Ysidro Lane, Santa Barbara CA 93108 www.immaculateheartcenter.org (805) 969-2474

St. Meinrad Archabbey, Illinois 800 581-6905 www.saintmeinrad.edu

Holy Trinity, St. David Arizona (Charismatic Catholic) Benedictine, (520) 720-4642

St. Augustine's House, Oxford, Michigan, (248) 628-5155

Assumption Abbey, Ava, MO Remote Ozark Mountain Location, Trappist Monastery, (Thomas Merton Style) (417) 683-5110

Little Portion Hermitage, The Brothers and Sisters of Charity, Eureka Springs, AK
John Michael Talbot Leader, charismatic Catholic www.john-michael-talbot.org (501) 253-7710

Christ-centered social and spiritual activism resources

Acres4Life –www.acres4life.org is an African-US based ministry that purchases land in starving African villages and then brings the science of self-sustainment through *farming* to local communities, all in the Name of Jesus.

Cambodian Foursquare Missions – Director Ted Olbrich and his team have seen God transforming a nation! In ten years, church membership has gone from 25 to almost 1 million through serving the cultural and social needs of orphans and the impoverished!
www.warmblankets.org and www.missionreports.com/cambodia

Care Now Foundation - www.carenowfoundation.org focuses on providing access to healthcare for the world's least served people. They are currently working in Africa and partner with organizations in who run medical clinics, but need assistance. CareNow also organizes and funds shipments of medical supplies, instruments, equipment, and medicines as well.

Gospel Light Worldwide – gospellightworldwide.org There are three things that set GLWW's children's ministry apart from other missionary efforts:
      1) Focused Exclusively on Children
      2) No Western Missionaries
      3) Built-In Sustainability

Ignite the Nations - www.reacheveryvillage.com is focused on evangelism and church planting in South Asia using indigenous believers to bring the gospel to unchurched villages.

World Vision, Appalachia - Your group will work alongside local youth and adults to encourage, inspire, and build relationships that have lasting impact. Trips for adults, youth, and families are available. www.worldvisionusprograms.org/#/Appalachia

The Hole in Our Gospel, by Richard Stearns, Thomas Nelson 2009, pp-221-225

End Notes

Prologue

[1] Statistics from Focus on the Family Publishing, "Promise Keepers at Work."
[2] Source www.churchformen.com/allmen.php
[3] Exodus 15:3 "Yahweh is a warrior; Yahweh is his name."
[4] Agape Press by Jim Brown, August 7, 2006
[5] Engagement, Art Hobba, 2008

Chapter One - Beginnings

[1] Isaiah 14:12-14 and Luke 10:18
[2] Patrick Lencioni's Speaker's notes, Maximum Impact Leadership Conference, May 2005
[3] Zechariah 13:7 (Note Hebrew word puts for 'Scattered' means to break, scatter, crush or dash to pieces)
[4] DiSC is a common tool used to identify the four common types of behaviors. The **D**river (Director), the **I**nfluencer (persuader-talker), the **S**erver (supporter-team builder), and the **C**ontroller (analyzer). Everyone has some components of each type but one or two are more dominant than others. The DiSC assessment is an integral part of the third The Warrior series workshop. More info can be found at www.core300.org/DiSC)

Chapter Two – Gideon: Alone, Hiding and Disqualified

[1] Ephesians 5:25
[2] Yahweh is the personal name of the one true God who delivered Israel from Egypt and gave the Ten Commandments, a Hebrew vocalization of the Tetragrammoton
[3] **The Friendless American Male**, David W. Smith, Regal Books, 1984

Chapter Three – Blood on the Floor

[1] Biblical Discernment Ministries, 2003,
http://www.rapidnet.com/~jbeard/bdm/BookReviews/jabez.htm
[2] **Silence, Solitude, Simplicity**, Sister Jeremy Hall, OSB, Liturgical Press, 2007, page 19
[3] **Crazy Love, Overwhelmed by a Relentless God**, by Francis Chan, David C. Cook, 2008
[4] Malachi 3:10b-12
[5] Psalm 106:9; Nahum 1:4
[6] Matthew 5:20, Romans 13:10-since most or all of what we give to God ends up helping others, our giving should begin at a level of 10%. This is not yet another legal formula, however! Each believer must start somewhere and there are good resources and guidelines on Biblical giving that are available to those desiring to move forward with greater levels of giving over time. See www.crown.org for helps and resources on stewardship and worshipful giving.
[7] **Dune**, Frank P. Herbert, Chilton Book Company, 1965, page 19

Chapter Four – A Primer on Spiritual Warfare

[1] 2 Corinthians 2:10-12
[2] Luke 10:17-19, Isaiah 14:12-14
[3] Genesis 3:1-7
[4] Ephesians 1:19-22 and 2:5-7, Colossians 3:1-3
[5] Psalms 55:21, New Living Translation (new)
[6] Revelation 12:12
[7] Isaiah 14:11-13, New King James Version
[8] Revelation 1:18; Matt 16:19
[9] Genesis 3:19
[10] Wisdom 2:24, The New American Bible, Oxford University Press (Apocrypha)
[11] Jude 1:9
[12] Matthew 16:19
[13] Yet you have the power in you– the Spirit - to overcome the world, flesh, and devil. (Mark 8:36; Gal 5:17; Eph. 6:12)
[14] **Revolution**, George Barna, page 19-20, Tyndale House Publishing, 2005

[15] Tactical Advisory – the chief driving goal of the enemy is to be glorified. This is also behind the world spirit and the carnal nature. Be graciously thankful for accolades that may come your way, but never, ever contrive for or receive any of the glory for it. God is jealous of this glory because it is always due Him, but also because He knows that in our present form, it is poison to the soul and feeds only the hearths of pride.

[16] Tactical Advisory - This, along with drinking alcohol later in the evening is a sure fire method employed by the carnal mind and lawless spirits to take a man down. If you are married, go to bed with your wife! If not, don't drink and find a good book to read in bed.

[17] **The 33 Strategies of War**, Robert Greene, Penguin Books, 2006

Chapter Five – From Fearful Farmer to Baal Buster

[1] The Seven Names of the Lord from
http://www.votbg.org/tja/jehovah.htm

    Jehovah-jireh: The Lord will provide. Genesis 22:14
    Jehovah-rapha: The Lord that heals. Exodus 15:26
    Jehovah-nissi: The Lord our banner. Exodus 17:15,16
    Jehovah-shalom: The Lord our peace. Judges 6:23,24
    Jehovah-ra-ah: The Lord my shepherd. Psalm 23
    Jehovah-tsidkenu: The Lord our righteousness. Jeremiah 23:6
    Jehovah-shammah: The Lord is present. Ezekiel 48:35

[2] Luke 8:26-35

[3] The Greek word *phragellion* (φραγἐλλιον) is used to describe the scourge that Jesus made himself prior to and for the purpose of cleansing the Temple in John 2:15. It is the same name used for the Roman lash that was used for public punishment

[4] The Jewish Encyclopedia,
www.jewishencyclopedia.com/view.jsp?letter=B&artid=2

[5] 1 Kings 18:25-29

[6] *Encyclopedia Mythica*, www.pantheon.org/articles/b/baal.html

[7] *The New Bible Dictionary*, Tyndale House Publishers, 1982, p. 1230

[8] Expert psychiatrists and psychologists agree that certain professions are at higher risk of burning out from their jobs. Higher stress jobs (like most places we work) and occupations that care for or protect others, are in need of more frequent "away times," marked with prayer and solitude.

[9] **The Spirit of the Disciplines,** Dallas Willard, Harper San Francisco, 1988, page 102
[10] Mark 4:19
[11] 2 Corinthians 10:12
[12] Matthew 6:24

Chapter Six – From Asherah to Ashes

[1] Matthew 4:3-6
[2] Jeremiah Chapters 7 and 44
[3] No Babies, New York Times, June 28, 2008, www.nytimes.com/2008/06/29/magazine/29Birth-t.html?pagewanted=2&_r=1
[4] Proverbs 6:27-29; 1 Timothy 4:1-2;
[5] The Great Divorce, C.S. Lewis, Chapter 11, Harper Collins, 1946
[6] 2 Timothy 4:2
[7] Exodus 20:5
[8] Luke 8:5-15
[9] 2 Corinthians 9:6-12; I John 3:9

Chapter Seven – Blowing Your Own Horn

[1] For research and more information, see www.hartmaninstitute.org
[2] The Emergence of Positive Psychology: The Building of a Field of Dreams, Shane J. Lopez, PhD, American Psychological Association, *Summer 2000, Vol. 12(2)*
[3] The Hartman Value Profile-for more information, go to www.transcende.net/PBLprofile.html
[4] **Spiritual Leadership: Moving People on to God's Agenda**, Henry and Richard Blackaby, Broadman and Holman, 2001, page 93
[5] **The Leadership Secrets of Billy Graham**, by Harold Myra and Marshall Shelley, Christianity Today International, Zondervan 2005, page 22-23
[6] Judges 7:12
[7] **Spiritual Leadership: Moving People on to God's Agenda**, ibid, page 119
[8] John 11:14-16

Chapter Eight – All Other Ground is Sinking Sand

[1] The Influential Leader, Maximum Impact Simulcast: Apr 28, 2005

[2] Mark 14:31

[3] John 4:23

[4] Miriam-Webster's Online Dictionary, http://www.merriam-webster.com/dictionary/worship

[5] **Becoming a Healthy Church**, by Stephen Macchia, Baker Books, 1999

Chapter Nine - The Twelve Strategies of Defensive Warfare

[1] Genesis 6:4

[2] Though theories abound, it is unclear as to who these "sons of God" were and exactly how it was that they mated with human women, but it did happen. Some of the Apocryphal books touch more in detail on these super-human creatures. Some scholars believe that some of the mythological stories of half-god half men like Achilles and Hercules were actually Nephilim who were mighty on the earth for a season in ancient history.

[3] **The Endless Knot**, Stephen R. Lawhead, Zondervan Pub. House, 1998, pp 285-287

[4] 1 Peter 3:7 and 1 Corinthians 7:4-6

[5] 2 Chronicles 5:11

[6] 2 Chronicles 20:15-28

[7] Try reading the song of Moses and of Miriam in the desert (Exodus 15), David's Praises (2 Samuel 22), Solomon's dedication prayer (**1 Kings 8:22-30**) or any one of dozens of Psalms like 9, 21, 34, 63, 103, 134

[8] **Lectures in Systematic Theology**, Henry Thiessen, Eerdmans Publishing, 1976, pp 202-203

[9] Revelation 12:10, one of the names used for Satan

[10] Luke 23:34

[11] Hebrews 5:8

[12] **The 33 Strategies of War**, Robert Greene, Penguin Books, 2006

Chapter Ten – Dressed for Success – Body Armor

[1] Ephesians 4:21

[2] John 14:17

[3] John 17:15-17

[4] Strong's Concordance with Hebrew and Greek Lexicon, www.eliyah.com/lexicon.html

[5] Source Hadrians.com,
www.hadrians.com/rome/romans/clothes/roman_soldiers_clothes.html
[6] *Pax Deo* – Latin for Peace of God
[7] Ephesians 6:17
[8] I Corinthians 2:16

Chapter Eleven – Total Annihilation

[1] Judges 7:14
[2] 1 Samuel 2:19
[3] 2 Samuel 1:22
[4] Exodus 18:4
[5] Hebrews 4:12-13
[6] Tanlladwyr- also called "Brightkiller," the sword of Lancelot in Bernard Cornwell's *The Warlord Chronicles*
[7] Genesis 3:24 - *possibly* the same two-edged sword John saw coming out of the mouth of Christ in Revelation 1:16 and 19:21
[8] Judges 7:20
[9] **Strong's Concordance and Lexicon**, www.eliyah.com/lexicon.html
[10] Matthew 8:29
[11] Colossians 1:27
[12] "And having disarmed the powers and authorities, he made a public spectacle of them, triumphing over them by the cross." Colossians 2:15
[13] Ephesians 1:5
[14] John 14:12
[15] Revelation 19 – compare versus 7-8 with verse 14 to show that the church is the same as His army
[16] Intercessory prayer is a kind of prayer that steps into the gap on behalf of someone else and intercedes…appealing to God in fervent prayer to intervene, deliver, rescue or heal another person in need.
[17] Core 300 coin can be ordered at www.core300.org/Store.htm.

Chapter Twelve – To Know Me Is To Love Me

[1] **IMdbPro**, Bruce Willis Biography, www.imdb.com/name/nm0000246/bio
[2] **Secrets to Lasting Love**, Gary Smalley, Fireside, 2000

[3] 1 Samuel 18:1-3

[4] 2 Samuel 2:26

[5] Judges 6:13

[6] Hebrews 4:15-16 - For we do not have a High Priest who cannot sympathize with our weaknesses, but was in *all points* tempted as *we are, yet without sin. Let us therefore come boldly to the throne of grace, that we may obtain mercy and find grace to help in time of need.

[7] **Strong's Exhaustive Concordance of the Bible**, by James Strong, Royal Publishers

[8] Tetanus is a potentially deadly nervous system disease due to the bacteria *Clostridium tetani (C. tetani).* Tetanus often begins with spasms in the jaw muscles (**lockjaw**).

[9] Wayne Cordeiro, Lecture on Servant Leadership, Simi Valley, CA, December 2009

[10] 911s are 2 to 3 men close to you who know when you are in need of prayer, protection (lock shields), or in pain...or out of town. They have the right to challenge you at any time regarding your spiritual walk...and *vice versa.*

[11] Colossians 1:24; 1 Peter 4:13

[12] Philippians 1:6

Epilogue

[1] God's Peace

[2] **The Hole in Our Gospel**, Richard Stearns, Thomas Nelson 2009, pp-221-225

About the Author

Art Hobba has had his feet firmly planted in both the world of ministry and business for over thirty years.

With two decades of pastoral and men's ministry experience, he Founded **Core 300** (www.core300.org) where he serves the Body of Christ by calling men out of the stands of mediocrity, into the arena of their destiny.

In the world of enterprise, he leads **Transcende** (www.trancende.net), a management consulting company that helps organizations "raise performance to the next level."

Art lives in the Los Angeles area with his wife, Sharon, and he enjoys writing, speaking and everything about the sea, including spear fishing, diving and boating. Most of his five sons still remain close enough to enjoy regular "refrigerator rights."

CPSIA information can be obtained at www.ICGtesting.com
Printed in the USA
LVOW112238080412

276726LV00001B/5/P